Principles and
for Response i
Language Writing

Based on the assumptions that students expect feedback and want to improve, and that improvement is possible, this book introduces a framework that applies the theory of self-regulated learning to guide second language writing teachers' response to learners at all stages of the writing process. This approach provides teachers with principles and activities for helping students to take more responsibility for their own learning. By using self-regulated learning strategies, students can increase their independence from the teacher, improve their writing skills, and continue to make progress once the course ends, with or without teacher guidance.

The book focuses on the six dimensions of self-regulated learning—motive, methods of learning, time, physical environment, social environment, and performance. Each chapter offers practical activities and suggestions for implementing the principles and guidelines, including tools and materials that teachers can immediately use.

Maureen Snow Andrade is Associate Vice President for Academic Affairs/Academic Programs, Utah Valley University, USA.

Norman W. Evans is Associate Professor in the Department of Linguistics and English Language, Brigham Young University, USA.

ESL & Applied Linguistics Professional Series
Eli Hinkel, Series Editor

Nunan/Choi, Eds. • Language and Culture: Reflective Narratives and the Emergence of Identity

Braine • Nonnative Speaker English Teachers: Research, Pedagogy, and Professional Growth

Burns • Doing Action Research in English Language Teaching: A Guide for Practitioners

Nation/Macalister • Language Curriculum Design

Birch • The English Language Teacher and Global Civil Society

Johnson • Second Language Teacher Education: A Sociocultural Perspective

Nation • Teaching ESL/EFL Reading and Writing

Nation/Newton • Teaching ESL/EFL Listening and Speaking

Kachru/Smith • Cultures, Contexts, and World Englishes

McKay/Bokhosrt-Heng • International English in its Sociolinguistic Contexts: Towards a Socially Sensitive EIL Pedagogy

Christison/Murray, Eds. • Leadership in English Language Education: Theoretical Foundations and Practical Skills for Changing Times

McCafferty/Stam, Eds. • Gesture: Second Language Acquisition and Classroom Research

Liu • Idioms: Description, Comprehension, Acquisition, and Pedagogy

Chapelle/Enright/Jamison, Eds. • Building a Validity Argument for the Test of English as a Foreign Language™

Kondo-Brown/Brown, Eds. • Teaching Chinese, Japanese, and Korean Heritage Students: Curriculum Needs, Materials, and Assessments

Youmans • Chicano-Anglo Conversations: Truth, Honesty, and Politeness

Birch • English L2 Reading: Getting to the Bottom, Second Edition

Luk/Lin • Classroom Interactions as Cross-cultural Encounters: Native Speakers in EFL Lessons

Levy/Stockwell • CALL Dimensions: Issues and Options in Computer Assisted Language Learning

Nero, Ed. • Dialects, Englishes, Creoles, and Education

Basturkmen • Ideas and Options in English for Specific Purposes

Visit **www.routledge.com/education** for additional information on titles in the ESL & Applied Linguistics Professional Series

Principles and Practices for Response in Second Language Writing

Developing Self-Regulated Learners

Maureen Snow Andrade
and Norman W. Evans

Routledge
Taylor & Francis Group

NEW YORK AND LONDON

First published 2013
by Routledge
711 Third Avenue, New York, NY 10017

Simultaneously published in the UK
by Routledge
2 Park Square, Milton Park, Abingdon, Oxon OX14 4RN

Routledge is an imprint of the Taylor & Francis Group, an informa business

© 2013 Taylor & Francis

The right of Maureen Snow Andrade and Norman W. Evans to be
identified as authors of this work has been asserted in accordance with
sections 77 and 78 of the Copyright, Designs and Patents Act 1988.

Library of Congress Cataloging in Publication Data
Andrade, Maureen S., 1961–
Principles and practices for response in second language writing :
developing self-regulated learners / by Maureen Snow Andrade and
Norman W. Evans.
p. cm.
Includes bibliographical references and index.
ISBN 978-0-415-89701-3 — ISBN 978-0-415-89702-0 (pbk.) —
ISBN 978-0-203-80460-5 (e-book) 1. English language—Rhetoric—
Study and teaching—Foreign speakers. 2. Academic writing—Study
and teaching. 3. Second language acquisition. I. Evans, Norman W.
II. Title.
PE1128.A2A538 2013
428.0071—dc23   2012019159

ISBN: 978-0-415-89701-3 (hbk)
ISBN: 978-0-415-89702-0 (pbk)
ISBN: 978-0-203-80460-5 (ebk)

Typeset in Bembo
by HWA Text and Data Management, London

Printed and bound in the United States of America on acid-free paper

SUSTAINABLE
FORESTRY
INITIATIVE

Certified Sourcing
www.sfiprogram.org
SFI-00555
The SFI label applies to the text stock.

Printed and bound in the United States of America by
Walsworth Publishing Company, Marceline, MO.

Contents

Preface

Most educators are familiar with the proverb often attributed to Chinese wisdom: "Give a man a fish and you feed him for a day; teach him how to fish and you feed him for a lifetime." The principle captured in this adage has broad teaching applications and serves as the foundation for this volume. As ESL (English as Second Language) teachers for most of our careers, we are acutely aware of the importance of helping language learners develop skills and strategies that will allow them to continue learning and improving long after they leave our classrooms.

We have spent much of our careers providing feedback to learners in L2 (second language) writing classrooms to help them develop effective writing skills. We are convinced that feedback is central to learning and writing improvement. In fact, it is by means of feedback, both direct and indirect, from our students that we have learned one vital lesson: the way feedback is provided is critically important to its effectiveness.

Corrective feedback is a long-standing practice in both first and second writing pedagogy. Writing teachers share their insights, perspectives, and suggestions with novice writers with the aim of helping them develop effective writing skills. This feedback is provided by means of marginal notes, rubrics, error codes, and writing conferences to name but a few. Much has been said about the methodologies for offering corrective feedback. So what sets the approach described in this volume apart from these methods?

The purpose of this book is to bring a new perspective to long-standing feedback practices in second language writing. To our knowledge, this is the first time the principles of self-regulated learning have been applied to second language writing pedagogy. In fact, one of the reviewers who read a draft of the original manuscript proposal captured our intent exactly: "The significant feature of the book is its combination of writing research and autonomous learning. This is the first treatment that I have seen of these two major areas of applied linguistics being brought together in such a practical and helpful way."

A substantial research base demonstrates that self-regulated learners, specifically those who apply the primary tenets of self-regulated learning—motive, method, time, physical environment, social environment, and performance—have stronger academic performance than learners who do not. Six of the nine chapters in this book are focused on each of these principles. The principle is first defined and then its application to language learning and second language writing is explained. The chapters also include numerous practical activities and approaches to help teachers respond to second language learners in ways that help them become self-regulated writers.

Joy Reid (1993) once said that written corrective feedback ought to lead to "long-term improvement and cognitive change" (p. 229). Ken and Fiona Hyland (2006b) similarly suggest that feedback should point "forward to the student's future writing and the development of his or her writing process" (p. 83). Our experience tells us that feedback based on the six self-regulated learning principles presented in this book points forward to improved second language writing and lasting change. As one of our reviewers noted, "This book provides an excellent description with very practical suggestions on how to help learners take control of the development of their own skill in writing … with an excellent model of how the ideas of self-regulated and autonomous learning can be implemented in a particular language skill." This was precisely the objective we had in mind when we undertook this project.

Acknowledgments

We are especially grateful to those who reviewed our book proposal. They caught the vision and paved the way for it to be realized. We are also in debt to Laura Rawlins and the Brigham Young University Faculty Editing Service team, Mel Thorn from Brigham Young University Humanities Publications Center, Anthony Perez from Brigham Young University Publications and Graphics, and Elizabeth Gillis for their expertise and hours of support as we wrote and refined the manuscript and prepared it for publication. Naomi Silverman, our editor from Taylor and Francis, was enthusiastic and encouraging throughout the process, as was Eli Hinkel, editor for the ESL & Applied Linguistics Professional Series. We also recognize our institutions—Utah Valley University and Brigham Young University—for their support in terms of time and resources to enable us to complete this book. Without these dedicated individuals and favorable circumstances, this work would not have come to fruition.

Chapter 1

Response to Second Language Writing and Principles of Self-Regulated Learning

Objectives

This chapter:

- discusses the history of response to writing in first language (L1) and second language (L2) contexts;
- reviews key terms related to response to writing;
- examines the debate regarding responding to form and responding to meaning;
- explores why and how teachers respond to learners' writing;
- introduces research-based principles of response to writing;
- defines self-regulated learning and explores its dimensions;
- provides an overview of research supporting self-regulated learning theory and resulting practical classroom applications;
- connects self-regulated learning to the concept of autonomy and language learning; and
- explains the rationale for adopting self-regulated learning as a guiding framework.

A Theoretical Framework

Second language writing teachers recognize that learner improvement is gradual and requires much effort on the part of both teacher and learner. This book introduces a framework that assists teachers in guiding learners to take more responsibility for improving their writing skills. Although the framework does not speed up the process of learning to write or decrease the amount of effort required, it does result in the development of effective writing habits by outlining methods of teacher response and describing how learners can use that response to become more independent writers. The framework applies the concept of self-regulated learning to L2 writing.

The goal of this approach is to develop writers who can effectively use self-regulatory strategies throughout the writing process to produce clear, accurate written texts. Achievement of this goal is contingent upon carefully designed teacher response. Reid (1993) has suggested that ESL teacher objectives should be "long-term improvement and cognitive change" (p. 229) when responding to L2 learners' writing. Others have expressed similar ideas, advocating that feedback should point "forward to the student's future writing and the development of his or her writing process" (Hyland & Hyland, 2006b, p. 83). This is the principal aim of this book—to help L2 learners become better writers and continue to improve over time, with or without teacher guidance, by teaching them how to use appropriate strategies motivated by response to their writing.

Achieving this objective requires an understanding of the history of writing feedback in L1 and L2 language contexts. It is also critical to understand what it means to respond to L2 learner writing, as terminology is not consistent. Not only do terms need to be clear, but so does understanding why teachers go to such lengths to respond to their learners' writing, and what methods they employ to provide meaningful feedback. Furthermore, although research findings are far from conclusive regarding the efficacy of teacher response, it will be helpful to know what the research suggests about the practice.

As the practice of responding to L2 writing has matured, principles of good practice have emerged that are informative and helpful for achieving "long-term improvement and cognitive change" (Reid, 1993, p. 229), one of this book's primary purposes. With these elements clarified, the chapter next discusses the principles and practices of self-regulated learning and how these can be coupled with writing response principles to help learners become self-regulated writers.

Responding to L2 Writing

To understand current feedback practices in L2 writing, one must consider two significant points. First, as a language skill, writing has not always had the prominence it has today. Sometimes referred to as the "last language skill" (Leki, 1992, p. 4), writing has been viewed as the skill "that lends itself to advanced-level training and use in specialized situations" (Bowen, Madsen, & Hilferty, 1985, p. 278) rather than an essential part of language learning. The second important point to consider is that L1 writing practices have been highly influential in L2 pedagogy, and it can be argued that nothing has been more influential than the process approach (Ferris & Hedgcock, 2005; Grabe, 2001; Hinkel, 2004; Silva, 1993). A brief discussion of these points will be helpful to our understanding of current feedback practices in L2 writing.

Where and When: Origins

Not until the 1970s, when English language teaching pedagogy was transitioning from grammar-based language teaching methodologies to communicative language teaching (CLT), did writing assume a position of importance as a skill in its own right (Bowen et al., 1985; Ferris, 2003; Leki, 1992; Matsuda, 2003). Prior to the advent of CLT, writing was a means of reinforcing structural patterns; it was limited in scope, and generally quite controlled. Feedback was often focused on surface-level features of the language aimed at eliminating grammatical, lexical, and mechanical errors (Ferris, 2003, 2004; Hyland, 2003; Leki, 1992). This narrow view of writing changed, however, as the principles of CLT started to take root in L2 teaching and, coincidently, as L2 learner populations changed.

The 1960s and 1970s were a time of marked increases in international student enrollments in U.S. institutions of higher education (Brawner, Bevis, & Lucas, 2007). As the number of international students seeking admission to universities in English-speaking countries increased, so did the number of students needing the ability to write text that required more fluency than the guided and controlled approaches to writing which were developed in earlier times. Learners found that they needed to compose purposeful, meaningful prose for academic and professional purposes; this created a need for ESL writing teachers to reconsider how "the last skill" should be taught (see Ferris, 2003 and Leki, 1992 for a detailed history).

While shifting trends in language teaching methodology and student demographics impacted the teaching of L2 writing, one of the most influential elements of change in pedagogy has been the adoption of L1 practices related to the process approach (Ferris, 2003; Ferris & Hedgcock, 2005; Hyland & Hyland, 2006b; Leki, 1992; Zamel, 1976, 1985). In the early 1970s, English composition theory called into question the long-standing practice of responding to writing in its final form—the product. Prior to process writing, teachers typically commented only on a final product to justify the assigned grade (Ferris, 2003; Hyland & Hyland, 2006b).

The research of Emig (1971) and others in the late 1960s shifted focus from a product orientation to a process orientation. As Kroll (2001) notes, "One of her [Emig's] watershed observations was the fact that writers do not, in general, produce text in the straightforward linear sequence that the traditional paradigm outlined" (p. 220). In short, the traditional or product approach did not seem to be based on how most writers really write. From this work emerged the concepts that writing is: (1) a process, (2) a method of discovering meaning, (3) a way to develop personal voice, and (4) a recursive, multiple-draft endeavor. The process approach suggests less focus on form and more on meaning and the discovery of meaning. In Kroll's (2001) words, the process approach has come to mean that "student writers engage in their writing tasks through a cyclical approach rather than through a single-shot approach" (p. 221). As such, she points out that writing by nature goes through stages and drafts wherein writers receive feedback "from peers and/ or teacher, followed by revision of their evolving texts" (p. 221).

The process approach (in a variety of forms) swept across the United States through the 1970s and 1980s and became a central component of English composition instruction and research. Second language writing pedagogy was not far behind. Zamel's (1976) article "Teaching composition in the ESL classroom: What we can learn from research in the teaching of English" is often cited as the first major introduction of the process approach for L2 writing (Matsuda, 2003). An overview of presentation titles at annual TESOL, Inc. conferences in the early 1980s reveals a growing interest in process writing issues. By 1985, the number of papers presented on process writing had increased dramatically over previous years. In fewer than 10 years, process had become a central topic in ESL writing circles and an essential tenet in L2 writing pedagogy. The popularity of process writing has continued, and is now a generally accepted practice in ESL composition (Ferris & Hedgcock, 2005; Kroll, 1990, 2001; Matsuda, 2003; Reid, 1993).

The characteristic of process writing most germane to this discussion is, as Kroll (2001) points out, that process writing requires feedback (or response) from "peers, and/or teachers" (p. 221) to help writers improve their skills. Feedback, or response, is the next point of discussion. Because terminology is inconsistent and pedagogical processes vary, the next section defines *response* and discusses what forms of response are typically used in ESL writing.

What: A Clarification of Terms and Practices

Practitioners use a number of terms when discussing response to L2 writing, including expressions such as *feedback*, *response*, *written commentary*, *error correction*, *written corrective feedback*, and *formative* and *summative evaluation*. In an effort to understand these terms, it is helpful to first identify an umbrella term. Typically, *feedback* and *response* are the most broadly used terms when discussing the act of teachers or peers offering helpful suggestions to developing writers (Ferris, 2003; Hyland & Hyland, 2006a; Leki, 1992). While some speak of *feedback* (Harmer, 2004; Hyland & Hyland, 2006b), others use *response* (Ferris, 2003; Leki, 1992), and still others use *feedback* and *response* interchangeably (Ferris, 2003; Reid, 1993). Little exists in the literature that contradicts Reid's (1993) interchangeable use of these terms. She notes that "response, or 'feedback' can be defined as any input from the reader to writer that provides information for revision" (p. 218).

Research (e.g., see Ferris, 2003; Hyland & Hyland, 2006a, 2006b; Leki, 1992; Reid, 1993) and personal practice also suggest that *feedback* and *response* have essentially the same meaning. Therefore, this book uses these terms interchangeably to refer to the act of offering suggestions to L2 writers. In other words, *response* covers guidance or direction given to the writer at any stage in the writing process; this includes, for instance, response related to brainstorming, planning, drafting, revising, and editing; response for the purpose of building motivation, determining purpose, and understanding grading criteria; and other types of teacher direction. Thus, responding is not limited to what happens when learners submit their writing to the teacher, but extends to all stages and aspects of writing.

The varied methods of responding to L2 writing also require clarification. This can best be accomplished by first discussing the means by which response can be provided and then considering what kind of response is offered. Feedback is typically provided in three ways: in writing, electronically, or orally. Written feedback, where a teacher, tutor, or peer makes suggestions on the learner's manuscript has been the most common form of feedback (Hyland & Hyland, 2006b). Written feedback is quickly being replaced, however, by electronic feedback (e.g., see Ware & Warschauer, 2006; Warschauer, 1995). Technological advances have made it possible to respond to L2 writing electronically by such means as in-text comments, blogs, or e-mail. The immediacy of this feedback can be a great advantage to learner and teacher alike. Finally, oral response is commonly practiced and can be delivered in several ways. Most often, teachers or tutors will conference in person with a learner, offering feedback as the two discuss the merits and needs of the manuscript. An alternative to personal contact with the writer is to make an audio recording of responses to the learner's writing (Ferris & Hedgcock, 2005). The practice saves time by not having to compose carefully worded responses, and the comments have the potential to be more detailed than if they were written.

Each method, whether written, electronic, or oral, has advantages and disadvantages, and, deciding which form of feedback to use depends on a number of factors. Harmer (2004) suggests that "the ways we react to students' work will depend not only on the kind of task the students are given, but also on what we want to achieve at any one point" (p. 108). One useful distinction to make when determining what type of feedback should be provided is to ask if the intent is to focus on form or meaning.

What: Form and Meaning

One of the most contentious aspects of process writing over the years has been the appropriateness of form-focused feedback. Many have argued that feedback on surface-level errors has no place in a process writing curriculum. This is certainly the position taken in L1 composition pedagogy (Hartwell, 1985). In L2 writing, the debate is far from certain and is a considerably more complex question. One of the liveliest exchanges in L2 writing literature was over the practice of feedback focused on form. Horowitz (1986a, 1986b) and Liebman-Kleine's (1986) debate over this issue drew considerable attention to the merits of responding to form and meaning. A brief discussion of the issues as they apply to today's feedback practices in L2 writing is warranted.

The process and product orientations were often conceived of as a dichotomy, which led to a series of debates. Kamimura (2000) points out that as "the process orientation gained primacy in ESL/EFL writing, attention to product, including both linguistic and rhetorical forms, began to be criticized" (p. 2). Those most vocally opposed to the process approach seemed to be advocating a shift in focus from the writer to the reader, or, as Kroll (1990) notes, "the academic discourse community" (p. 7). Others suggest that feedback on form indeed has a place in process writing. Harmer (2004), for instance, suggests that feedback can be offered in two ways: response and correction. The distinction between these two can be seen when he notes "in early drafts, responding may be more appropriate than correcting" (p. 109). Ferris and Hedgcock (2005), on the other hand, maintain that content and form feedback is a false dichotomy. They maintain that language and content cannot be separated, and, indeed, some research suggests that learners can improve their writing while focusing on both simultaneously (e.g., see Ferris, 2003).

Another controversial aspect of form-focused feedback that was first raised in L1 writing and is now prominent in L2 writing literature is whether written corrective feedback has any positive effects. Truscott (1996) is credited for beginning this discussion when he suggested that written corrective feedback was not only not helpful, but perhaps even harmful to L2 writers. This launched a wave of research and debate spanning over a decade, aiming to disprove Truscott's claim (Bitchener, Young, & Cameron, 2005; Chandler, 2003; Ferris, 1999, 2003, 2004; Guénette, 2007; Polio, Fleck, & Leder, 1998). The results are far from conclusive, but well-designed research is beginning to emerge suggesting that form-focused feedback can indeed make a positive difference in the accuracy of L2 writing (Bitchener, 2008; Bitchener & Knoch, 2008; Ellis, Sheen, Murakami, & Takashima, 2008; Evans, Hartshorn, McCollum, & Wolfersberger, 2010; Hartshorn et al., 2010; Sheen, 2007; Storch, 2010). One final point is that teachers, despite the decade of debate and uncertainty, consider written corrective feedback an essential aspect of L2 writing and a responsibility of the L2 writing teacher. Evans, Hartshorn, & Tuioti (2010a) found that nearly 95% of all writing teachers questioned in a large, international survey indicated that they provide students with written corrective feedback, and many say that they do this because their students need it.

To bring focus to this debate between from and meaning, Hamp-Lyons (1986) offers a voice of reason. She argues that the Horowitz (1986a, 1986b) and Liebman-Kleine (1986) exchange created a false dichotomy and that viewing these methods as competing paradigms is no way to resolve the issue. She advocates "a descriptive model which will allow us to reconcile the 'product approach,' (as characterized in the descriptions of current-traditional rhetoric) and the 'process approach.' Such a reconciliation would be to the support of teachers and the benefit of learners" (p. 794). In other words, there is a need and place for both form- and meaning-focused feedback. The balance depends on what teachers are focusing on and what they expect of learners. In many ways, the reconciliation that Hamp-Lyons calls for can be found in the genre-focused pedagogy that has become prevalent in L2 writing (Johns, 2003). Specifically, the type of writing or genre greatly influences the kind of feedback learners receive and when in the process they receive it.

Why: Purposes and Efficacy of Feedback

The question of why teachers should respond to learners' writing can be answered on several levels. First, common sense dictates that teacher response is necessary (Bruton, 2009, 2010). Responding to learners' writing is how teachers help learners improve. As Hyland and Hyland (2006b) suggest, "Feedback has long been regarded as essential for the development of L2 writing skills, both for its potential for learning and for learner motivation" (p. 83). Furthermore, learners expect it (e.g., Cohen & Cavalcanti, 1990; Ferris, 1995; Guénette, 2007; Hedgcock & Lefkowitz, 1994; Leki, 1991; Truscott, 1996). One might logically ask, if learners receive no feedback how will they improve? Nearly everything individuals learn, including writing, is based on some form of feedback (Evans et al., 2010a; Hattie & Timperley, 2007).

Another way to consider this question is not nearly as straightforward. Many teachers ask why invest so many hours responding to writing when some learners show no apparent improvement in their writing ability. Advocates of this viewpoint cite the lack of definitive evidence in the research as support for limiting the amount of response given (Hyland & Hyland, 2006b). In other words, if it does not work, why bother?

One way to respond to this dilemma is to consider all related factors. First, many variables can impact the efficacy of written feedback. These include learner, situation, and methodological variables (Evans et al., 2010a; Hattie & Timperlye, 2007). Furthermore, the concept of improvement must be clear (Casanave, 2003; Leki, 1992). A growing body of literature suggests that when properly provided, feedback can indeed make a positive difference in the quality of student writing (Ferris, 2003; Hyland & Hyland, 2006b). Said another way, learners demonstrate improvement when their teachers utilize principles of effective feedback. These principles are the focus of the next section.

How: Approaches to Feedback

The phrase *best practices* is commonly used in educational discussion when speaking about the most effective ways to help learners achieve their potential.

A problem with the idea of best practices is that it assumes that all learners are the same, when in fact, learners are remarkably different and practices of necessity must be modified to meet differing needs. Rather than suggesting best practices for written feedback, a more reasonable approach is to identify sound principles on which teachers can base their feedback. When a reliable principle is in use, educators can develop practices specifically tailored to their learners' needs.

For this reason, the following 10 writing response principles, identified through personal practice and reviews of research, are effective in guiding teacher responses to writing. This is not intended to be an all-inclusive list, but it is a good base for the practices found in subsequent chapters of this book. Furthermore, these principles are not mutually exclusive. There is, in fact, considerable overlap among them. For instance, the principle that response should be interactive also reinforces the principle that teachers should avoid appropriating student writing. The following descriptions of written response principles have been adapted from the work of Ferris (2003), Harmer (2004), and Hyland and Hyland (2006b), as well as the authors' years of practice. They are also summarized in Figure 1.1.

Clarity is Paramount

This is intentionally listed first because learners' most often cited criticism about their teachers' feedback is that it is unclear (e.g., see Ferris, 2003). Lack of clarity can result from various factors such as sloppy writing, unfamiliar symbols, vague wording such as *awkward*, or ambiguous suggestions to name a few. Writing improvement requires communicating what the writer needs to consider for revisions. Unclear comments will derail an effective response, ultimately defeating the purpose of giving feedback.

The Teacher is Not the Only Respondent

Each learner is surrounded by individuals who can serve as respondents to a learner's ideas and organization. With minimal amounts of training or well-designed rubrics, teachers can effectively draw on other readers such as tutors, classmates, and even roommates to help guide learners in their writing development.

Written Response is Only One Option

Oral and electronic comments can also be effective response method choices. As noted earlier, oral response allows for more detail and clarity without requiring the time needed to compose written comments, while electronic feedback can take on a number of forms, each offering unique alternatives.

Stephen Ruffus

English

For instance, multiple respondents can post responses to a piece of writing on an online blog.

Respond Selectively

This principle should remind teachers that too much feedback can be both overwhelming and discouraging. In addition, this principle can be applied in various ways. First, a teacher may choose to respond only to those elements of writing that have been covered in class, thus helping learners focus on a limited number of features in their writing. Alternatively, a teacher may decide to respond only to certain drafts of a paper, allowing others to help shape the learner's improvement.

Customize Response to Individual Learner Needs

This principle, frequently noted in the literature (Ferris, 2003, 2004; Hyland, 2003; Hyland & Hyland, 2006b; Leki, 1992; Reid, 1993), suggests that writers learn from and respond to feedback differently. L2 writers develop in different ways and have different needs based on education, culture, personality, and linguistic background to name a few. Each of these must be considered when offering feedback. Neglecting any one factor or assuming that all writers need the same assistance is misguided.

Response Needs to Be Interactive

When response is interactive, learners can assume ownership of their ideas. Too often L2 learners perceive the teacher's comments as commandments rather than suggestions. When response is seen as being nonjudgmental, the opportunity for dialog between the writer and teacher improves, and the possibility of negotiating improvement also increases.

Do Not Adhere to Rigid Response Prescriptions

Rigid, formulaic approaches to response presuppose that all writers have the same needs and respond to the same kinds of feedback. This simply is not the case. This principle overlaps considerably with the principle related to customizing response, which suggests that response needs to be customized to individual writer's needs. The practice of responding only to linguistic needs on final drafts, for instance, suggests that writers do not need or want feedback on their linguistic accuracy early on in the writing process, but substantial research suggests just the opposite is true (Cohen & Cavalcanti, 1990; Ferris, 2003; Ferris & Hedgcock, 2005; Guénette, 2007; Hedgcock & Lefkowitz, 1994; Leki, 1991; Truscott, 1996).

Improvement Takes Time

The work of Cummins (1980, 1981, 1996) and other more recent research tells us that L2 acquisition, especially for academic purposes, takes considerable time (Omaggio Hadley, 2000). This insight shows that improvement in writing is, as Reid (1993) has suggested, "a process not an event" (p. 139). It also offers a partial response to the question of why teachers should respond to a learner's writing when improvement is not always apparent.

Appropriately Balance Critique and Praise

This has sometimes been referred to as the "sandwich" (Ferris & Hedgcock, 2005, p. 198) approach to feedback. Such an approach suggests that feedback is most effective when three or four focused areas for improvement are sandwiched between sincere, encouraging remarks. Students need and expect constructive criticism without being overwhelmed by only negative comments.

Find Balance Between Giving Clear, Specific Response, and Appropriating Student Writing

This can sometimes be a difficult task when working with L2 learners who see their teacher's input as definitive. Care has to be taken to ensure that a learner's writing is exactly that—the learner's. While many teachers make honest efforts to help learners find their voice in writing, some become overbearing in their responses, thereby appropriating student writing. Also, some research suggests that L2 learners are likely to change their work to match as closely as possible what their teacher has suggested (Hyland & Hyland, 2006b; Tardy, 2006).

It is important to restate that these principles intentionally lack some degree of detail. Each learner and context is different, and practices must be adapted accordingly. The details are in the practices that teachers employ.

Using a broad definition of response, which includes written commentary and corrective feedback, based on principles derived from years of research and practice, teachers can help L2 learners improve their writing. The possibility of learners improving is even greater if they themselves apply sound principles of self-regulated learning. A discussion of what it means to be a self-regulated learner and how related principles can be applied to an L2 writing context follows.

Self-Regulated Learning

Self-regulated learning is "the ability of learners to control the factors or conditions affecting their learning" (Dembo, Junge, & Lynch, 2006, p.

Clarity is paramount
- Unclear comments hinder effective responses.
- Be abundantly clear what students should do.
- Use tools such as cover sheets and rubrics to clarify meaning.

Teacher is not the only respondent
- Use tutors, peers, and classmates.

Written response is only one option
- Provide oral response in
    o small group discussion
    o tutorial sessions
    o writing conferences
    o audio recordings.
- Use electronic feedback for timely responses.

Respond selectively
- Select elements for comment that will most benefit the writer.
- Don't respond to some drafts.

Customize response to individual learner needs
- Vary feedback according to
    o assignment type
    o time in the semester
    o student level.

Response needs to be interactive
- Build a productive interpersonal relationship with the writer.
- Carry on a dialog with the learner about the writing without judging it.

Do not adhere to rigid response prescriptions
- Match response to
    o individual assignment
    o student differences (see *Customize* in this table).

Improvement takes time
- Remember that writing improvement is a process not an event.
- Help students recognize progress.
- Offer consistent, clear, and encouraging advice.

Appropriately balance critique and praise
- Use praise, criticism, and suggestions.
- Provide constructive criticism not simple platitudes.
- Sandwich substantive suggestions between sincere praise.

Find balance between giving clear, specific response, and appropriating student writing
- Guide, don't control.
- Allow students a sense of ownership throughout the revision and response process.

Figure 1.1 Writing Response Principles

188). Learners who are self-regulated "are distinguished by their systematic use of metacognitive, motivational, and behavioral strategies; by their responsiveness to feedback regarding the effectiveness of their learning; and by their self-perceptions of academic accomplishment" (Zimmerman, 1990, p. 14). The presence of cognitive processes that aid understanding and remembering information are an additional characteristic (Wernke, Wagener, Anschuetz, & Moschner, 2011). Educators are familiar with learners who make insightful comments, are well-organized and prepared for class, meet assignment deadlines, and ask for help when they do poorly on their work or do not understand a concept—self-regulated learners. Equally common are those who fail to apply knowledge, do only enough work to get by, and persist with the same behaviors regardless of outcomes.

What may not be so well-known is that teachers can influence these behaviors in positive ways. Self-regulated learning has been viewed both as a set of teachable skills and as a developmental process that emerges from experience (Paris & Paris, 2001). These perspectives are not mutually exclusive. Both support the idea that educators can help learners become more effective. Logically, behavior changes take time. A classroom of learners will be at all points on the continuum with regard to self-regulation. Teachers are not likely to take learners from a complete lack of self-regulation to full self-regulation over the time period of a single course, but they can help learners make progress. For the teacher, this progress depends on their response practices that are aimed specifically at developing learner self-regulation.

The next section further defines self-regulated learning and explores its dimensions. It provides a brief overview of research supporting self-regulated learning theory and resulting practical classroom applications. The discussion connects self-regulated learning to the concept of autonomy and language learning and explains why self-regulated learning is an effective guiding framework.

Defining and Exploring

Self-regulated learning and its related strategies are comprised of four categories:

- metacognitive (planning, setting goals, monitoring, evaluating)
- motivation (the ability to self-motivate, taking responsibility for success and failures; developing self-efficacy)
- cognitive (understanding and remembering information), and
- behavior (seeking help, creating a positive learning environment) (Dembo et al., 2006; Wernke et al., 2011; Zimmerman & Risemberg, 1997).

Learners who are self-regulated utilize a combination of strategies from these areas. All of these strategies can be taught and learned. Additionally, based on classroom research, six specific dimensions of self-regulated learning have been identified:

- motive
- methods of learning
- time
- physical environment
- social environment, and
- performance (Zimmerman & Risemberg, 1997).

The dimensions correspond to the questions why, how, when, where, with whom, and what. Each is associated with one or more of the four categories of self-regulated learning, and work in concert to help learners become self-regulated.

The Six Dimensions

The six dimensions of self-regulated learning form the framework for this book, with a chapter devoted to each. The chapters apply the dimensions to language learning and L2 writing. The primary focus of each chapter is on activities for teacher response to help learners become self-regulated writers. The six dimensions have been applied to distance language learning (Andrade & Bunker, 2009; Andrade & Bunker, 2011), although not to language learning in general or to writing specifically, until now. Discussions of strategy use for learning languages is plentiful but has not been conceptualized within the theory of self-regulated learning and its dimensions. The latter provide specificity regarding the nature of self-regulated learning and the components necessary for its achievement.

Motive is related to the reasons for learning (*why*) and involves setting realistic goals, examining self-talk (the positive or negative internal comments that individuals make about themselves), and managing emotions. Motivation in language learning may be integrative (a desire to associate with L2 speakers) or instrumental (the need to achieve a specific goal) (Gardner & Lambert, 1972). Indicators of motivation include choice, effort, and persistence (Pintrich & Schunk, 2002). The freedom to choose activities and assignments can support effort and persistence when learning becomes difficult or boring. Motivated learners set and attain goals, thereby further increasing motivation. Managing emotions lowers the affective filter (Krashen, 1981), or factors that interfere with language acquisition, including anxiety, inhibitions, and personality characteristics.

Method focuses on the cognitive aspect of self-regulated learning and refers to *how* learners learn, including approaches such as summarizing, note-taking, asking questions, rehearsing information, and using visual representations (e.g., charts, maps, pictures, etc.). The more strategies learners have, the more successful they can be, because if one strategy is not effective, they can implement another. Learners can be introduced to a variety of strategies for deliberate language study (referred to by Nation, 2009, as language-focused learning, one of four strands, or components, critical to language learning). Examples of these strategies include techniques for remembering vocabulary, applying grammar rules, or using teacher feedback. A rehearsal strategy for vocabulary learning, for instance, is distributed retrieval—studying words for a set period of time and then returning to them later for further study (Nation, 2001). Timed writing activities are a method of learning that results in the ability to write more and faster. This builds fluency, another of the four strands for a balanced language learning approach (Nation, 2009).

The third dimension, time, involves consideration of *when* to study and for how long (Dembo et al., 2006). It comprises both the metacognitive (i.e., monitoring, evaluating) and behavior aspects of self-regulated learning. Learners who demonstrate good time-management skills are aware of deadlines, begin working on assignments early, set priorities, and accurately evaluate both the difficulty of tasks and the amount of time needed to complete them. Generally, learners need assistance in planning, self-monitoring, and adjusting their use of time. A first step for L2 writing is developing awareness of the writing process and of the need to allow sufficient time to address the stages of prewriting, planning, writing, revising, and editing. Learners who take short cuts will produce a less effective composition than those who fully address each stage. Teachers can help learners avoid procrastination by requiring evidence of the completion of each part of the writing process, such as multiple drafts demonstrating response to feedback. Learners also need to consider their time (i.e., how long it takes them to read and write in comparison with native speakers) as they build fluency in the language (e.g., see Nation, 2009).

Physical environment (*where*) involves the self-regulated learning aspects of metacognition (i.e., monitoring, evaluating) and behavior to ensure that a learner's surroundings support effective study (i.e., are quiet, free of distractions, comfortable). Learners need to become aware of how the environment affects learning and how to restructure it as needed—moving to a different location, turning off the television, or avoiding places where they will encounter friends. Physical environment also involves the opportunity to access information related to learning. Language learners need rich resources to provide input and focused learning. Nation (2009) suggests that four strands are required for a balanced approach to language learning (meaning-focused input, meaning-focused output, language-focused learning, and fluency). Two of these, meaning-focused input through reading and listening (see also Krashen's input hypothesis; Krashen, 1985) and language-focused learning through deliberate study (related to methods of learning), require the availability of appropriate and plentiful resources. These could include textbooks or course materials, graded readers, Internet sites, or academic support facilities. Learners need to know what exists in the environment and how to access and use available resources.

The social environment (*with whom*) refers to the learner's ability to seek, find, and evaluate help. Potentially, it involves all four categories of self-regulated learning (motive, cognition, metacognition, behavior). Specific to language learning, it encompasses opportunities for interaction and practice, or what Nation (2009) calls meaning-focused output, achieved through speaking and writing. Achieving communicative competence, which consists of grammatical (understanding syntax, vocabulary, grammar), sociolinguistic (using language appropriately in a given context), discourse (connecting language components), and strategic competence (repairing communication breakdowns) (Canale & Swain, 1980), depends on the interaction and the cues learners receive about their output. Within the classroom, learners need a safe environment that supports risk-taking and making mistakes. This also requires having a low affective filter—levels of anxiety and inhibitions (Krashen, 1981), and is related to the dimension of motive discussed earlier.

Performance, the last dimension, primarily involves the motive, metacognitive, and behavioral features of self-regulated learning to examine *what* is learned. As learners acquire knowledge or language skill, they observe their actions, reflect on outcomes, evaluate performance, and revise goals. Tools such as skills audits, action plans, self-assessment sheets, reflective journals, and tips sheets have been used to help distance and web-based language learners successfully summarize feedback, identify needs, and modify goals to increase independence (Baggetun & Wasson, 2006; Dembo et al., 2006; Murphy, 2005; van den Boom, Paas, & van Merrienboer, 2007). As is true for the social environment dimension, interaction helps learners notice gaps between their language skills and effective communication (e.g., see Swain, 1995). They can then reflect on and analyze their performance and identify areas for improvement. Figure 1.2 depicts the six dimensions of self-regulated learning and how they interact to develop self-regulated writers.

Supporting Research and Applications

Self-regulated learning is particularly appealing because it is a worthy goal for learners of all ages in all disciplines (Paris & Paris, 2001). The principles of self-regulated learning have been applied in a variety of contexts to improve the learning experience. These include web-based learning (Bell, 2007; Chang, 2005; Dembo et al., 2006), distance language learning (Andrade & Bunker, 2009, 2011), face-to-face learning in middle schools (Dembo &

Figure 1.2 The Inter-Related Principles Applied by a Self-Regulated Writer

Eaton, 2000), learning in higher education (Bail, Zhang, & Tachiyama, 2008; Schloemer & Brenan, 2006; Tinnesz, Ahuna, & Kiener, 2006), and lifelong learning (Caneiro & Steffens, 2006). Years of research support the efficacy of the theory of self-regulated learning and its dimensions (see Zimmerman & Risemberg, 1997 for a thorough review of research in the 1980s and 1990s that supports the six dimensions of self-regulated learning). This research demonstrates that learners who possess self-regulated behaviors (i.e., set goals, use and modify learning strategies, and monitor their progress) are higher achievers than are those who do not (e.g., see Borkowski & Thorpe, 1994; Zimmerman, 1994; Zimmerman & Martinez-Pons, 1986).

Teachers can support the development of self-regulated learning by discussing learning strategies with students—what they are, how they work, and when to use them; designing open-ended activities (with appropriate scaffolding) that involve collaboration rather than focusing only on rote exercises; and minimizing objective assessments in favor of portfolios and projects that motivate and provide opportunities for creativity (Paris & Paris, 2001). Indeed, classroom observations demonstrate that children become more self-regulated when teachers engage them in complex and open-ended tasks, offer choices, allow them to control the level of challenge, and provide opportunities for self and peer evaluation (Perry, VandeKamp, Mercer, & Nordby, 2002). Undergraduate students who set goals; exercised choice;

monitored, evaluated, and modified strategy use; and received feedback from peers and instructors had higher cumulative GPAs, higher graduation rates, and fewer failing grades than did students with similar academic backgrounds who did not receive self-regulated learning instruction (Bail et al., 2008).

As evidenced by these studies, self-regulated learning is more likely to occur when teachers create appropriate conditions and environments. The ultimate goal of self-regulated learning instruction is to develop active learners who are confident, resourceful, diligent, and seek help when needed. They understand the processes that result in these behaviors and engage in systematic use of metacognitive, cognitive, motivational, and behavioral strategies. The goal of this book is to provide L2 writing teachers with the tools to establish such a learning environment.

Self-Regulated Learning, Autonomy, and Language Learning

The terms *self-regulation* and *autonomy* are often used synonymously; however, they have distinct characteristics. Because autonomy is a more commonly used term in language learning than self-regulated learning, which is based in educational psychology, a discussion of autonomy, its relation to self-regulated learning, and the rationale for using self-regulated learning as a guiding framework in this book are critical.

Autonomy and Language Learning

The concept of autonomy is "elusive" (Hurd, 2005, p. 1). It has been depicted as a learner attribute consisting of the capacity for taking responsibility for learning (Holec, 1981), as a situation in which the learner is responsible for making and implementing decisions related to learning (Oxford, 2008), and as the "freedom and ability to manage one's own affairs, which entails the right to make decisions" (Scharle & Szabó, 2000, p. 4). Descriptors associated with autonomy reflect diverse learner characteristics and behaviors. These descriptors include decision-making, choice, control, independence, capacity to learn, self-direction, self-awareness, active learning, taking responsibility, strategic competence, motivation, metacognition, behavior, reflection, goal-setting, time management, and self-assessment (e.g., see Garrison, 2003; Holec, 1981; Hurd, 1998a, 1998b, 2005; Hurd, Beaven, & Ortega, 2001; Little, 1991; Peters, 1998; Scharle & Szabó, 2000; White, 2003).

Learners do not develop autonomy simply by being placed in situations where they have no other choice (Benson, 2007), nor does autonomy entail complete independence or a lack of support. Instead, it reflects a state of interdependence between teachers and learners (e.g., see Burge,

1988; Garrison & Archer, 2000; Little, 1995; White, 2003). In other words, achieving autonomy is not an automatic or solitary process, but one that can be positively affected through formal learning. In fact, models of autonomy related to language learning are based on the premise that learners possess autonomy in varying degrees (e.g., see Benson, 2001; Littlewood, 1997; Macaro, 1997; Nunan, 1997; Scharle & Szabó, 2000), and that it can be developed and increased over time.

Nunan's (1997) five-stage model (awareness, involvement, intervention, creation, transcendence) takes a learner from being a recipient of information—and largely dependent on a formal learning system—to the ability to create new knowledge and teach others. Scharle and Szabó's (2000) three-stage training process (raising awareness, changing attitudes, and transferring roles) aims to decrease passive learning and overreliance on a teacher. Learners must understand the role of their own contributions to learning, practice being responsible, and take on some teacher roles, such as choosing materials. These models emphasize a gradual process and support the idea that the development of autonomy can and should be a part of regular classroom instruction.

Cultural issues must also be considered. One cannot assume that autonomy is equally familiar, valued, or desirable in all contexts. Learners will vary in their desire to have choices in the learning process and to accept responsibility for learning. Language educators must demonstrate awareness that autonomy is not a universal or neutral concept, and consider its possible applications and limitations within given contexts (Schmenk, 2005). However, distinctions must also be made between an acceptance of the principle of autonomy and the teaching methods associated with it (Benson, 2007). For instance, even if the means of achieving autonomy in a specific context, perhaps through self-access centers or online course components, may be inappropriate, the goal of autonomy remains worthwhile. Another consideration is the many faces of autonomy and the corresponding difficulty that exists when sorting through them as the teacher tries to determine the best way to support autonomy for a particular learner and in specific contexts.

Increasing numbers of scholarly publications and presentations on the topic of autonomy are evidence of growing interest in the topic (Benson, 2007). This interest is at least partly due to a greater use of technology for language learning, which typically necessitates some degree of independent learning. Modes of technology-based learning include hybrid courses, distance learning, and self-access centers. These forms of learning have the potential to develop learner autonomy, but this is not likely to occur without related support being built into the course. Some explorations of autonomy and language learning have considered face-to-face classroom learning (Miller, 2006; Palfreyman & Smith, 2003) although Oxford (2008) observes that autonomy is not as widely focused on in the classroom as it should be compared to learning in less formal contexts (i.e., out-of-class learning or self-instruction) (Gardner & Miller, 1999; Hyland, 2004; Murray, 2004).

In distance learning, for example, White (2003) refers to the idea of "collaborative control" (p. 149) through which autonomy can develop. Learners collaborate with peers and teachers to control (i.e., explore and make choices) and manage learning tasks. This interaction encourages language practice and builds learner capacity and competence. Collaborative control depends on strategy training through course materials, and allowing learners to select and access meaningful opportunities for learning. Using a related approach, Andrade and Bunker (2009, 2011) present a model for distance language learning based on the six dimensions of self-regulated learning. The model supports the need to consciously train learners to become self-regulated, and guides course designers in building components that assist learners in managing their own learning; the latter is critical to success as a distance language learner.

Empirical evidence on the topic of autonomy and language learning remains weak, largely due to the desire to demonstrate the effectiveness of initiatives to promote learner autonomy rather than to critically analyze teacher and learner response to these initiatives and how autonomy develops across contexts (Benson, 2007). However, the area of autonomy and distance language learning offers a growing body of literature that supports the value of autonomy and how that value can be increased through course instruction and materials. Support for this claim is apparent in a number of studies. Distance learners of French increased their self-awareness and confidence through participation and risk-taking, and acquired new skills such as self-monitoring, reflection, planning, prioritizing, self-discipline, and responsibility (Hurd, 2000). Motivation improved through positive self-talk, goal setting, interaction with French native speakers, and reading. Malaysian distance students of English increased their confidence and understanding of goals and expected standards, had better attitudes about staff, and preferred more freedom than did on-campus learners (Thang, 2005).

Distance learners of French, German, and Spanish were active, involved, sought interaction opportunities, demonstrated the ability to critically reflect, and took control through the use of supplementary materials (Murphy, 2005). Using the language was motivating and helped them recognize progress. Student success in an independent study Russian class was positively affected by an internal locus of learning (i.e., the belief that learning occurs within the learner rather than on the transfer of knowledge from an expert), self-motivation, and self-encouragement (Bown, 2006). Online learners studying biblical Greek and Latin improved their levels of motivation and interest (Harlow, 2007). These studies demonstrate positive trends in the development of autonomy. In most cases, however, increased autonomy has not yet been linked to proficiency gains or achievement.

As discussed previously in this chapter, various strategies are associated with the six dimensions of self-regulated learning. Related strategies are associated with autonomy and language learning. Oxford (2008) categorizes these into four groups: (1) metacognitive strategies that guide the learning process through planning and evaluation, (2) affective strategies for managing emotions and developing motivation, (3) cognitive strategies related to mental processes such as analyzing and synthesizing, and (4) social-interactive strategies including collaboration and noticing sociocultural factors. Oxford links the use of various strategies within these categories to learner autonomy. In later work, Oxford (2011) retains the three categories of affective, cognitive, and sociocultural-interactive, but broadens metacognitive strategies into metastrategies, which refer to ways in which learners manage their learning in all three areas. These form the basis for the strategic self-regulation model of L2 learning (S^2R). Oxford's model is based on the four components of self-regulated learning—metacognitive, motivation, cognitive, and behavior—but is specifically applied to language learning.

Rationale for Self-Regulated Learning as a Guiding Framework

While similarities between autonomy and self-regulated learning are evident, particularly in Oxford's (2008) categories of language learning strategies and Zimmerman and Risemberg's (1997) categories for self-regulated learning, there are distinctions between the two concepts. Two primary components stand out in definitions of autonomy: (1) the learner's capacity for taking responsibility, and (2) choice in what, where, and how to learn (e.g., see Holec, 1981; Hurd, 1998b, 2005; Little, 1991; White, 2003). Self-regulated learning places less emphasis on learner attributes and choice, and more on *how* learners can be effective by taking control of the learning process. Self-regulated learning also focuses predominantly on how to teach and monitor the strategy use of learners (Dembo et al., 2006). As such, it is a particularly useful concept for classroom teachers.

Research on autonomy and language learning has been closely associated with learning strategies (Benson, 2007) although autonomy is a broader concept (e.g., see Little, 2000; Palfreyman, 2003): "The use of learning strategies can strongly both reflect and further promote learner autonomy" (Oxford, 2008, p. 43). Some scholars advocate abandoning the focus on language learning strategies in favor of self-regulated learning, which is considered to be a more versatile term (Dörnyei & Skehan, 2003; Dörnyei, 2005). This has merit, although it is still necessary to determine *what* strategies learners use to be self-regulated (Griffiths, 2008). Self-regulated learning encompasses specific learning strategies. The term self-regulated learning is also preferable for other reasons, which make it preferable as a guiding framework rather than autonomy.

Much can be learned from the literature on autonomy and language learning. Similarities between self-regulated learning and autonomy are readily apparent, and both concepts potentially offer positive direction to language teaching and learning. Although both have been defined as learners taking responsibility for their own learning (Dembo & Eaton, 2000; Holec, 1981; Muller-Verweyen, 1999; Vanijdee, 2003), the concept of self-regulated learning, particularly the six dimensions—motive, methods, time, physical environment, social environment, and performance—offer specific processes and strategies (Dembo et al., 2006) upon which instruction can be based. In contrast, the multiplicity of definitions of autonomy and its related characteristics makes it difficult for teachers to structure the curriculum in ways that will help learners increase their levels of responsibility.

Self-regulated learning has much to contribute to the field of language learning. It has been referred to as "one of the most exciting developments in second or foreign language (L2) teaching" (Oxford, 2011, p. 7). All of the characteristics associated with autonomy are conceptualized within the framework of self-regulated learning and its six dimensions. In contrast to autonomy, self-regulated learning places less emphasis on giving the learner choices and more emphasis on guiding them toward being effective learners without reliance on teacher-imposed structure and control. It focuses on *how* learners can take control of the learning process. These six dimensions provide a framework and process that help teachers to structure assignments and response to develop self-regulated L2 writers. Although other models and frameworks exist (e.g., Oxford, 2011), the six dimensions offer a straightforward and transparent means of implementing self-regulated learning into L2 writing instruction.

Using Teacher Response to Develop Self-Regulated Writers

As the discussion in this chapter has indicated, responding to L2 writers and identifying approaches that help learners become self-regulated are multifaceted topics of high interest. Both areas have potential to help teachers assist L2 learners in strengthening their writing skills, and this potential is even stronger when findings from the two lines of research are integrated. Our premise in this book is that teachers can successfully facilitate the development of self-regulated writers (defined as L2 learners taking responsibility for the factors affecting their ability to write), by using key principles as a framework for response. Although the literature on self-regulated learning refers to motive, methods of learning, time, social/physical environment, and performance as psychological dimensions, in this book they are referred to as principles. This term is commonly used in L2 teaching literature to represent constructs that inform classroom practice and are based in theory and research (Brown, 2007; Ellis, 2005; Kumaravadivelu, 1994, 2006; Larsen-Freeman, 2011; Nunan, 1999; Richards, 2001). The principles establish a foundation for teaching L2 writing from which classroom practices and related activities can be derived.

The framework explored in upcoming chapters addresses common problems relating to L2 writing, such as learners not utilizing teacher comments, lack of learner interest in writing, and teacher investment of large amounts of response time for little return (Gebhard, 2006; Snow, 2006). In exchange, learner responsibility, motivation, and use of strategies throughout the writing process, combined with strategies of response employed by the teacher support incremental and steady improvement. As learners engage in real-world writing tasks, exercise choice, and apply the principles of self-regulated learning, they can overcome the disadvantages of limited class time and short-term formal learning opportunities. Teachers can encourage independence, learning outside of the classroom, and ongoing progress through their methods of response and deliberate learner training in the application of self-regulated learning principles.

The activities in this book are most appropriate for learners with intermediate and advanced levels of proficiency. Language learners need a base line of proficiency to communicate and produce some quantity of writing. Quality of writing can be improved through the application of the approaches explored in each chapter. Chapter 9 provides guidelines for synthesizing all of the principles for a coherent and sustained approach to developing SRL writers. Additionally, it explains how activities can be adapted to various environmental constraints such as teacher experience, individual learners, proficiency levels, and contexts. As stated earlier, best practices in one situation may not be best practices in another. This suggests the need to base practices on sound principles, adapt them appropriately, and create context-based best practices for a specific learner, classroom, program, or institution.

Summary

This chapter has:

- introduced key terms—feedback, response, self-regulated learning, self-regulated writers;
- outlined research-based principles of response to L2 writing and explained the effectiveness of self-regulated learning approaches; and
- established an interdisciplinary theoretical framework of response to aid teachers in facilitating the development of self-regulated writers.

The next chapter:

- explores the self-regulated learning principle of motive, especially why motive is important to self-regulation and how it can benefit language learners generally and L2 writers specifically;
- discusses pedagogical practices that help learners assess, explore, and improve their motivation; and
- shares activities and approaches that teachers can use to respond to learners in ways that will increase their motivation and lead to the development of better writing skills.

Chapter 2

Motive

Objectives

This chapter discusses the principle of motive and its application to L2 writing, and outlines practices and activities for helping learners:

- assess their current levels of motivation;
- adopt strategies for improving motivation;
- understand why a command of written English is important to them personally;
- identify authentic purposes for communicating in writing;
- diagnose their strengths and weaknesses in writing; and
- set goals for improving effective written communication.

Definitions and Applications

Motive, or motivation, refers to reasons for learning. This principle of self-regulated learning examines the question "Why?" Motivation involves internal processes such as goals, beliefs, views, and expectations that shape and direct behavior (Dembo & Seli, 2008). It is related to learners' perceptions of their abilities and how they view past successes and failures—specifically, whether they attribute these outcomes to factors within their control (e.g., diligent study or lack of study, good time management or procrastination) or to factors outside their control (e.g., the teacher, grading practices, luck). Successful learners can motivate themselves even when they do not feel like completing a task. They take responsibility for their own learning, and practice self-regulated learning strategies.

Strategies for improving learner motivation include goal setting, verbal reinforcement, and rewards and punishments (Dembo & Eaton, 2000). Setting goals results in attentiveness to instruction, increased effort, and greater self-confidence when goals are met. Verbal reinforcement consists of positive self-talk related to desirable learning behaviors (e.g., "Great! The new strategy I used allowed me to finish my timed essay in 30 minutes"). In contrast, negative self-talk does not result in improved behavior (e.g., "I can never finish my timed essay in 30 minutes; it's not enough time. The teacher should allow more time"). The latter is not only an example of negative self-talk but attributes failure to an external factor—the teacher. Self-regulated learners also give themselves rewards for positive outcomes and punishments for lack of success on academic tasks. A learner may treat himself to a special dessert for decreasing the number of errors in a composition, or punish himself by not attending a movie with friends for not achieving his goal. Learners who practice these strategies enjoy higher academic performance.

When applied to teaching L2 writing, motive has two primary components: (1) the learner's motivation for learning English, and (2) the learner's motive, or reason, for learning to write in English, including writing a particular composition. The writing teacher needs to address both of these factors when responding to and interacting with learners.

Motive and Language Learning

Motivation in language learning is often described as instrumental or integrative. Instrumental motivation involves learning a language for its practical value, such as to earn a higher salary or pass an exam, whereas integrative motivation focuses on the learner's desire to be involved with the culture and people of the target language (Gardner & Lambert, 1972; Gardner, 1985). Motivation may be influenced by the learning context. In EFL situations, learners may be studying English for instrumental reasons, such as admission to an educational program in an English-speaking country. Those in ESL situations may demonstrate integrative motivation by seeing first-hand the desirability of cultural adjustment and interaction with target language speakers. Both types of motivation can be powerful. However, an integrative motivation potentially leads to greater interaction with the target language group, which positively affects acquisition. Ideally, learners would admire the target language and culture, see value in studying the language, and be eager for the benefits of being bilingual (Cook, 2008).

Although the concepts of instrumental and integrative motivation are specific to language learning, they have not yielded much practical classroom application (Ushioda, 2008). Consequently, cognitive theories of motivation, specifically intrinsic (learning as an end in itself) and extrinsic (learning as a means to achieve a separate outcome) motives, have more appeal. Cognitive theories focus on setting goals, learner self-perceptions, self-efficacy, locus of control, and causal attributions (Pintrich & Schunk, 2002). Both views of motivation provide lenses through which to understand and affect learner behavior. Learning is most effective when motivation originates from the learner rather than being externally imposed (Ushioda, 2008).

Motivation may also be influenced by sociocultural factors such as family background (e.g., being a first-generation student, desiring to meet parental expectations) (Dembo & Seli, 2008), or cultural background (e.g., views toward achievement in higher education, beliefs about teacher and learner roles). In the case of language learning, factors like the importance of the language in the learner's society, the status of the target language, positive and negative images of the culture, attitudes of family and peers toward the target language, and curiosity toward the teacher or the language, potentially impact motivation (Harmer, 2007). Some learners believe that learning a language adds new skills and experience and does not detract from current knowledge (i.e., additive bilingualism), while others believe learning the language threatens what they already know, and subtracts from their cultural identity (Cook, 2008). Those who hold the latter belief will not succeed in learning the language.

Motive and Writing

When learners understand the expectations for written communication in terms of content, organization, and accuracy, and identify why learning to write is important for them personally, they will be motivated to invest the time and effort needed to become effective writers. Similarly, for individual writing assignments, learners must have a clear purpose and conceptualize a specific audience. Learners also need a real interest in the topics they are writing about and need to be involved in authentic communication to the extent possible. The teacher and the classroom environment are important factors in achieving these outcomes.

Teachers need to help learners sustain motivation if they already have it, and increase it if it is initially weak (Harmer, 2007). They can guide learners in ways that assist them in changing their beliefs about motivation, and orchestrate a classroom environment that supports learners taking responsibility for their own learning. In such an environment, the teacher acts as: (1) a motivator who creates conditions to help learners generate ideas, persuades them about the usefulness of an activity, and encourages effort; (2) a resource for providing information, suggestions, and guidance; and (3) a source of feedback to indicate progress, give positive comments, and determine the amount of feedback learners need at various stages of learning and for specific tasks (Harmer, 2004, 2007).

Guiding Classroom Practices

The following set of guiding classroom practices is designed to assist teachers in helping learners understand the principle of learner motivation and how it must be managed so they can develop into self-regulated learners and effective L2 writers. The succeeding section then presents activities that are informed by these guiding practices and that help learners increase their motivation. Although we discuss the practices and activities separately, they work synergistically to influence motivation.

Assess attitudes and needs

Teachers must consider the "reservations and preconceptions of their students" (Cook, 2008, p. 149) as these relate to students' knowledge of the writing process, their reasons for learning to write, their past successes and failures with writing in English, their personal interest in writing, and their L1 writing backgrounds. All of these factors potentially affect motive, which can impact performance. Teachers can use the information they collect to help learners develop specific writing goals. For example, if learners have had little experience writing in their L1 and in English, they may need to set goals related to the writing process. Learners who have had negative experiences with writing may need to identify which part of the writing process led to these experiences, and so on.

Communicate High Expectations

Learners report being motivated to excel by teachers who communicate high expectations (Dembo & Seli, 2008). Achievement is motivating, but it has to be earned and cannot be too easy (Harmer, 2007). Writing requires effort for native and nonnative speakers alike. To communicate successfully, writing must be clear and accurate, thus expectations are naturally high. In speaking, an accent can be considered charming, and communication failures can often be immediately resolved by interlocutors. Not so in writing. Teachers must guide and respond to learners in ways that motivate them to reach expected standards.

Select Motivating Materials and Content

Success in achieving goals creates motivation. Teachers must select materials that are level-appropriate and set manageable assignments in terms of amount and difficulty. Particularly important to motive, writing topics should be of high interest, and the types of writing should be relevant to the learner. Activities and instruction must be meaningful and related to findings of the initial needs analysis. Motivation related to daily classroom activities is short-term but important (Cook, 2008), and over the weeks of a course, it can make a significant difference in learners' attitudes toward writing. As teachers consider topics, materials, and course content, and help learners set and achieve appropriate goals, they can have a positive influence on learners' motivation.

Guide Learners at All Stages of the Writing Process

Teacher response is not limited to comments and grades on final writing products. Teachers must guide and respond along the way to encourage self-regulation. Once information is obtained from the needs analysis, teachers should help learners identify their strengths and weaknesses related to each stage of the writing process (i.e., pre-writing, planning, drafting, revising, editing), and help them set appropriate goals. Then strategies should be taught, practiced, and evaluated. Motivation increases when learners have goals and when these goals are achieved.

Serve as an Audience

The teacher serves as an audience by responding to ideas in a learner's paper (Harmer, 2007). Other members of the class may also act in this role. Having a real audience is critical in providing a motive, or a reason for writing, and for motivating learners to communicate effectively.

Create a Positive Classroom Environment

Learners' views toward the teacher and the course affect learner success (Cook, 2008). Teachers who care, show respect, listen, and offer help will build learner self-esteem (Harmer, 2007). Although the classroom environment is critical to the development of all the components of self-regulated learning, setting high expectations and creating a positive environment in which sharing and support are encouraged provide a foundation for motivation. The teacher's expertise also increases learners' confidence and engagement in their learning process (Harmer, 2007).

Activities and Approaches

The following activities provide practical ways to positively affect learner motivation in the writing classroom. These activities correspond directly to the learning objectives introduced at the beginning of the chapter and support the guiding classroom practices presented in the last section.

Assess Current Levels of Motivation

A number of instruments are available or can be adapted or created to assess learners' motivation. The instruments can focus on motivation for language learning in general or specifically for L2 writing. Beyond these assessment tools, teachers should observe learners' behaviors and comments on an on-going basis to identify their attitudes and help them overcome those that cause them to disengage from the writing process.

Instrumental versus Integrative

The Attitude Motivation Test Battery (AMTB) (Gardner, 2004) measures motivation related to language learning. Example questions include "Studying in English is important because I will be able to interact more easily with speakers of English," "When I am studying English, I ignore distractions, and pay attention to my task," and "I wish I were fluent in English." Most response choices are based on a 6-point Likert scale that ranges from strongly disagree to strongly agree.

This assessment provides a greater understanding of the learner's motivation for learning English, although it is not specifically related to writing. Teachers can explore the concepts of instrumental and integrative motivation with learners and how their motivation affects learning. The findings also provide insights into learner behaviors, some of which are related to self-regulated learning, such as "When I have a problem understanding something in English, I always ask my teacher for help." (This question addresses use of the social environment, the topic of Chapter 6.) Results may be used for learner self-analysis, reflection, and goal setting. (For detailed information about the AMTB, including scoring procedures, search the term *Attitude Motivation Test Battery* using an Internet browser.)

Extrinsic versus Intrinsic

Extrinsic motivation for learning English might be to pass a test in order to get admitted to a university. The reward is admission to the university. The learner does not derive satisfaction from the task of learning English itself. The latter would be considered intrinsic motivation because the learner derives pleasure from the task itself rather than from an external reward.

Various measures of extrinsic and intrinsic motivation related to English language learning are available (e.g., see Carreira, 2005; Kimura, Nakata, & Okumura, 2001; Schmidt, Boraie, & Kassabgy, 1996; Takagi, 2003). Test items are similar to those in the AMTB. Examples are "Being able to speak English will add to my social status," and "One main reason I learn English is that I can meet new people and make friends in my English class" (Schmidt et al., 1996). Teachers should review possible measures to identify one that best fits their learners and classroom context. (For additional ideas related to assessing learners' needs and attitudes, see Scharle & Szabó, 2000.)

Beliefs and Experiences

Early in the course, the teacher can ask learners to reflect on their beliefs and experiences with writing in English and writing in their first language. Learners can respond to questions such as the following, discuss their responses in pairs and small groups, or use the questions as prompts for journal writing.

- How do you feel when you write?
- Have you ever written anything you are proud of?
- Have you had any writing disasters?
- What have you been taught about successful writing?
- What do you believe makes successful writing?
- How much do you like writing in your own language?
- How much do you like writing in English?
- What are the features of a well-written text? (Reid, 1993, p. 165)

The activity guides learners in reflecting on their writing experiences and provides writing practice at the same time. An adaption of the activity follows.

> Write for 5 minutes about your feelings and experiences with writing in both your own language and in English. How do you feel when you write? Have you ever written anything you are proud of? Have you had any writing disasters? What have you been taught about successful writing? What do you believe makes successful writing?

The time limit (e.g., 5 minutes) for the adaptation is designed to build fluency (e.g., see Nation, 2009) and confidence. Learners should be instructed to focus on expressing their thoughts in English without worrying about using correct grammar and vocabulary.

Both versions of the activity allow teachers to examine learner motivation for writing in English and the influence of their past experiences. They also build connections among the teacher and learners, which is conducive to forming a strong classroom environment.

Adopt Strategies for Improving Motivation

A variety of activities for teacher response related to improving learner motivation are next described. These focus on helping learners have positive feelings about themselves and their abilities and adopt behaviors conducive to successful learning.

Positive Self-Talk

One strategy that learners can adopt is to change their verbalizations about their abilities. For example, instead of entertaining defeating thoughts such as "I hate writing," and "I know I'm not going to get a good grade on this assignment," learners should practice positive self-verbalizations. These need

Table 2.1 Positive and Negative Self-Talk

Joshua	Ariel
I'm terrible with grammar. I keep making the same mistakes over and over and I don't understand why. I've heard that university professors just care about your ideas anyway, especially if you're a nonnative speaker.	On my last two papers, I made a lot of verb phrase errors. Looking at these errors, I can see a pattern. Maybe I should ask my teacher or find a tutor at the Writing Center who can explain what I'm doing wrong and suggest some grammar books for me to study.

Discussion Questions

1. How might the self-talk of these writers affect their success in improving their writing?

2. How could Joshua change his self-talk so that it leads to improvement?

3. What types of self-talk do you experience related to writing? What changes can you make so that your attitude is more positive?

4. Write in your journal about your understanding of self-talk. Give examples of your own self-talk related to writing and explain why you think this way. How can you replace negative self-talk with positive self-talk?

to be honest. Learners who convince themselves that they get better grades when they do assignments at the last minute need to understand that this is likely not accurate. If they look at the situation truthfully, they probably feel rushed and stressed and know they can do better.

To address this, teachers can find a reading, create a handout, or give a short presentation on the topic of self-talk. They can also prepare examples of positive and negative self-talk related to writing (see Table 2.1). This should be followed by pair, small group, or whole class discussion based on questions designed to help learners analyze their self-talk. Individual self-reflection, such as journal writing, can also be used.

Internal Attributions

Just as learners need to learn to replace negative self-talk with positive self-talk, they also need to understand that they are in control of their attitudes and emotions, rather than these being determined by other people and events. Learners who attribute their failures to external causes, such as poor teaching or lack of intelligence (e.g., believing they were born with limited intelligence and cannot change this), typically think that change or improvement is outside their control. Attribution theory suggests that when learners believe they are in control of the factors affecting their learning, they are more motivated and able to make the changes needed to be successful (Weiner, 1986).

To aid the development of internal attribution, teachers should lead learners through the writing process to help them see that it takes time and effort (Gebhard, 2006), and that they can be successful if they are willing to invest the time and effort required to be successful. Learners need to be able to see that they are making progress. Portfolio writing is often helpful because learners can see improvements in individual drafts, as well as overall improvement in the work from the beginning to the end of the course. (Portfolios will be discussed in more detail in Chapter 7.) Grading scales that allow learners to see incremental improvements on various aspects of writing (e.g., topic sentences, supporting examples, sentence structure, etc.) are more conducive to showing improvement than holistic evaluations (e.g., assigning a single grade or score to a paper).

Teachers also need to be aware of the kinds of statements learners make, as these show causal attributions. Do they attribute success to luck or failure, to not being smart enough, or to the course being too difficult? These are uncontrollable attributions. To address this, teachers need to be careful about the kinds of comments they make to learners, and they should also practice attribution retraining. For example, instead of saying, "This material is easy," causing learners who are having difficulty to doubt their ability, teachers can say, "You all have the ability to do well in this course" (Perry, 1999). Teachers can respond to learners' comments about the learners' lack of ability by redirecting their focus. When learners say, "Learning to write in English is too hard," teachers can respond with, "You just need to take it a step at a time." Examining the types of verbal comments teachers make and ensuring that those comments are encouraging will help create a positive learning environment and build learners' self-esteem.

Another tool for determining learners' attributions is to have them participate in a self-assessment to help them gain awareness of their beliefs about learning to write. This could consist of a series of statements such as the following, accompanied by a Likert-like scale.

- My successes in writing have been the result of hard work.
- My worst writing experiences were due to a lack of effort.
- Learning to write in English is a skill that can be developed over time.
- I have the ability to learn to write well in English.
- I learn best when my teacher tells me what to write and corrects my errors.

These questions could also be used as prompts for a writing assignment or journal entry. Learners could be asked to agree or disagree with a statement and support their position. The responses will help the teacher understand learners' beliefs about writing and how they view their own abilities.

Rewards and Punishments

Most people like to celebrate their accomplishments with some type of reward. Teachers can build this into a course by publishing class writing. One professor had his students write about a theme related to the institution's 50th anniversary. He compiled the compositions into a small booklet, and each student received a copy. Another semester, students wrote about a folk tale from their countries, and these were published in booklet form. Another teacher organized her writing class around the publication of a newsletter. The learners were responsible for the topics, selection of papers, design, and editing. Some schools sponsor writing contests with categories for both native and nonnative speakers.

All of these activities provide a real-life purpose for writing and a genuine audience. They also reward good writing. Obviously, the teacher should not punish learners for not meeting their goals or for poor writing. The idea is that learners should become responsible for their own learning outcomes. If they do poorly on a test or assignment, then they might choose to forego a leisure activity in order to study. When they do make progress, they may want to treat themselves in some way such as having an ice cream cone or going to a movie.

Understand Why a Command of Written English is Important to Them Personally

Learners need to identify why learning to write in English is important to them, and teachers also need to be aware of this information. It may be that some learners have not taken the time to contemplate how writing might be valuable to their futures. Teachers should guide and respond to learners in ways that help them explore their reasons for learning to write.

Survey or Reflection Paper

The motivation instruments referenced earlier could be a source of questions for a teacher-designed survey to help learners determine their motive for learning to write in English. For example, teachers could create a 10-item survey (see Table 2.2) that learners would take individually, followed by pair or small group discussion or teacher conferencing. Learners might be asked to write about their thoughts as they relate to their survey responses in a journal entry or in a letter to the teacher. The results could be the basis of the first writing assignment for the course.

A questionnaire such as the example in Table 2.2 can be designed to examine motivation and writing, and can be adapted to the teaching context, learners' proficiency levels, and course objectives.

Table 2.2 Determining Motivation for Writing

1. Writing in English is important to me so that I can obtain a good-paying job.

| *Strongly Disagree* | *Moderately* | *Slightly* | *Slightly* | *Moderately* | *Strongly Agree* |

2. I enjoy writing in English.

| *Strongly Disagree* | *Moderately* | *Slightly* | *Slightly* | *Moderately* | *Strongly Agree* |

3. I need to learn to write in English to be successful at school.

| *Strongly Disagree* | *Moderately* | *Slightly* | *Slightly* | *Moderately* | *Strongly Agree* |

4. My parents expect me to learn good writing skills.

| *Strongly Disagree* | *Moderately* | *Slightly* | *Slightly* | *Moderately* | *Strongly Agree* |

5. I need to learn English writing to pass the TOEFL.

| *Strongly Disagree* | *Moderately* | *Slightly* | *Slightly* | *Moderately* | *Strongly Agree* |

6. I don't think I will do much writing in English in the future.

| *Strongly Disagree* | *Moderately* | *Slightly* | *Slightly* | *Moderately* | *Strongly Agree* |

7. Writing in English will help me communicate with native speakers.

| *Strongly Disagree* | *Moderately* | *Slightly* | *Slightly* | *Moderately* | *Strongly Agree* |

8. I prefer learning about and practicing writing more than other language skills, such as listening, speaking, and reading.

| *Strongly Disagree* | *Moderately* | *Slightly* | *Slightly* | *Moderately* | *Strongly Agree* |

9. Learning how to write in English will help me understand written texts in English.

| *Strongly Disagree* | *Moderately* | *Slightly* | *Slightly* | *Moderately* | *Strongly Agree* |

10. I feel proud when I work hard and receive praise on my writing assignments.

| *Strongly Disagree* | *Moderately* | *Slightly* | *Slightly* | *Moderately* | *Strongly Agree* |

Testimonials

Teachers can use role models to get learners to consider why writing is important and to motivate them to excel. The teacher can invite former learners to share their experiences with writing in English while they were enrolled in L2 coursework and in their current situations. Some of these learners may have gone on for further education and can share information about the expectations of their current teachers. Others may be in employment situations where writing in English is required. In both cases, current learners will increase their understanding of the value of writing by listening to those who share similar cultural and linguistic backgrounds and have similar educational and professional goals. Teachers can provide directive questions to the presenters, such as those listed in Table 2.3. An alternative would be to have current learners draft the questions and interview the former learners when they visit the class. The latter leads to greater learner involvement.

If inviting former learners to class is not possible, teachers could gather written or video-taped testimonials and share these with the class.

Regardless of format, follow-up activities might involve having learners discuss in pairs or groups what they learned and how they can apply it. A number of writing assignments could be derived from this activity, such as a comparison/contrast paragraph or essay about two of the guests, or about the writing experiences of both the guest and the learner writing the paper. Learners could interview a former student outside of class, share information about the person with the class, and then write a brief newsletter article about the person. These activities are rich in language learning opportunities, allowing the practice of multiple skills and providing authentic communication situations. They are also fun and build motivation.

Table 2.3 Interviewing Former Learners

1. Share your experiences with learning to write in English. For example, what surprised you? What did you find particularly difficult? What was rewarding?

2. What motivated you to improve your writing in English?

3. Share two or three strategies that have worked well for you as you have learned to write in English.

4. In what ways do you currently use what you have learned about writing? How much do you write? How often do you write? Who is your audience?

5. How do you use the writing process—prewriting, planning, organizing, drafting, revising, editing—to your advantage?

6. What advice do you have for the learners in this class?

Experience Authentic Purposes for Communicating in Writing

Less proficient writers benefit from having a real audience (Gebhard, 2006), and all writers benefit from having a "message-focused purpose" (Nation, 2009, p. 94). Learners need to understand that they are communicating with a reader, and this reader should be someone other than the teacher.

A Real Audience

As a first step to learning how to communicate with a real audience, teachers can incorporate strategic questions to see what learners know about their topic and what additional information is needed in order to communicate effectively with an identified audience. Learners can be questioned about their goals for writing, who might want to read what they are writing, and what information these readers need (Gebhard, 2006).

Beyond helping learners explore reasons for writing and ideas for content, teachers can also organize activities such as dialogue journals to provide learners with an actual audience. Two teachers can arrange for learners in their classes to exchange journals on a weekly basis. In collaboration with the learners, teachers must design journal topics, create guidelines for length, and explain expectations for peer response. The activity motivates learners to write so that they can receive comments from their partners. This experience gives them a real reason for communicating and doing so clearly. At the end of the semester, the learners can meet each other in person at a class party. E-mail exchanges, blogs, and online discussion groups can be used in similar ways depending on the teaching context and availability of technology.

The projects discussed earlier about creating a class newsletter, compiling compositions into a booklet for distribution, or holding a writing contest, also focus on writing for a real audience. Learners recognize that these situations are designed so others can read what they write. Therefore, they understand that they must consider the content needs and expectations of their audience, and convey this information as clearly as possible.

Although writing for the teacher may not be perceived as writing for a real audience, in reality, teachers will often be the sole audience. This has some disadvantages. Learners may write about what they think the teacher wants to hear, or the higher status of the teacher may create social distance (Gebhard, 2006), making it difficult for some learners to express themselves comfortably. To address this, teachers can set up assignments and topics that create real information gaps (Snow, 2006), such as having learners write about information that is known to them and is unknown to the teacher. Examples include subjects such as the learners' countries, families, or childhoods. Teachers can respond in ways that demonstrate interest in and a sincere desire to obtain the information. For example, a teacher might ask questions about advice for tourists visiting the learner's country, such as "What traditional dishes would you recommend to someone visiting your country who does not like spicy food?" or "What activities are available for those who cannot do much walking?" Teachers must help learners understand that they are writing to communicate their ideas about the topic, not simply to fulfill the assignment requirements.

High Interest Topics

Related to an authentic purpose for writing is choosing topics that interest and motivate the writer. When one has little to say about a topic, writing is nearly impossible. Learners can create an issue log on a topic of interest and follow the topic over the semester (Nation, 2009). They become an expert on that topic by gathering information from newspapers, magazines, TV, and other sources. They provide weekly oral reports to classmates and write a weekly summary. This activity creates a strong knowledge base. It builds schema about topics of interest and engages others in the class who are eager to hear the next installment. Authority lists perform a similar function. Learners create a list of topics on which they are experts (or at least have some background knowledge), and draw from this list for writing assignments during the semester (Reid, 1993).

Diagnose Strengths and Weaknesses in Writing

Teachers typically have learners write something within the first few days of class to determine what they know and where they need help. Diagnosing strengths and weaknesses is important to motivation in that it is needed before learners can set goals for improvement; learners with goals are more academically successful than those who do not have goals.

Teachers will need to determine a philosophy of feedback, the degree to which they will focus on content or form, and how various elements of the writing will be weighted for grading purposes. (The literature related to response was reviewed in Chapter 1.) Consideration must also be given to the learner's future needs for writing in English. A balanced approach to content and form is likely appropriate.

Diagnostic Tools to Focus on Form

Teachers can use tools such as tally sheets to help learners set goals related to accuracy. Grammar correction symbols can be used to mark errors, and learners can tally the number of each type of error on each assignment during the course. Many writing textbooks contain a system for marking grammatical errors. It is helpful to have examples of the errors for the

Table 2.4 Grammar Correction Marks

_♂_	omit	He needed books, papers and pens ~~and etc.~~
⌃	something missing	During class ⌃fell asleep.
inc.	incomplete sentence	(Because he wanted to go.) [inc.]
ro	run-on sentence	My friend was studying in his room from his [ro] desk he could see the tennis courts.
ss	sentence structure	(They brought the man who they him found.) [ss]
t	verb tense	He is here since June. [t]
vp	verb phrase	It was happened yesterday. [vp]
sv	subject–verb agreement	The three boys on the bus goes to town. [sv]
∿	word order	I saw five times that movie.
wf	word form	We enjoy to play tennis. [wf]
wc	word choice	It was raining, then I took my umbrella. [wc]
d	determiner	We climbed mountain every day. [d]
pp	preposition	She arrived at Honolulu yesterday. [pp]
spg	spelling	I go to class evreyday. [spg]
c	capitalization	The Aloha center is closed for a week. [c]
p	punctuation	What else could I say. [p]
s/pl	singular/plural	We have been here for six month. [s/pl]
c/nc	count/non-count noun	We need a lot of informations for the report. [c/nc]
?	meaning is not clear	(He borrowed some smoke.) [?]
awk	awkward wording	(He will have five years) on his next birthday. [awk]
¶	new paragraph	

Table 2.5 Error Tally Sheet

	Assignment #1	Assignment #2	Assignment #3	Assignment #4	Assignment #5	Assignment #6
ℓ						
∧						
inc						
ro						
ss						
t						
vp						
sv						
⌒						
wf						
wc						
d						
pp						
spg						
c						
p						
s/pl						
c/nc						
?						
awk						
¶						

Note: Adapted from "Effects of Dynamic Corrective Feedback on ESL Writing Accuracy," by K. J. Hartshorn, N. Evans, P. Merrill, R. Sudweeks, D. Strong-Krause, and N. J. Anderson, 2010, *TESOL Quarterly, 44*, p. 108. Copyright 2010 by TESOL, Inc. Adapted with permission

learners. Table 2.4 provides a possible symbol system, and Table 2.5 provides a sample tally sheet. On the tally sheet, the assignment number, a description of the assignment, the date, or a combination of this information can be recorded at the top.

The tally of errors on the first few writing assignments helps determine if learners have recurring or widespread errors. The former might be the result of a pattern having not yet been acquired by the learner, and the latter by carelessness. In either case, teachers can work with learners to analyze the tally sheet and determine specific goals.

Diagnostic Tools to Focus on Meaning

Less proficient writers tend to begin a writing task without pre-writing and may focus on form too quickly, rather than examining meaning (Gebhard, 2006). As teachers respond to learners' work, stressing content over form will encourage the learner's desire to communicate (Gebhard, 2006). One means of achieving a balanced approach to content and form is to use a checklist or feedback sheet for each assignment. In this way, teachers can determine the emphasis of content and form based on course objectives and learner needs. Learners can use checklists to review their work prior to submission, and the teacher can use them to provide feedback and assign grades. Checklists can also be used for peer review (see Chapter 7).

Most writing textbooks have examples of checklists or scoring sheets. These, however, often have yes/no questions such as, "Do you have a topic sentence?" "Have you used transition words correctly?", or "Is your spelling and capitalization correct?" Most learners simply circle "Yes" and submit their papers to the teacher. Checklists with open-ended questions that require comments are more effective learning tools than those of the yes/no variety. An example for paragraph writing is provided in Table 2.6. The form can be adjusted for varying levels of proficiency. An example for teacher use, which includes a scoring scale, is included in Table 2.7.

Learners will need teachers to model how to use feedback sheets such as those shown in Tables 2.6 and 2.7. Teachers should complete an example with the class and provide good samples for the learners to review. Learners may need guidance the first few times they complete the form. A cautionary note: If time is not given in class for training and modeling, the form will be completed superficially and have limited value. It may be helpful to use a standard feedback sheet for each assignment so that learners grow accustomed to it.

The teacher feedback sheet in Table 2.7 can help learners identify weaknesses in specific areas. The comments are particularly important because learners will need to know the rationale for their scores—why they received a 3 as opposed to a 2 or 4, for example. Grading criteria always needs to be explained. Additionally, feedback that motivates will help the learner write more and learn to enjoy writing (Nation, 2009).

Conferences

To help learners identify strengths and weaknesses in their writing, teachers should conference with the learner briefly in class, or for a longer period of time outside of class. Teachers will need to determine the number of conferences they are able to have with each learner during a course, but some type of initial one-on-one interaction is critical in the diagnostic stage.

Table 2.6 Learner Feedback Sheet

Writing Feature	To Do—Check the box when you have completed the item
Topic Sentence	☐ Write your topic sentence below.
	☐ Explain how the topic sentence helps narrows the topic.
Supporting Details	☐ List the examples, reasons, and facts in the paragraph.
	☐ Explain why you think you have enough support for the topic sentence.
Concluding Sentence	☐ Write your concluding sentence below.
	☐ Explain how the concluding sentence restates the topic sentence.
Paragraph Format	☐ Have a friend or classmate check that the first line of the paragraph is indented and that margins are used correctly.
	☐ Ask your friend or classmate to sign below.
Punctuation and Spelling	☐ Use the spell checker. Read each sentence carefully and look at your punctuation and spelling.
	☐ Write any words or sentences you have questions about below.
Sentence Structure and Verb Forms	☐ Use the grammar checker. Read each sentence carefully. Have a classmate read your paragraph and tell you about any sentences that are unclear. Revise those sentences.
	☐ Put the original and the revision of at least one sentence below.
Transition Words and Connectors	☐ Check that you have used correct transitions and correct punctuation.
	☐ Write an example of a sentence using a transition word below.

Table 2.7 Teacher Feedback/Scoring Sheet

Topic Sentence—introduces the topic of the paragraph and has a controlling idea.			
1	2	3	4
Ineffective			Effective

Comments:

Supporting details—uses a sufficient number of examples, reasons, opinions.			
1	2	3	4
Ineffective			Effective

Comments:

Concluding sentence—restates the topic sentence.			
1	2	3	4
Ineffective			Effective

Comments:

Paragraph format—indents first line; uses margins correctly.			
1	2	3	4
Ineffective			Effective

Comments:

Punctuation and spelling—verify correct usage.			
1	2	3	4
Ineffective			Effective

Comments:

Sentence structure and verb forms—correctly used with few errors that interfere with meaning.			
1	2	3	4
Ineffective			Effective

Comments:

Transition words and connectors—correctly used.			
1	2	3	4
Ineffective			Effective

Comments:

Furthermore, whenever assignments are returned, teachers should allow class time for learners to review comments and ask questions. (We provide further discussion of conferencing and its various purposes in Chapters 4 and 6.) A key guideline for successful writing conferences is for the teacher to encourage learners to take responsibility for asking questions. This requires that learners identify the purpose of the conference and the questions they need to ask. Once again, effective use of conferencing takes training and modeling because it is unfamiliar to many learners.

Set Goals for Improving Effective Written Communication

The goal-setting stage is an opportunity for teachers to emphasize high expectations for the course. That learners are required to set goals, which are regularly reviewed and reflected on, sends a clear message that progress and improvement are expected. Learners who have difficulty identifying goals may benefit from examples. They also need to understand that writing does not begin with the first sentence or end with the last word (Snow, 2006). They must be introduced to the writing process. Goals can potentially be set for various parts of the writing process, depending on learners' strengths and weaknesses.

Choice and Autonomy

Although teachers can guide, direct, and facilitate goal-setting, learners must choose their own meaningful goals. The teacher's goal is to help learners become self-regulated; this entails allowing and encouraging learners to take ownership for what they need to work on. Generally, the goals will be short term, over the time of the course. Goals should focus on application of course content. Class time needs to be allowed for regular review of goals and modification.

Accuracy Goals

A primary focus for goal-setting is accuracy. Readers expect writing to be accurate, and although some argue for the acceptance of a variety of Englishes (Matsuda, 2006), our position is that in most cases this can be a disadvantage to learners, who must be able to hold their own in academic and professional arenas. The use of tally sheets, described earlier, can help learners identify grammatical challenges. A first step is to identify frequently occurring errors with a simple activity such as the one on the next page.

Based on your writing this semester, identify three grammar errors that you frequently make and that you would like to focus on during the semester. Your tally sheet may be helpful to you in identifying the types of errors you make most often.

1.

2.

3.

The next step is to set specific goals related to these errors, such as in the following example:

To improve accuracy in using the present perfect tense, I will:

- review two grammar books to gain a better understanding of how to use the present perfect tense;
- complete six different grammar exercises based on usage of perfect tenses;
- rewrite sentences with present perfect tense errors in my current essay;
- underline all verb phrases in my next composition and study them carefully to determine if correct verb tenses and forms have been used; and
- make an appointment with a tutor or native speaker and ask that person to review all verbs in my next essay.

Teachers need to provide examples of goals and ideas for how to achieve them, such as familiarizing learners with available resources (e.g., textbooks, websites, tutoring services).

Writing Process Goals

Learning goals can be derived from all aspects of the writing process and from all components of writing. As teachers work with learners and observe their writing strategies, they can provide feedback regarding various parts of the writing process or components of good writing that learners may be neglecting. Throughout the course, teachers should focus on various strategies related to the writing process such as brainstorming, mapping, and cubing for pre-writing; outlining or diagramming for planning; and underlining sentence parts that may be troublesome, such as subjects, verbs, or articles for editing.

Teachers may also want to give learners a self-assessment on their familiarity with and ability to use various aspects of writing. A possible survey to this effect is provided in Table 2.8, based on a vocabulary survey (Read, 2000). Any writing concept can be slotted into the survey; we provide just a few examples. The survey allows teachers and learners to explore leaners' previous knowledge about writing and to help them set goals in areas that are less familiar or need mastery.

Table 2.8 Writing Concepts Familiarity Survey

Pre-writing

1. I have not seen this term before.

2. I have seen this term before, but don't know what it is.

3. I have seen this term before, and I think it means _____

4. I know this term. It means _____

5. I know how to do this in writing and do it regularly.

Unity

1. I have not seen this term before.

2. I have seen this term before, but don't know what it is.

3. I have seen this term before, and I think it means _____

4. I know this term. It means _____

5. I know how to do this in writing and do it regularly.

Outlining

1. I have not seen this term before.

2. I have seen this term before, but don't know what it is.

3. I have seen this term before, and I think it means _____

4. I know this term. It means _____

5. I know how to do this in writing and do it regularly.

Topic Sentence

1. I have not seen this term before.

2. I have seen this term before, but don't know what it is.

3. I have seen this term before, and I think it means _____

4. I know this term. It means _____

5. I know how to do this in writing and do it regularly.

Coherance

1. I have not seen this term before.

2. I have seen this term before, but don't know what it is.

3. I have seen this term before, and I think it means _____

4. I know this term. It means _____

5. I know how to do this in writing and do it regularly.

Drafting

1. I have not seen this term before.

2. I have seen this term before, but don't know what it is.

3. I have seen this term before, and I think it means _____

4. I know this term. It means _____

5. I know how to do this in writing and do it regularly.

Strategic Questions

Strategic questions can be used to get learners to identify possible goals. Teachers can give learners a list of concepts related to writing in general and specifically to course objectives—such as writing a topic sentence, the controlling idea, the thesis statement, supporting details, transitions, planning, drafting—and ask learners the following questions.

- In which of these areas of writing do you feel you need to practice?
- What is your goal? What do you need to find out?
- How will you get this information?
- How will you improve your skill in this area?
- How can I help?

Questioning their own writing helps learners self-assess and puts them in charge of their learning. This activity can be done when the teacher returns the first or second assignment, complete with feedback.

Awareness of New Approaches to Writing

To help learners become familiar with a variety of approaches, teachers can ask them to answer specific questions about their habits, motives, and methods related to writing or have them describe these in a composition or journal. For instance, learners can write about the steps they take in approaching an assignment. How do they begin? How do they generate ideas? How do they organize their writing? What strategies do they use for revision and editing? How do they motivate themselves to start writing and to finish an assignment before the deadline? This information can be shared and a master class list of strategies compiled. The list can then be discussed and amended as the teacher introduces concepts and approaches throughout the course. Learners can use the list to generate goals.

Language Learning Plan

The goal of this book is to help learners become self-regulated and take responsibility for their own learning. In order to do this, learners should have a definite plan. Learners may be unsuccessful in language learning because they do not see any progress, lack opportunities to use the language, and find learning more work than fun (Snow, 2006). Given this, teachers need to help learners get to the point where they can use the language in a meaningful way, and achieve their goals for studying the language. Seeing progress and using the language for a real purpose is extremely motivating. Goals should be narrow and specific; learners should share information with the teacher about the goal, their reasons for choosing it, and a method for how they will accomplish it (Snow, 2006).

The suggestions in this chapter guide learners through the process of determining their reasons for learning to write in English, assessing their strengths and weaknesses, and setting goals. In essence, this is their language learning plan. Subsequent chapters will help learners address all aspects of becoming self-regulated writers. (We will specifically address how to help learners be accountable for their goals in Chapter 7.)

Summary

This chapter has:

- defined and explored the concept of motivation generally as it relates to language learning and to L2 writing specifically;
- identified key pedagogical practices involved in guiding and responding to writing to improve learner motivation; and
- provided a range of learner activities and approaches designed to improve motivation and writing skill and to develop self-regulated L2 writers.

The next chapter:

- explores the self-regulated learning component of methods; in this case, methods of response to writing and how various response techniques can benefit language learners generally and L2 writers specifically;
- discusses pedagogical practices to guide teachers in using different methods of response and in modeling how learners can use feedback to facilitate the development of self-regulated L2 writers; and
- shares activities and approaches that teachers can use to assist learners in understanding and benefiting from various types of teacher response.

Chapter 3

Methods of Learning

Objectives

This chapter discusses the principle of methods of learning and its application to L2 writing, and outlines practices and activities for helping learners:

- improve their ability to draft and revise;
- develop strategies for using form-focused teacher response;
- understand expectations and grading criteria;
- adopt new roles;
- identify preferences for types of feedback; and
- use self-evaluation tools.

Definitions and Applications

Methods of learning refer to *how* learners learn. They consist of the tools, techniques, and strategies learners use to acquire knowledge. Low-achievers typically use few learning strategies and may mistakenly attribute their lack of success to ability rather than recognizing the real cause—not knowing *how* to learn. In fact, they use the same one or two strategies for all tasks (Dembo & Eaton, 2000). Inherent ability is beyond one's control, but familiarity with learning strategies is not. Learners who have a wide array of strategies are higher achievers than those who possess a limited number of strategies (Zimmerman & Martinez-Pons, 1986). Successful learners also have the ability to apply strategies appropriately. When learners have been taught a range of strategies and are able to choose those most effective for a particular task, they are on their way to becoming self-regulated learners.

Effective methods of learning focus on the cognitive aspect of self-regulated learning and include practices such as rehearsal, elaboration, and organization (Dembo & Eaton, 2000; Dembo & Seli, 2008). Rehearsal might involve memorizing lists of words and definitions, underlining important information in textbooks, or taking notes from a lecture. Although appropriate for some learning tasks, these activities do not connect new information to knowledge held in long-term memory. This limits their value. Elaboration, which consists of activities such as summarizing, paraphrasing, asking and answering questions, and creating analogies, has more potential for long-term memory storage and retrieval. Learners who write questions based on their notes or compose a brief summary of the main points of a lecture, remember information better than those who write down only what the professor says and read through their notes the night before an exam. Similarly, organizing material into a chart or graph is an example of a strategy that aids the storage of information in long-term memory and facilitates information retrieval.

Much has been written about methods of learning that aid in acquiring a language and learning to write in a second language. We briefly examine these two areas as a foundation for the primary focus of this chapter—building strategies that help learners understand and benefit from teacher response to their writing. Because teacher feedback is designed to improve the writing of L2 learners, strategies for how learners can use this feedback leads to the development of self-regulated writers. Teachers should respond to learners at all stages of the writing process to guide and direct improvement.

Methods of Learning and Language Learning

Language learning strategies have been variously defined over the past several decades, as shown in Table 3.1. As indicated earlier, high-achieving learners in general possess a range of strategies and know how and when to use them. The same is true for language learners—proficient language learners possess a broad array of strategies and use them frequently (O'Malley & Chamot, 1990). They know how to combine strategies for more complex tasks, and they take an active approach to learning (Oxford, 2008). "It is not the *presence* or *absence* of a strategy that leads to effective learning; rather it is *how* that strategy is used (or not used) to accomplish tasks and learner goals" (Rubin, 2008, pp. 11–12). Teachers must consider differences in learners (e.g., age, L1 background, gender, learning styles, culture) and learning contexts (e.g., teaching methods, physical and social environment). Teachers must also keep in mind that a strategy that is effective for one learner or one situation may not be effective for all.

Language learning strategies which are aimed at promoting autonomy have been grouped into four categories: metacognitive, affective, cognitive, and social-interactive (Oxford, 2008), as discussed in Chapter 1. The self-regulated learning categories—metacognitive, motivation, cognitive, and behavior—are similar to these language learning categories, but with a few differences. For instance, Oxford's social-interactive category emphasizes the learner's environment and its importance for facilitating learning, as does the self-regulated learning category of behavior, although the latter has broader applications (i.e., physical environment, use of time, performance, etc.). The

Table 3.1 Language Learning Strategies Defined

Time	Definition	Source
1970s	"Techniques or devices which a learner may use to acquire knowledge"	Rubin, 1975, p. 43
1980s	"Set of operations or steps used by a learner that will facilitate the acquisition, storage, retrieval, or use of information"	O'Malley, Chamot, Stewner-Manzanares, Kupper, & Russo, 1985, p. 23
1990s	"Specific actions taken by the learner to make learning easier, faster, more enjoyable, more self-directed, more effective, and more transferable to new situations"	Oxford, 1990, p. 8
2000s	"Activities consciously chosen by learners for the purpose of regulating their own language learning"	Griffiths, 2008, p. 87

other three categories—metacognitive, affective/motivation, and cognitive—are essentially the same. However, the six principles of self-regulated learning further define the categories and offer a concrete, guiding framework. Each principle involves learning strategies; self-regulated learning is achieved through the application of these strategies. Our focus in this chapter is on a single principle, the methods or strategies for *how* to learn, specifically for *how* to use teacher response to achieve self-regulated learning skills.

Methods of Learning and Writing

ESL writing textbooks focus on various methods for learning how to write. They provide models of rhetorical patterns, activities for determining unity and coherence, and practice in writing thesis statements. They guide learners through strategies for prewriting and planning, such as brainstorming, concept mapping, and outlining. They help learners narrow a topic and identify different types of support. Strategies for learning how to write in a second language are plentiful for all stages of the writing process.

Our focus is on strategies associated with teacher response. We support the approach that "teachers should intervene with editorial comment, motivating suggestions, or language advice" (Harmer, 2004, p. 108) to produce short- and long-term improvement in writing. Feedback that directs learners to simply follow teacher suggestions and fosters dependency does not result in long-term gains (Gordon, 2008). To develop self-regulated learning, learners must be actively engaged in the decision-making processes related to revision and editing, and be helped to hold themselves accountable for using feedback.

Guiding Classroom Practices

The guiding classroom practices that follow offer a foundation for teacher response. They address methods of response, ways to encourage learners to use teacher and peer response, and learning approaches that can be used to achieve self-regulation. These are followed by corresponding activities and approaches in the next section.

Consider the Purpose for the Response

Assessment has four purposes: (1) to motivate, (2) diagnose problems, (3) improve quality, and (4) measure proficiency (Nation, 2009). The first purpose, motivation, can be accomplished through teacher response that provides learners with positive feedback. Motivation is also strengthened when response helps learners establish an authentic reason for writing and identify a specific audience (see Chapter 2). Another purpose for response is to diagnose problems in ways that help learners recognize and address error patterns. This is connected to the third purpose for assessment—improving the quality of writing. The latter occurs when learners understand problem areas in their writing and how to apply teacher response in their revisions. The last purpose of response, measuring proficiency, involves providing summative feedback, which is most appropriate on final drafts and is necessary to placement, grading, and advancement decisions. This type of response evaluates the learner's ability to address weaknesses identified by feedback during the course of study. While grades are easy to understand for exercises and single-answer tests, they are less easy to understand for creative work (Harmer, 2007). Thus, learners need to understand what their grades (numeric or letter) on writing assignments actually represent.

Response can take various forms such as oral explanations, margin and end notes, indirect correction (e.g., use of symbols), direct correction, rubrics, and comments made with software tracking systems. Teachers must consider the purposes for response, appropriate formats, how to use different types and combinations of response, and how to help learners understand them.

Allow Choice

Three ways to foster autonomy, or self-regulated learning, are: (1) allowing choice of materials, (2) changing teacher and learner roles, and (3) developing learner networks (Candlin & Byrnes, 1995). To create self-regulated writers, the role of the teacher is to encourage choice and expand options for learning. For this to be successful, the teacher must establish a supportive atmosphere and encourage risk-taking, make constructive judgments and evaluations, have learners communicate about their learning, and involve learners in posing problems and communicating with others to confirm their knowledge and abilities (Hurd, Beaven, & Ortega, 2001). Teachers act as facilitators and guides, with learners being actively engaged in decisions about their learning. Learner networks, including communicating with other learners, and collaborative reflection on learning processes, are the focus of Chapter 6.

Use a Variety of Methods for Response

Teachers need a collection of methods they can employ to help learners develop awareness of their strengths and weaknesses (Hyland & Hyland, 2006a), an important step in achieving self-regulation. Teachers should measure the effects of various methods for each learner, and determine what works best in specific contexts. All methods have advantages and disadvantages, and learners have personal preferences. For example, end notes are helpful for summarizing strengths and weaknesses, but they do not allow for making suggestions at relevant points in the paper. Asking questions orally or in writing about content can provide a sense of audience and place responsibility for changes on the learner, but may confuse those who expect more direct guidance. The use of symbols or underlining errors may be appropriate to learners less-skilled in editing, while noting the number of errors in a paragraph may assist those who are more advanced. Regardless of the method, feedback should be constructive, helpful, and clear (Hyland & Hyland, 2006a). Teachers must also balance the amount of praise and criticism they provide. Too much praise signifies that the learner is doing fine and does not result in change; too much criticism can lead to discouragement.

Determine the Focus and Extent of Response

Teachers must decide when to focus on form and when to focus on content. Although some scholars advise not focusing on form until the final draft so that learners are able to express their thoughts without concern for accuracy (Gebhard, 2006; Gordon, 2008; Harmer, 2007), we support the view that teachers should respond to what is relevant, regardless of the draft (Ferris & Hedgcock, 2005). Because meaning is affected by ungrammatical constructions, a focus on meaning alone is difficult to maintain. Ideas and language cannot be separated (Hyland & Hyland, 2006a). The end goal is to help learners communicate effectively; therefore, teachers need to tailor their approach for specific learners and drafts.

Teachers should also determine whether to adopt a selective or a comprehensive approach. The former involves responding to only parts of a draft or to only a few areas, while the latter includes responding to all areas needing improvement. Generally, learners will benefit more from a limited amount of response (Snow, 2006). Marking too many errors may be confusing (Gebhard, 2006). Selective methods include identifying two to four major feedback points, addressing persistent problems, commenting on areas of progress, or focusing on application of principles taught (Ferris & Hedgcock, 2005). Response may also be aimed at patterns of errors, serious errors, or errors that are difficult to self-correct (Snow, 2006). Errors that learners can correct based on grammar rules can be marked with symbols (indirect correction), while those that are idiosyncratic, represent exceptions to rules, or are beyond the learner's ability can be corrected by the teacher (direct correction). If response is selective, teachers should explain their rationale for not marking all errors. Learners may expect the teacher to mark everything that is "wrong" with their writing.

Ensure Learner Use of Teacher Feedback

The purpose of teacher response is to ensure that learners do something with the advice to improve their writing, rather than looking at the grade and setting the paper aside (Harmer, 2004; Snow, 2006). Teachers should explain error symbols, check lists, and response sheets; model how to respond to comments; allow class time for learners to review comments and ask questions; and require learners to include a cover memo with revisions explaining how they responded to feedback (Ferris & Hedgcock, 2005). Prior to submitting a writing assignment, learners might be asked to list points on which they would like feedback, or learners can be asked to keep a grammar notebook with examples of errors and corrections (Snow, 2006). Summary reports outlining achievements and strengths and areas for future improvement (Harmer, 2007) will help learners set goals and monitor their progress.

Activities and Approaches

Given that "the use of strategies embodies taking active, timely, coordinated responsibility for learning" and is "both learnable and teachable" (Oxford, 2008, p. 52), we propose the following activities and approaches for teacher response and for learners' implementation of teacher response to improve their writing.

Improve Ability to Draft and Revise

Learners who are unfamiliar with the writing process or who have different cultural approaches to writing may not understand why revision is necessary or how to do it. The ability to revise is crucial to becoming self-regulated and managing the writing process; however, it develops gradually. To help learners understand that writing involves more than simply putting words to paper in a single sitting, teachers should introduce them to multiple possibilities for exploring a topic and expressing their ideas.

Reformulation

One way to help learners understand the importance of revision and editing is to show alternatives for problematic expressions through reformulation. Teachers can select a paragraph from a learner's composition and rewrite it (Harmer, 2007). The reformulation can reflect improvements in content, organization, or grammar, or a combination of these depending on the learning objective or purpose for the activity. Learners then compare the reformulation with the original. As part of this process, learners should be given the opportunity to ask questions about the rationale for various aspects of the teacher's revision. This could occur in a class session, working with a peer, or in a one-on-one conference with the teacher.

Learners then revise the paragraph in their own way without referring to the reformulation. When the revision is submitted, learners can include a summary of what they learned and how the reformulation influenced their revision. Summarizing is a type of elaboration strategy that aids learning. For lower level learners, teachers can demonstrate how a sentence could be rewritten, after which learners compare their version to the teacher's version and redraft (Harmer, 2004).

Multiple Versions and Self-Evaluation

An alternative activity to reformulation is to have learners write three versions of a paragraph, letter, or other type of composition. Depending on the assignment, learners can consider changing different parts of an essay— such as the introduction, supporting examples, or conclusion—or modifying parts of a narrative—such as the events, climax, point of view, setting, or characters (Gebhard, 2006). The learner reviews the three versions and selects one for the teacher to respond to or grade, including a note about why it was selected. This activity not only helps learners explore the process of revision, but involves choice and develops self-evaluation skills.

Develop Strategies for Using Form-Focused Teacher Response

The act of editing for form (i.e., grammatical errors) in and of itself will not create self-regulated writers. Learners need to reflect on the editing process, identify gaps in knowledge, and set related goals. The ability of L2 writers to self-edit develops gradually; teachers need to guide learners, be patient, and help learners be patient. Guidance can occur as teachers help learners ask appropriate questions, determine error patterns, and identify how to correct errors. The following strategies demonstrate how teachers can facilitate learner use of form-related response.

Progressive Editing

In addition to revision, which involves content and organization changes, another stage of the writing process that needs to be addressed is editing for grammatical errors. Although reformulation can be aimed at improving accuracy, additional strategies are available. Chapter 2 introduced the use of grammar symbols and tally sheets for diagnosing weaknesses and setting goals. For learners to improve grammatical accuracy, they need to understand and know how to respond to the teacher's error-related markings. They also need to understand that focusing on editing really involves focusing on meaning, as grammar must be accurate in order for communication to occur.

Depending on the instructional objective, teachers can mark the majority of errors, or they might focus on errors that interfere with meaning (i.e., global errors), that are stigmatizing or distracting (i.e., local errors), or those related to what has been recently taught. As stated earlier when we reviewed guiding practices associated with methods of learning, teachers must evaluate what individual learners need to help them improve their writing throughout the writing process. Teachers must understand that the amount and difficulty of editing expected must be manageable and appropriate to the learner's proficiency level.

To support the development of self-regulated writers, teachers should gradually encourage learners to take more responsibility for finding and correcting grammatical errors. For example, as editing ability improves, teachers can decrease the specificity of their markings. Instead of indicating exactly what the error is (e.g., article, word form, etc.) and where it is located, they can underline the error, place a check mark at the beginning of the sentence or in the margin, indicate the number of errors in a sentence or paragraph, or comment at the end of the piece of writing on the types of errors needing correction. Each of these stages involves careful structuring by the teacher to guide the development of independent editing.

Ten-Minute Paragraphs

This activity involves progressive editing, but adds a specific structure for it. Learners are given a topic at the beginning of a class period and asked to write a paragraph within a 10-minute time limit (Evans et al., 2010a). Learners should focus on organization, content, and accuracy. The teacher collects the paragraphs, marks the errors with symbols (see Chapter 2, Table 2.4 for examples of error correction symbols), and assigns a score with a 75% weighting for accuracy and 25% for content. The teacher returns the paragraphs in the next class period. Learners tally their errors (see Chapter 2, Table 2.5 for an example of a tally sheet) and compile a list of their errors in context. They then correct their errors, type the paragraph, and resubmit it. The teacher indicates any remaining errors with a check mark, circle, or underlining, and returns it to the learner for further editing as needed. Error tallying and listing is repeated. The goal is to have an error-free paragraph. This can generally be accomplished within two drafts as learners increase their awareness of errors and their ability to edit.

Scaffolding

Vygotsky's (1978) zone of proximal development views learning as a social process whereby learners can move beyond their current level of development with guidance and collaboration. Scaffolding involves providing guidance to the learner through background information, modeling a strategy or task, whole class or small group work, and so forth. The scaffolding is gradually decreased so that the learner is able to assume greater responsibility for performing tasks independently. Successful scaffolding depends on building a community of learning in which learners are comfortable sharing their work, helping each other, and soliciting assistance from the teacher (see Chapter 6). Scaffolding is not limited to the editing stage but can be implemented for any component of the writing process and added to any activity.

With regard to focusing on form, the previous activities of progressive editing and 10-minute paragraphs are examples of teacher-led scaffolding. Scaffolding can also be implemented by partnering learners with a classmate possessing slightly more skill or a different linguistic background, so that L1 interference related to error correction is minimized. Learners can assist each other by sharing grammatical knowledge related to form-focused response. Learners can use highlighter pens in different colors to mark features of organization (topic sentences, transitions, supporting ideas) or grammar constructions (areas of weakness, structures recently taught). They could also be asked to find a certain number of errors (e.g., 10) in their partner's papers—limiting themselves to constructions that they know are incorrect, and that they know how to explain to their partners. In this way, the learners are stretched slightly beyond their ability to develop improved editing skills.

Scaffolding may involve methods of learning such as collaboration with peers, elaboration (summarizing, paraphrasing, and asking and answering questions), and application of concepts learned to subsequent work. Teachers may assign learners to take notes, provide oral or written summaries, or incorporate some personal reflection related to their writing and editing activities.

Hints

Regardless of the learning configuration (i.e., independent or peer-based) or activity, the teacher should be available to provide direction—generally with hints by way of questioning rather than by giving direct answers. For instance, depending on the error, a teacher might say, "Read the sentence aloud. Does it sound right? What do you think sounds strange?" "Use your spell checker." "You have two events in the past. One happened before the other. What tense do you use in this case?" "The word *they* is plural, so what form of the verb do you need?" This technique represents a facilitator role conducive to the development of self-regulated writers, as opposed to a teacher-centered role that encourages passive learning.

Modeling

Modeling demonstrates to learners what is involved in revision and editing, how to fix common problems, and what the teacher expects (Nation, 2009). This can be accomplished in a number of ways. Teachers can write sentences with errors on the board and guide learners through the editing process or have the class assist in editing the sentences and explaining the rationale for the changes. Handouts with selected sentences or paragraphs can serve the same purpose, as can overhead transparencies, PowerPoint slides, or Word documents projected on a screen. Computer classrooms allow the teacher and learners to view and work on the same document from different stations.

Throughout this process, teachers must be sensitive to the feelings of the author of the composition—emphasize the good points along with those needing improvement, ask for volunteers to have their papers discussed, and maintain confidentiality of the authors of example papers. Modeling is important not only for editing but for all aspects of the writing process. It can aid learners in becoming self-regulated writers, but needs to be ongoing and with continual practice.

Resources and Guides

In editing-related discussions, references can be made to grammar lessons previously given, textbook explanations, online help, and so forth. A number of books focus specifically on editing, and include grammar explanations, related exercises, and flowcharts (e.g., Lane & Lange, 1999; Raimes, 2004). Online writing labs, often called OWLs, are also excellent sources of information and are often more accessible, convenient, and easier to search than traditional textbooks. Class time should be provided so that learners can look up answers to their questions online and in books and get assistance from the teacher until they develop greater independence. Teachers should help learners identify specific questions and how to access the relevant sources of information.

Teachers can also design their own guides, such as the one in Figure 3.1. The guide shown in Figure 3.1 is a general example and can be adapted for different proficiency levels. It is most useful if introduced after a review of the appropriate grammar rules or a presentation of examples, and when it is

Answer the questions to help you determine correct article usage. Remember, these are general rules; be aware of exceptions.

1. **Is the noun proper or common?**

   Proper

   - Use Ø article for singular names of people, singular country names (e.g., George, Annette; England, Samoa).

   - Use *the* for plural family names (e.g., the Browns); oceans, rivers, mountain ranges, public buildings (e.g., the Thames, the Himalayas); names of plural countries and those that contain words such as *united, union, kingdom, republic* (e.g., *the* United States, *the* Kingdom of Tonga).

   - Use Ø article for states, cities, streets, universities unless *City of* or *University of* precedes the name (e.g., Elm Street, *the* University of Idaho).

   Common

2. **Is the noun identified or not identified?**

   Not identified

3. **Is the noun countable or uncountable?**

   - Use *a* for singular countable nouns (e.g., I ate *a* banana for lunch today.)

   - Use Ø for uncountable and plural nouns (I bought furniture for my living room. Tomorrow, I will eat two oranges for breakfast).

   Identified

   - Use *the* when mentioning the noun a second time (e.g., I bought *a* coat at the store. I wore *the* coat to school today).

   - Use *the* for singular or plural, countable or uncountable nouns if the noun is a ranking adjective (e.g., He is *the* tallest person in the class).

   - Use *the* if the noun is identified through shared knowledge (e.g., I am meeting my friends at *the* library after class), by a modifying phrase (*The* car that I want to buy is too expensive), or by quantity + of (e.g., most of *the* book).

Figure 3.1 Editing for correct use of articles

used in conjunction with practice exercises. Depending on the language level of the learner and the degree of self-regulation the learner already possesses, teachers can determine the amount of guidance needed for learners to access resources and use editing guides.

Understand Expectations and Grading Criteria

Learners should always know how they will be evaluated before beginning an assignment. This will help them be more responsible for assessing their own writing prior to submission. Scoring rubrics should reflect the key points emphasized in class, such as the elements of a good thesis statement, paragraph unity, or use of transitions. Providing learners with access to example writing assignments scored with the rubric of choice is also valuable as are handouts that explain the grading system or rubric. The following methods of learning will aid teachers in helping learners identify expectations.

Class and Small Group Scoring

Reviewing and scoring an example composition together as a class with a checklist or rubric helps learners understand the criteria used for grading. After the class agrees on a score, the teacher can also assign a score, and differences between the two scores can be discussed. Learners can also evaluate sample essays in small groups, discuss their scores, and try to reach consensus. These activities create awareness of different interpretations of checklists and writing guidelines, and familiarize learners with teacher expectations. The activity also gives teachers the opportunity to clarify and revise the scoring rubrics as appropriate.

Whole Class Reflection

To create awareness of common challenges across a group of L2 writers, teachers can provide a handout that engages learners in a whole class reflection. The handout summarizes what was done well on a particular assignment, common errors and weaknesses, and suggestions for improvement (Nation, 2009). The teacher can engage the class in a discussion during which learners identify what they feel comfortable with and what is still unclear to them related to the writing assignment. They can examine their own compositions based on the content of the handout and determine how the feedback applies to their papers. The handout can also serve as a record and be referred to when determining whether progress has been made by the class and individually. This technique builds learner collaboration and a sense of group responsibility.

Adopt New Roles

Because many learners are not accustomed to being responsible for their learning but are dependent on a teacher, the new role of being self-regulated must be introduced and modeled. As learners begin to understand the concept of self-regulation, the teacher can gradually delegate more tasks to the learner. This occurs most effectively in a loosely structured classroom that provides learners with the freedom to determine and complete activities and apply and discuss various methods of learning.

Neutral Questions

Teachers should focus on helping learners make decisions about their compositions so they understand that they are responsible for all aspects of their writing. Harmer (2004) suggests that teachers visit with learners about their compositions by asking neutral questions, such as what the meaning of a sentence is, or why the paper begins the way it does, or by indicating the need to recheck information. By asking questions—Why did you do this? What do you want to say in this part?—learners become responsible for making decisions rather than merely following teacher commands.

Requests for Help

Teachers may have difficulty restraining themselves when learners request help because it is often much easier to tell them what to do, point out their errors, or rewrite their sentences. It takes much more skill to lead learners in making their own choices and revisions than it does to take over the drafting, revision, or editing process. However, the former is critical in developing self-regulated writers. To this end, and again to emphasize responsibility, learners can have a sign on their desks saying if they want intervention—"No, thanks" or "Yes, please" (Harmer, 2004). Learners may be more accustomed to taking a passive role and expect their teacher to direct them. To change this, teachers need to demonstrate the expectation that learners should make their own decisions about their writing and transfer responsibility for revision to the learner.

Choice

Transferring roles occurs most effectively when learners understand expectations and goals, but have the autonomy to make choices. This might include choosing topics, experimenting with different methods of brainstorming, determining how many drafts are needed, or selecting the writing samples to be graded (such as in portfolio writing). Choice also involves learners identifying the type of response they prefer and what they would like teachers to comment on related to their writing assignments.

Identify Preferences for Types of Feedback

Learners have their own perspectives on feedback—some do not like positive comments while others do (Hyland & Hyland, 2006a). Learners who receive only positive feedback will have unrealistic views of their writing and will not see the need to improve, but too much criticism will discourage them. Response must be individualized and must place responsibility on the learner. The following activities are useful methods of learning.

Preference Surveys

An important step in helping learners understand teacher response and what to do with it is to help learners understand the methods of response being used on specific assignments. Surveying learners about methods of response provides the teacher with information about learner preferences, emphasizes learner responsibility, and gives learners choice (see Table 3.2).

Such a survey could be administered by e-mail, in individual learner–teacher conferences, or in a class focus group. These focus groups could be led by learners or involve someone other than the teacher so that responses are completely open. The teacher can continue to invite response throughout the course by trying different methods and helping learners recognize which are most helpful.

Negotiation

Self-regulated learning is encouraged when the learner and teacher negotiate the kind of response given on a composition. Based on preferences, learners can choose what response method they want the teacher to use on the next assignment, either individually or as a class. The latter approach would likely

Table 3.2 Response Survey

On our first in-class essay, I marked all your grammar errors using symbols and asked you to identify the errors you would like to work on this term. I also asked you to revise the essay and make grammar corrections. I would like you to answer a few questions about this process.

- Do you find it helpful to have all your grammar errors marked? Why or why not?
- Does having all your errors marked help you understand the kinds of errors you make?
- Does having all your errors marked help you do better on your next writing assignment?

I evaluated your second essay using a scoring rubric with points for different aspects of your writing. How helpful was this form in giving you feedback about your essay and suggesting ways you can improve?

be simpler for the teacher. Teachers will need to guide learners, point out advantages and disadvantages of various approaches, and perhaps indicate the degree to which learners seem to be benefiting so that adjustments can be made. Learners must consider teacher workload in their requests for various types of response, and also understand that the goal is to become less dependent on teacher feedback.

Use Self-Evaluation Tools

One source of annoyance for a writing teacher is having a learner ask in the final weeks of the course, "What are my weaknesses?" Or, when asking a learner to self-identify weaknesses, to hear the very general response, "Grammar." The first response indicates that the learner has not internalized the comments provided on each writing assignment during the course, and the second response indicates that the learner lacks self-awareness of specific strengths and weaknesses. In other words, the learner is expecting the teacher to bear the burden for improvement and tell the learner what is wrong and how to fix it. Teachers need to place the burden for improvement on the learner.

Self-regulated writers must increase their awareness of how teacher response is aimed at directing their improvement, and how to take responsibility for using the response. Self-evaluation emphasizes the active involvement of the learner with the teacher taking a facilitator role. Opportunities for learner self-evaluation can occur through course materials and formal assessment. When learners relate what they are learning to what they know, they create deeper connections, helping them understand and remember information—the goal of the methods of learning principle.

Record of Achievement

One method of learning aimed at self-evaluation is having learners complete a record of achievement (ROA) (Harmer, 2007). The ROA contains the following learner information: name, subject, comments about progress, signature, and date. The comments focus on self-assessment of successes and challenges, and outline plans for future progress. Teachers add their assessment, reply to the learner comments, and assign a grade. Self-assessment increases awareness of the learning process and leads to greater understanding of teacher feedback. ROAs encourage both teachers and learners to think about writing strengths and weaknesses and to determine future actions.

Categorization

When compositions are returned to learners, they may simply see a multitude of comments and may not know how to evaluate the purpose of the comments or respond to them. Depending on the response strategy of the teacher, comments likely cover an array of issues encompassing content, organization, and form. One way learners can begin to manage these is with categorization, or creating a list with specific categories. These categories can be as simple as *content, organization,* and *form* (or grammar). In the form column, learners can summarize information from a tally sheet like the one introduced in Chapter 2 to give them an overall view of grammatical weaknesses. The categorization activity encourages learners to track teacher comments on assignments over the course of the semester and identify strengths, weaknesses, and areas of improvement (see Table 3.3). The listing should be reviewed periodically throughout the course so the learner understands where to focus.

If this activity is adopted, teachers may need to adjust the level of detail of their comments. Rather than writing "good introduction" or "nice ending," they will need to be more specific. Examples of specific feedback are included in Table 3.3. Teachers must be aware of their responses, how those responses affect the learner, and how the responses can lead to improvement and increased self-regulation. As teachers provide assistance in the categorization process, they will want to help learners understand the purposes of their feedback—to improve content, organization, or accuracy, or as general encouragement, for example. A category could be added to the chart for "purpose" of response so that learners can learn to value both praise and criticism.

Table 3.3 Comment Categorization

Assignment	Content Strengths	Content Weaknesses	Response / Strategy
#1	An attention-getting introduction.	Unsupported general statements in supporting paragraphs.	I will use more specific examples, facts, or statistics to support my ideas.

Assignment	Organization Strengths	Organization Weaknesses	Response / Strategy
#1	Thesis statement clearly identifies the topic and states an idea, opinion, or attitude about the topic.	Some sentences are off the topic in the supporting paragraphs.	I will ask my roommate to read my paragraphs to see if any sentences are off topic and ask him to explain why.

Assignment	Grammar Strengths	Grammar Weaknesses	Response / Strategy
#1	Vocabulary choices are appropriate and in the correct form.	Confusion about the simple past and past perfect.	I will look for clues in the sentence that show a specific time in the past.

Table 3.4 Cover Sheet

Strengths	The first sentence contains the author's name, the date of the publication, and the main idea of the article.
How I applied feedback from previous compositions	I did not include my own reaction or view, just the author's ideas.
Things I am not sure about	I think my summary might have too much detail rather than only the main points.

Cover Sheets

To help create language awareness, learners can attach a check list or cover sheet with their first drafts and revisions, such as the one in Table 3.4 that accompanies a first draft of a summary assignment. Cover sheets related to revisions may include information about how the learner responded to teacher comments.

Reflective Notebooks

Learners can use notebooks to record thoughts about the learning process. The format and content of these can vary as illustrated in Table 3.5.

Although we have described a variety of activities, teachers will need to select a limited number of these so that the feedback they provide and what learners are required to do with it does not become overwhelming. We advise consistency in the approach selected as learners need time to adapt to and benefit from various methods for response. For instance, grammar notebooks, tally sheets, and a comment categorization chart may be too much and too similar in purpose. Managing all of these methods may also prove difficult for the teacher. However, teachers may want to introduce options and allow learners to choose. This is very much in the spirit of self-regulated learning and encourages experimentation. If one method is not proving effective, learners can choose another. Reflection will aid this process.

Several practices can help teachers maintain a manageable work load. One approach is to not require all parts of the writing process for each assignment but to practice the stages separately (e.g., outlining, planning, editing) (Snow, 2006). On some assignments (e.g., journals, personal stories, position papers, newsletter items), the teacher may give no feedback or may arrange for a peer audience (Snow, 2006). Learners must understand that becoming a good writer requires practice in the same way that learning a musical instrument or playing a sport does, and that writing is valuable even without teacher feedback. Many learners will expect teacher comments on all their work. Helping learners understand the value of other sources of response or even

Table 3.5 Types of Reflective Notebooks

Format	Purpose
Learner Journals	Reflection on successes with writing. Identification of strategies used and description of use. Assessment of the effectiveness of strategies used. Plans for modifications. Summaries of class activities with an evaluation of their effectiveness. Specific ideas for improvement on next assignment.
One-Minute Papers	A one-minute reflection at the end of a class session. Identification of how well material was understood. Comments on familiarity with a particular aspect of writing being taught (e.g., transitions, unity, sequence).
Editing Journal	Sample sentences with errors and corrections. Notes about relevant grammar rules. Identification of possible strategies to try. Reflection on the effectiveness of strategies. Summaries of what was learned from editing a paper.

practicing writing with no response will assist them in becoming more independent and self-regulated.

Summary

This chapter has:

- defined and explored the concept of methods of learning generally and as it relates to language learning strategies and L2 writing specifically;
- identified key pedagogical practices involved in guiding and responding to writing to improve the learner's ability to use methods of learning related to teacher feedback; and
- provided a range of learner activities and approaches designed to improve methods of learning and writing skill and to develop self-regulated L2 writers.

The next chapter:

- explores the self-regulated learning principle of time, specifically how time management is important to self-regulation and how it can benefit language learners generally and L2 writers specifically;
- discusses pedagogical practices that help learners implement effective time management strategies; and
- shares activities and approaches for learner improvement in time management that leads to improvement in writing.

Chapter 4

Time Factors

Objectives

This chapter discusses the principle of time and its application to L2 writing, and outlines practices and activities that help learners:

- develop time management strategies;
- identify procrastination factors that may affect their productivity as writers;
- determine a reasonable amount of time to complete a given writing task;
- increase their ability to write within time constraints; and
- understand the time required to significantly improve their writing skills.

Definitions and Applications

The principle of time in self-regulated learning determines *when* and for *how long* learners apply themselves to learning tasks. The process of estimating and budgeting how to use time is often associated with successful leaning (Dembo & Seli, 2008; Zimmerman, 1990, 1998; Zimmerman & Kitsantas, 1997). A useful way to consider the principle of time is by dividing it into the self-regulatory skills of time management and procrastination avoidance (Dembo & Eaton, 2000).

Time management is really a matter of task management (Dembo & Eaton, 2000). Being able to prioritize tasks and allocate the time needed for each is a skill that has application not only in academic settings but also in most aspects of life. Factors that contribute to poor time or task management include a lack of goals or an uncertainty of what is to be accomplished, a failure to break goals into several tasks, a lack of understanding of how to manage time, and a lack of knowledge of how much time is needed to accomplish a task (Dembo & Seli, 2008). Several key processes associated with a learner's effective use of time include time planning, time management, and self-belief (Zimmerman,

1998). While time management abilities can be taught and learned, not all learners have these skills, and some have them in greater degrees than others. It is important for teachers to help learners acquire these abilities.

Procrastination, while clearly related to time management, is something that must be understood independently. Simply defining procrastination as "the process of postponing tasks" inadequately describes this complex phenomenon. An alternate definition suggests that it is "a needless delay of a timely and relevant activity" (Knaus, 2010, p. 3). Furthermore, it must be understood that procrastination is much more than a behavioral problem. It has a complex interconnection among cognitive, emotional, and behavioral factors that must each be considered when attempting to correct it (Knaus, 2010).

Procrastination in an academic setting has serious consequences. Some estimates suggest that 70–90% of all college students procrastinate to one degree or another such academic tasks as writing papers, completing homework, studying for exams, and registering for classes (Knaus, 2000). Learners who procrastinate are more likely to perform poorly than those who do not procrastinate (Dembo & Seli, 2008; Zimmerman, 1998).

Time Factors and Language Learning

Time, how it is measured and what it means, is a factor frequently used when comparing cultural differences. Not all cultures view or value time in the same ways (Samovar, Porter, & McDaniel, 2009). A colleague once shared an interesting perspective on how time is viewed differently in two cultures. His Sioux Indian friend had told him, "You look at your watch not to tell what time it is, but to tell what time it is not quite yet." It is extremely important to understand different perceptions of time while working with international students. Their perceptions of time may have a huge impact on how they treat time in their host culture. In fact, one of the case studies on procrastination patterns in this chapter has much to do with the conflicting values of time between certain island nations in the South Pacific and the United States. Knowing how learners perceive time will be essential to successfully orienting them to alternative concepts and uses of time.

The views and values of time presented in this chapter and incorporated in the activities are all based on a Western concept of time. It is to this concept that learners must adapt if they are going to become self-regulated learners in their new surroundings.

Research specifically documenting the effects of time management and procrastination on language learning is nonexistent. However, current research on the time required to learn a language suggests that these factors are important. Learning a language takes time and much learner effort to achieve advanced proficiency levels. Foremost among this research is Cummins' (1980, 1981, 1996) work, which suggests that it takes ESL learners from five to seven years to gain proficiency sufficient for university-level study, called cognitive academic language proficiency (CALP). Additional research extends that developmental time beyond seven years (Collier, 1987; Collier & Thomas, 1989).

A similar line of research has shown that time to acquire a second language is related to the distance between the first and second languages (R .Clifford, personal communication, September 2008; Omaggio Hadley, 2000). The greater the distance between the two languages, as measured by such factors as syntactic, morphological, or phonological differences, the longer it takes to acquire the second language. While this research is not directly related to time management and procrastination, the findings are helpful for teachers working with language learners to help them understand how much must be learned and what a realistic learning time-frame might be. Such information will be essential to students becoming self-regulated L2 writers.

Time Factors and Writing

While there is no specific literature base for time management and language learning, much can be said about time and its appropriate use in L2 writing. For example, writing "tests produced by L2 writers are generally shorter, less cohesive, less fluent, and contain more errors" than those by first language (L1) writers (Hyland, 2003, p. 34). Research also suggests that L2 writers tend to plan less and produce shorter texts, have difficulty setting goals and generating material, revise more but reflect less on what they have written, and are less fluent and less accurate in what they write (Hyland, 2003). Each of these insights becomes more significant when considered in the context of two common causes of procrastination: lack of conscientiousness and avoidance (Ferrari, Johnson, & McCown, 1995). Avoidance in particular, which is often a result of insecurity about one's ability, seems especially applicable to an L2 learning context. Anyone who has attempted to write in a second language understands how feelings of insecurity about articulating complex ideas using an entirely new syntactic, lexical, and discourse system might lead to procrastination.

Another factor to consider is time constraints. Some have suggested that timed writing exams, which are common in an L2 context, are contrived and not "real writing"; it's not how we write (Horowitz, 1986a, p. 141). Such a statement is simply not accurate. Writing within time constraints occurs regularly in academic settings. For instance, the most common method for assessing L2 writing proficiency both for placement and achievement purposes is a timed essay (Ferris, 2009). Major standardized English proficiency exams (TOEFL, IELTS) require writing under time constraints. University students frequently take examinations that include timed essay and short answer questions (Horowitz, 1986a). Furthermore, other university assignments such as term papers, lab reports, and critiques of plays or performances all require writing, and while the time limits extend beyond a few hours such as timed exams, each has imposed deadlines. All of these academic writing tasks require learners to be able to manage their writing time appropriately.

An additional aspect of time as it relates to L2 writing is the way the process incorporates time factors into writing. Since the early 1980s, process writing has become an integral part of L2 writing instruction (Ferris & Hedgcock, 2005; Matsuda, 2003; Zamel, 1983). One of the great advantages of this approach is that it divides a writing task into sequential, manageable steps. The processes of generating ideas, drafting, revising, conferencing, and editing, all recognized aspects of process writing, lead to a better final paper. Furthermore, such a system is consistent with the principle of time management and self-regulated learning (Dembo & Seli, 2008; Zimmerman, 1998). Process writing can be used to teach multiple concepts at once—good writing, time management, and self-regulated learning.

Guiding Classroom Practices

The following set of guiding classroom practices is designed to assist teachers in helping learners understand the principle of time and how it must be managed so they can develop into self-regulated learners and effective L2 writers. The succeeding section then presents activities that are informed by these guiding practices and that help learners regulate their use of time.

Maintain a Reasonable Homework Expectation

It is not uncommon to hear students say that they wished their teachers would realize that they have other classes to tend to as well. "This is not our *only* class you know." While such a declaration may in part reflect a learner's misunderstanding of how much work is required in a given academic context, it certainly may include a degree of truth. Teachers must carefully consider what they expect learners to do given their schedules and language learning levels. Observations suggest that a common practice among novice teachers is to overestimate what L2 learners can do in a given time (Tsui, 2003). Generally, the lower the level of the learner, the longer the task is likely to take.

A teacher can help learners manage time by establishing a realistic weekly time frame for homework in the class. For instance, a writing teacher may estimate that a learner will need to spend approximately 10 hours each week on the assignments for the class to make significant gains as L2 writers. With that as a guide, a teacher could then set reasonable time estimates for each assignment that fit within the 10-hour time frame. If a journal is required for the class, the teacher may determine that 2 of the 10 hours will be used for writing journals. This should then be communicated to the learners at the beginning of a course and as each task is assigned. Such a practice helps teachers maintain a reasonable workload, and it provides learners with time parameters for their work.

Provide Timely Feedback and Expect Prompt Revisions

An important way to instruct learners on the careful use of their time is to expect prompt revision and response to teacher feedback. Too often the writing/learning process is left half-finished. Typically a teacher will assign a writing task with a set deadline. The assignment is completed, submitted, read, responded to, and returned to the writer. It is expected that learners will take that feedback, internalize it, and improve on subsequent writing assignments. While this would be ideal, what generally happens is learners look at the feedback, and file or throw the assignment away.

Feedback neglect happens for several reasons. First, the teacher may have not established a system that requires learners to be responsible for improving an assignment based on feedback. A second possible cause is the teacher does not return the assignment promptly, making the feedback only remotely relevant to the learners who are likely immersed in a new, demanding writing task. Finally, learners may not understand what the teacher's feedback means (see Chapter 1). In order for learners to take advantage of a teacher's feedback, revision and accountability need to be built into the system. Providing timely feedback and expecting prompt revisions develops more time-responsible, self-regulated learners.

Provide Fluency-Building Activities

As has been noted, L2 writers tend to write significantly less than their English-speaking classmates (Hyland, 2003; Purves, 1988; Silva, 1993). One way to offset this limitation is to incorporate fluency-building activities and assignments into the curriculum (Ferris, 2009; Harmer, 2004; Nation, 2009; Nation & Macalister, 2010). A basic premise of skill acquisition theory suggests that learners need repeated procedural experience for automaticity to occur (Brown, 2007; DeKeyser, 2001, 2007). Activities that build fluency generally consist of repetition and writing on topics and material that are "easy and familiar" (Nation, 2009, p. 95). Activities like journal writing allow learners to focus on meaning rather than form, thereby developing greater fluency.

Divide Tasks into Manageable Parts

Because poor time management and procrastination tend to be common problems with all learners, teachers need to help them develop strategies to avoid these pitfalls (Dembo & Seli, 2008; Knaus; 2000). One such strategy that addresses an oft-cited cause for poor time management is to break a large task into smaller parts (Dembo & Seli, 2008; Knaus, 2010). Each time teachers help learners see smaller parts of the whole, they are helping them see how such a strategy can make an assignment more manageable (Nation, 2009).

Communicate Realistic Time Frames for Writing Improvement

Most language learners do not have a reasonable sense of how long it takes to develop strong writing skills (Cummins, 1980, 1981, 1996; Collier, 1987). This lack of understanding can lead to unrealistic expectations, frustration, and, ultimately, discouragement. Teachers should build goals and objectives into their courses that communicate what can be realistically achieved over the duration of the course. Teachers should discuss these goals and objectives with learners to ensure that they understand the incremental steps needed to achieve desired levels of proficiency.

Allow for Incremental Progress to be Measured

There is no fast and easy route to language proficiency; learning a second language simply takes time. Moving from one level to the next is not a linear, direct track. As learners move up in proficiency, the amount of material to be learned and remembered expands exponentially. This phenomenon is often depicted by means of an inverted pyramid where the point of the pyramid represents the narrow, limited language of a novice learner, and the broad base indicates the expansive language range of an advanced or superior learner (Buck, Byrnes, & Thompson, 1989; Savignon, 2001; Snow, 2006). A consequence of this fact is that it is easy for learners to get discouraged, especially at the intermediate levels (Snow, 2006). A number of elements can be worked into writing class materials and activities that help learners understand and measure their progress as writers. Such things as writing fluency progress charts, error tally sheets, edit and revision logs, and writing portfolios can make incremental progress visible (also see Chapters 2 and 7). Stevick (1988) refers to this as "providing snacks and water to sustain them [language learners] along the path" (p. 128).

Activities and Approaches

The activities that follow are designed to be incorporated into the classroom to help learners develop self-regulated learner strategies associated with time and time management. As in other chapters, the activities are directly linked to the objectives stated at the beginning of the chapter and support the six guiding classroom practices just discussed.

Develop Time Management Strategies

Important or Urgent

It is quite possible that learners are not aware of how time and tasks can be effectively managed. A short lecture of 5 to 10 minutes could be developed to help learners understand when tasks are "important, urgent, both, or neither" (Dembo & Seli, 2008, p. 145). With a lecture that focuses on Covey's (1989) time management matrix (see Figure 4.1), learners could be provided with a copy of the matrix that contains key words, but no specific examples of what belongs in each quadrant nor any indication of how the matrix should be divided. Most tables using Covey's (1990) time management matrix divide the table into four equal quadrants. As the lecture progresses, each learner could be asked to fill in information in the appropriate spaces and determine if each quadrant should be equal in size. The presentation could include descriptions of the different quadrants and what each represents and that items in Quadrant IV ought to be the smallest. Sizing the quadrants should illustrate where good time managers spend their time. For instance, successful time managers set time aside each day for Quadrant II activities (Dembo & Seli, 2008). The more time a person spends on Quadrant II activities, the more likely it is that he or she will manage time and tasks well.

Several ways to reinforce the ideas taught in this lecture would be through pair or group discussions and individual writing tasks. For a group task, the teacher might use jigsaw puzzle groups in which the class is divided into four groups. Each group could be assigned to one quadrant and asked to write a description of their quadrant using examples from the lecture, or their own

		Urgent	Not urgent
Important		I **True emergencies** Types of events: • Crises • Pressing problems • Deadline-driven projects	II **Proactive power** Types of events: • Planning • Long-term projects
Not important		III **Deception** Types of events: • Interruptions (e.g., scheduling conflicts)	IV **Waste** Types of events: • Busywork • Time wasters (TV, Internet)

Figure 4.1 Time Management Matrix (adapted from Covey, 1990)

experiences. Once this is completed, the class is re-divided into four new groups, each of which has representatives from the original four groups. The task is then for each group member to teach the others in the group about their quadrant. This could be followed up with a full class discussion of how all four quadrants can be properly balanced.

An alternative or follow-up to this group activity would be to assign learners to write a brief definition paper in which the four quadrants are defined and illustrated by their personal experiences. Such an assignment is valuable for several reasons. First it allows students to write for content learning (Dean, 2011). In this case they would be learning more about the content of time management. The second valuable aspect of this assignment is that it is based on personal experiences. The more the writing is associated with a learner's personal experiences, the more meaningful the activity will be.

24-hour Evaluation

An additional activity to follow the time management matrix lecture and help learners see how they use their time would be a 24-hour evaluation. For this activity, students divide a paper into three columns. In the first column, they make a list of the tasks they performed in the past 24 hours. They then fill in the second column with a number indicating which quadrant from the matrix this task represents. Once this list is completed, they fill in the third column with comments on how they might have prioritized their activities differently to make better use of their time. As usual, group and class discussions are excellent ways to reinforce and clarify what has been learned.

A, B, C; 1, 2, 3

A frequently used method for prioritizing tasks is the A, B, C system (Dembo & Eaton, 2000; Smith, 1994). In this activity, a person designates each task that needs to be accomplished as an "A" for the most important; a "B" for those that are less important, and a "C" for tasks that are the least important. These can be further ranked using a 1, 2, 3, numbering system, which allows for multiple tasks with the same letter to be further prioritized. An "A-1" task is the most important and must be accomplished before beginning the next most important item, which is labeled as an A-2 and so forth (Dembo & Seli, 2008).

Once learners have identified and ranked their upcoming activities, they should be assigned to review their progress through the week. Progress can be tracked in several ways. A simple task-tracking sheet such as the one in Figure 4.2 works well. An alternative or supplement to the task tracking sheet would be to have the learners monitor their progress in a learner journal in which they reflect briefly at the end of each day how well they managed their time and what could be done better the following day.

Priority A, B, C / 1, 2, 3		Task	Date completed
Future tasks			

Figure 4.2 Task Tracking Sheet

Reporting on Success

After learners have had a week to try their time management skill using an activity like one of those described above, they should be given opportunities to report their successes, shortcomings, and lessons learned. This can be accomplished in several ways. A written report at the end of the week could be assigned that asks learners to assess their successes and failures and conclude with a "lessons learned" section. Alternatively, the class could be divided into small groups, and learners asked to share their individual strengths (successes) and weaknesses (shortcomings). The group could then offer suggestions on how to build on the strengths and avoid the weaknesses. These group discussions could then be followed up with a class discussion where the teacher asks members of each group to share what they learned about proper time management.

An important point to consider with any strategy training is that repetition and reinforcement are essential to acquisition (DeKeyser, 2007; Oxford, 2011). Instruction should ideally be followed up and reinforced over prolonged periods of time. The more that time management strategies are incorporated into class assignments, the greater the chances are for learners to practice them to the point of developing "fluent, spontaneous, largely effortless, and highly skilled behavior" (DeKeyser, 2007, p. 97). Such automaticity is essential for self-regulated learning.

Identify Procrastination Factors

Common Causes

Before learners can begin to improve their tendencies to procrastinate, they must know what the common causes of the behavior are. This can be accomplished by viewing various video clips available online. The quality and quantity of documents and videos on the Internet have increased dramatically in recent years, making it a valuable resource for teaching and learning. With that as a given, the dynamic nature of the Internet makes it impossible to determine what sites will be viable in the future. Based on the assumption that Internet sources will continue to grow in quality and scope, with a minimal amount of effort, a teacher could select video clips on the causes of procrastination for viewing in class or as homework.

Information Gap Writing

One way to use the videos about procrastination would be to create an information gap where one half of the class views one video and the other half views another video. Learners are then given a partner who has viewed a different video, and they each share their observations on what causes procrastination. As with all group work, having clear learning objectives and tasks are essential. The objective of this activity should be for learners to identify key factors that contribute to procrastination. For instance, a worksheet could be developed beforehand that asks group members to list the most common causes of procrastination, possible solutions to it, and natural consequences following it, as presented in the two different videos. Such an activity could be the precursor to writing tasks.

Depending on the content of the videos, a writing task could be given for the following types of papers:

- a short paper discussing the causes and effects of procrastination
- a problem-and-solution paper outlining the problems procrastination causes in an academic setting, and some possible solutions, or
- a compare-and-contrast paper that discusses the differences between the two videos.

To further strengthen the learner's background knowledge before writing, short reading passages could also be read and discussed.

Case Studies

An equally valuable approach to teaching common procrastination factors is the use of case studies (Dembo & Eaton, 2000; Dembo & Seli, 2008; Zimmerman & Risemberg, 1997). Brief paragraph descriptions of learners who avoid procrastination and those who do not can be used for instruction, discussion, and writing purposes. The samples in Table 4.1 illustrate two such case studies: Victor, a non-procrastinator, and Marinoa, a chronic procrastinator. Once a basic introduction to procrastination has been provided, learners can then be asked to read each case study and identify the causes of Marinoa's procrastination and Victor's non-procrastination. A follow-up to reading the case studies might be to ask learners to write a brief, reflective five-minute paragraph (see "Increase writing ability within time constraints" later) on the following statement: "My procrastination habits are most like Victor/Marinoa or neither because …"

An excellent way for learners to understand how the common causes for procrastination are related to their own tendencies is to write a case study about themselves. Once learners have seen several examples of case studies, such as Marinoa's and Victor's, they can then be assigned to write their own. To help the learners focus, they might be instructed to write about a particularly challenging time, such as the beginning or end of a semester in school.

Procrastination Survey

Once learners have a grasp of some of the more common causes for procrastination, they need to understand their own personal procrastination tendencies. Everyone procrastinates to one degree or another. Various procrastination surveys have been developed to classify the causes of and the severity levels to which one procrastinates (Lay, 1986; Tuckman, 1991). One such scale, the procrastination scale, provides a basic measure that can be used for classroom purposes (Lay, 1986). Samples and variations of the scale can also be found on the Internet. One advantage to using online versions is that some sites actually format the scale as a scored survey. Once the survey is taken, an instant ranking or description of tendencies is provided: Not a Systematic Procrastinator, Mild Procrastinator, and Procrastinator. With the survey results, learners can then participate in various discussions and writing tasks.

For instance, groups could be formed in the class. One group could be assigned to identify the statements on the survey that define a non-procrastinator, while another group finds statements that define procrastinators. A follow-up to these discussions might be to assign an analysis paper in which learners analyze the questions on the self-ranking

Table 4.1 Procrastination Case Studies

Case Studies: Two Classmates

Marinoa and Victor are classmates in their first year of university study in the United States of America. Each is an international student from very different backgrounds. Each deals with time and challenges in very different ways. Read these brief accounts to see if you can decide how each manages time differently and why.

Marinoa grew up on a small Pacific island where life was demanding but not governed by clocks. Her parents never had the chance to complete a high school education, so they worked very hard to make it possible for their children to get the education they never had. They would kindly remind Marinoa every day how important school was.

When Marinoa came to the USA to study, she knew it would be hard, but she had been a good student at home—why should that change now? She was surprised by the strict homework schedule for her classes; due dates seemed so absolute. Her teachers back home had given assignments, but the due dates did not seem to be so demanding.

Marinoa quickly learned that she had to work twice as hard in English. She could not speed through any assignment. She had to labor over each assignment until she understood the English words she was using. Before long, Marinoa fell behind in her studies. She felt ashamed for being a bad student. She felt like she couldn't ask her teacher for help. She felt that she should write better. The more Marinoa struggled in her writing, the less she wanted to write and the more she spent time with her distractors: Internet, cell phone, and friends. Sometimes after spending time with her friends and then coming home to her unstarted assignment that was due the next day, Marinoa wondered why she was even in the United States, wasting her time and her parents' money on something she obviously couldn't do. At these times, she felt like packing up and going home.

Victor was born and raised in a large city in South America. He received an uninterrupted education in some very good schools. His family had sacrificed much to send him to study in the United States. He was the type of person who couldn't enjoy activities until his homework was done. He felt haunted by unfinished tasks.

When Victor started his schooling in the United States, he knew it would be hard for him. He had taken English classes in high school, but they had always been difficult for him. But now he was in the United States, and he knew that if he wanted to succeed in school and make a life for himself, he needed to learn English well.

Victor felt overwhelmed by the amount of time required to do good work in his classes. He decided to sacrifice like his family did to get him here. He was determined to do the assignments right after class each day and only spend time with his friends after his homework was finished. Sometimes he would feel frustrated by an assignment and go do something else for a while, but because he had started it early, there was time to go back to it. Victor knew he missed many activities, but that was his sacrifice for his education. His future in the United States was more important than having fun in the moment. Eventually, Victor felt great satisfaction when he finished an assignment early, even if he wasn't particularly interested in it. However, Victor had learned how to find interest in almost every assignment.

survey that show their strengths or weaknesses, such as "I usually start a task I am given shortly after I'm given it" or "I usually accomplish all the things I plan to do in a day."

Metacognitive Paper

An additional assignment to help learners see their own procrastination tendencies would be for them to identify which of the most common causes of procrastination affect them. This can be done by setting up a two-column table. In the first column, learners list five tasks that they have procrastinated over in the past few months. Using the information they have gathered from the procrastination survey and common causes assignments discussed earlier, they can list in the second column the causes for their procrastination. This could then be used as the basis for a metacognitive paper in which learners reflect on personal experiences that exemplify their most common procrastination patterns. A less formal approach would be to assign journal entries in which students discuss their most common tendencies for procrastination and reflect on what might be done to remedy the tendencies.

80/20 Rule

A logical next step to identifying one's personal procrastination tendencies is knowing what to do about them—what strategies to employ to change them. It is important to point out that learner preferences for remedies vary considerably. No one strategy or solution will be appropriate to all. A variation of the A, B, C; 1, 2, 3 prioritizing technique discussed earlier is the 80/20 rule, sometimes called the Pareto Principle. This principle is based on an economic theory and has time management applications. The Italian economist Vilfredo Pareto found that 80% of all land in England (and every other country he studied) was owned by 20% of the population. Simply put, the principle specifies that the relationship between input and output is seldom in balance.

In time management, the 80/20 rule states that 20% of the tasks that a person spends time doing produce 80% of the desired results. The goal therefore must be to identify the actions that will yield the greatest results and make those a priority. Said another way, students should focus on the vital few tasks rather than the trivial many.

An activity that teaches the 80/20 rule is to have the learners use the list of tasks they generated in the A, B, C; 1, 2, 3, activity above. They should then identify 20% of those tasks that they deem to be most important. For instance, if they have 10 tasks on that list, they must identify the two tasks that will be the best use of their time. In many ways, this process is related to the time management matrix. Individuals who spend time in Quadrants III and IV are focusing on tasks that will not yield important results—the trivial many. The 80/20 rule teaches them to spend more time in Quadrant II—the vital few.

The Big Red X

Another valuable resource for helping learners manage time that is often overlooked is a writing teacher's own experiences. Teachers and their colleagues have many years of experience that can be used to help learners overcome procrastination. For example, a colleague suggests that a good way to help writers overcome one of the most common causes of procrastination—perfectionism—is to teach the concept of drafting early, clearly, and often. His approach is to require all his writing students to mark a big red X on each page of paper before writing, just to remind them that this is a draft; it won't be perfect, and that is acceptable. Many teachers build multiple drafting into their grading scheme, allowing learners to revise and improve a paper even after a grade has been assigned. Such a practice can help learners overcome the idea that writing has to be perfect on the first draft.

Determine Reasonable Time Limits

Timeline Cover Sheet

Two related and often cited causes for poor time management and procrastination are being overwhelmed by the size of a task and lacking the ability to estimate how much time will be needed to complete it (Dembo & Seli, 2008). Teachers often do not consider the principle of time as it relates to a writing task and how long it is likely to take. An effective way to help learners break a task into manageable parts and learn how to estimate time well is to use a cover sheet that includes a task title, a description, a final deadline, and a timeline for subtasks (see Figure 4.3). The cover sheet can be modified for almost any multifaceted writing task. Such a cover sheet can be prepared rather quickly, and because it results in learners starting to develop self-regulating strategies and skills, it is worth the effort.

There are several ways this cover sheet can be used to help learners determine time limits. First, the teacher could fill in the subtasks, subtask description, and estimated time boxes and tell the class why such estimates are reasonable. The teacher could then indicate what the due dates are for each subtask. Such an approach might be desirable for the first time the cover sheet is used. This would allow the learners to see how a task can be divided into manageable parts with reasonable time limits.

After completing the first assignment using the cover sheet that the teacher filled in, learners could fill in the amount of time it actually took and

Assignment: Natural disasters around the world
Description: *This is the kind of paper you will likely have to write once you begin your general undergraduate studies at the university. For this assignment you will first need to conduct some basic library research on the various types of natural disasters that occur around the world. You should select three destructive natural disasters and give a brief description of their causes and effects. It might be a good idea to include a specific example from recent history for each of the three types of disasters you write about.*
Length: 4–6 pages (approximately one introductory page, one page for each disaster, and a page to wrap up and conclude your findings)
Evaluation: As usual, the essay-scoring rubric used in this class will be used to evaluate your work
Due Date: Wednesday March 13, at the beginning of class

Subtasks	Subtask description Estimated time required		Due date
Research the topic			
Develop a thesis statement			
Outline key ideas/sections			
Write first draft			
Discuss draft with writing group			
Write second draft			
Revise			
Write final draft			
Submit final			March 13

Figure 4.3 Task Timeline Cover Sheet

reflect on why something took more or less time than the teacher's estimate. Small group discussions allowing learners to compare the time they took on a task with their classmates may help them make a more realistic estimate for completing their own time cover sheet on the next assignment.

Subsequent uses of the cover sheet might be to hand it out with the top section completed (i.e., Title, Description, Length, Evaluation criteria, Due date, and Subtasks). Learners could then be divided into pairs or small groups and asked to discuss and decide how much time will be needed for each subtask. They then determine what a reasonable due date might be for each subtask. This might be followed by a teacher-led class discussion of the groups' findings with the aim of reaching a class consensus on due dates.

The next time the cover sheet is used, the teacher would provide the title and description, leaving the subtask section blank. Learners might meet in small groups to describe the subtasks, estimate the time needed, and designate appropriate due dates. Again, a full class discussion could follow. Scaffolding the use of the cover sheet this way will allow learners to develop their own sense of time and modify self-regulated learning strategies to suit their personal preferences.

While the use of this cover sheet is intended to help learners understand how tasks can be divided into manageable sections, there are several indirect benefits. First, using this cover sheet helps teachers make more accurate estimates of the time required to complete a given task. In addition, as learners reason through the various subtasks on an assignment, they are also identifying key steps and principles in the writing process.

Assignment Time Log

While the timeline cover sheet helps learners estimate time and due dates, an important step to making accurate estimates is for students to be aware of how they use time or how long it takes them to complete a task. Learners can increase this awareness by simply recording in an assignment log how much time each writing task requires. Such a log could be as simple as a three-column document. In the first column the learner enters the assignment description or title. The second column is used to enter the approximate time that it took to complete the assignment. The third column is used to enter brief comments and reflections on the time required for the task, such as why it took longer than expected or why it was completed in less time.

To reinforce the learners' focus on time, a teacher might require learners to always write the amount of time they took to complete each assignment next to their name and date on the first page. An additional benefit of this practice is that it also helps a teacher understand how long given assignments take to complete.

Increase Writing Ability Within Time Constraints

Rush Writes

Nearly all academic writing has time constraints or deadlines that differ or are affected by the complexity of the assignment. Since all academic work has deadlines and L2 writers tend to write less and take more time to complete a writing task than other students, most L2 writers need opportunities to build their writing fluency skills (Hyland, 2003; Nation, 2009; Silva, 1993). The rush or quick write is a type of writing activity where the teacher assigns learners to reflectively write on a given topic for a brief time. The amount of time can be altered as needed, depending on the topic. This technique is useful for several reasons. First, it is often used at the beginning of a unit to help learners understand how much they know about a given topic, such as procrastination. It is also useful because it allows learners to build fluency within time constraints, without being overly concerned about linguistic accuracy.

10-Minute Paragraph

Already introduced in Chapter 3, the 10-minute paragraph also helps build fluency skills within a time constraint. Extensive experience teaches that when learners are asked to write a 10-minute paragraph at the beginning of nearly every class, invariably they express concerns that it is "very difficult" to try to think of something to say, and then write about it in only 10 minutes. Many struggle at first, but by the end of a 15-week course, not only have they improved their fluency but also their linguistic accuracy (Evans et al., 2010b; Evans et al., 2011; Hartshorn et al., 2010). Another advantage to this technique is that paragraphs must be resubmitted promptly after revisions have been made. The tasks are small but steady, thus teaching learners the importance of staying current with assignments by managing their time well.

Instant Writing

Harmer's (2004) "instant writing" is another technique that builds fluency. In such tasks learners are asked to write for a short period of time about such things as a weather forecast for the day, a description of what they think a piece of classical music portrays, a postcard being sent from the location depicted on the front of the card, letters to individuals in a portrait (for instance, the Mona Lisa), or acrostic/alphabet poems where the first word in each line begins with the letters of a selected focus word, such as *beach*. Each of these can be done within short time frames, usually within one class session, thus teaching learners how to judge time and complete tasks within a set time constraint, as well as building fluency.

Daily Writing

If class time does not allow for rush writes, 10-minute paragraphs, or instant writing activities, these can be assigned as homework, with some modifications where necessary. An alternative is to assign learners to write 15 consecutive minutes, five days a week on assigned topics. During a 15-week course, learners will have practiced nearly 19 hours of timed writing. Such practice can lead to more prolific writers who write with much less time-caused anguish as they develop greater fluency (Gray, 2005). Selecting topics that are interesting, relevant, and engaging (meaning they are intellectually as well as emotionally appealing) to a writer is important in this process (Harmer, 2004).

Understand the Time Required to Improve Writing Skills

Progress Conferences

Helping learners understand the considerable time that language acquisition takes is as much related to motive (Chapter 2), as it is to time. The realization that advanced competency may take years to achieve can be demoralizing. Teachers can help learners see that steady progress is possible by implementing activities, such as portfolios (see Chapter 7), into the class that help learners see the incremental progress they are making (Hamp-Lyons & Condon, 2000; Johns, 1997; White, 1994).

A variation of portfolios that allows learners to focus on their progress is the progress conference. For this activity, the teacher sets up three progress conferences with each learner throughout the course. The first conference should be set a few weeks into the course after the teacher has seen enough of the learners' work to be familiar with their strengths and weaknesses. The second conference is set at a date near the middle of the course, and the final conference is held during the final week or two of the course. Prior to the first conference, each learner is given a worksheet to complete that contains such questions as those listed in Table 4.2. Each of these questions is discussed in the three conferences with emphasis in the second and third conferences on the progress that has been made. Learners might even be

Table 4.2 Progress Conference Questions

Conference 1 (beginning of course)	Conference 2 (mid course)	Conference 3 (end of course)
1. What are your greatest strengths as a writer?	Use notes from Conference 1 to follow up on progress	Use notes from Conferences 1 and 2 to follow up on progress
2. What are your greatest weaknesses as a writer?	Use notes from Conference 1 to follow up on progress	Use notes from Conferences 1 and 2 to follow up on progress
3. What do you want to accomplish in this class to improve your writing skills?	Use notes from Conference 1 to follow up on progress.	Have you accomplished what you set out to do in this class?
4. Specifically, what are you going to do to improve your weaknesses as a writer?	Use notes from Conference 1 to follow up on progress.	Specifically, what have you done to improve your weaknesses as a writer?
5. What can your teacher do to help you achieve your writing goals?	Use notes from Conference 1 to follow up on progress.	What has your teacher done to help you achieve your writing goals?
6. What is something you have written in your second language that you feel good about? Why do you feel good about it?	What is something you have written during this course so far that you feel good about? Why do you feel good about it?	What have you written this semester that you are most proud of and why?

asked to come to the third conference having written a short paper on the progress they have made during the course.

Tally Sheets

Progress logs such as the tally sheets used with the 10-minute paragraphs also allow learners to see progress they are making by helping them keep track of grammatical errors marked by the teacher throughout the course (see Table 2.5, Chapter 2). A positive outcome from using error tally sheets is that the number of common, problematic errors learners make, such as with determiners or verb forms, diminishes with time. Typically, improvement begins to show after about six weeks into a course (Evans et al., 2011).

Edit Progress Log

An edit progress log generally indicates that, as a learner progresses through a course, the number of revisions needed to get a writing sample from a first draft to an error-free copy diminishes with each passing week (see Figure 4.4). While this log is associated with the 10-minute paragraph and 10 perfect sentences (see below), it can be modified to fit other writing tasks. The important point is that learners need to see their progress over time.

	Topic					# of revision
1.	Time	→	→	→	↓	3
2.	Success	→	→	→	↓	3
3.	Progress	→	→	↓		2
4.						
5.						
6.						
7.						
8.						

Figure 4.4 Ten Perfect Sentences Edit Log

Ten Perfect Sentences

This activity helps learners at lower levels see progress quickly (Henrichsen, 1981). The 10 perfect sentence activity actually has elements of the 10-minute paragraph process. Learners are given a topic, generally a one- or two-word prompt, and are asked to write 10 sentences on the topic. The only relationship among the sentences is that they all share the same topic, or perhaps the same grammatical structure, such as present progressive, passive voice, or future tense. The teacher collects and marks the sentences. Each sentence that is correct is marked with a check mark and is finished—*perfect*. The sentences that still have errors are marked by identifying where an error has occurred and are returned to the learners to revise. Each revision is then checked until it is error free. Once all 10 sentences are perfect, the learner moves on to the next set of 10 sentences. Using a simple table (see Figure 4.4), the teacher indicates by means of an arrow when a learner can move on to the next set of 10 sentences. The satisfaction of having a writing assignment "perfect" is quite motivating and helps the learners see that short steps of progress are possible in their long, language learning journey.

Summary

This chapter has:

- defined and explored the principle of time generally and as it relates to language learning strategies and L2 writing specifically;
- identified key classroom guidelines for responding to writing to improve the learner's ability to use time and task management feedback; and
- provided a range of learner activities and approaches designed to help L2 writers improve time management, avoid procrastination, develop writing skills, and build self-regulated learning strategies.

The next chapter:

- explores the self-regulated principle of physical environment, specifically how physical environment is important to self-regulation, and how a setting can benefit language learners generally and L2 writers specifically;
- discusses pedagogical principles that help learners implement effective physical environment strategies; and
- shares activities and approaches for learner improvement in physical environment that leads to improvement in writing.

Chapter 5

Physical Environment

Objectives

This chapter discusses the principle of physical environment and its application to L2 writing, and outlines practices and activities that help learners:

- understand how physical environment impacts writing performance;
- identify environmental factors that contribute to or distract from writing performance;
- clarify personal preferences for a positive writing environment; and
- develop strategies to avoid internal distractions.

Definitions and Applications

The physical environment principle of self-regulated learning focuses on location, or where learning takes place (Dembo & Seli, 2008; Zimmerman, 1998). Learners who are able to structure or adapt to their learning environment as needed perform better academically (Dembo & Eaton, 2000; Zimmerman, 1998; Zimmerman & Martinez-Pons, 1986). A detailed discussion and definition of the concept of physical environment will help learners understand physical environmental factors that impact learning. To understand how physical surroundings influence learning, it is first necessary to identify how they impact a learner's ability to concentrate on learning tasks. What physical elements disrupt concentration, causing learners to refocus attention?

Distracters may be external or internal. External factors are generally tangible and can be described using the senses of touch, sight, smell, and sound. External distracters may be in the form of a view out of a window or pictures hanging on the walls, the temperature of the room, the levels and frequency of noise, the type of furniture, the availability of needed materials (pencils, paper, books), the adequacy or lack of lighting, and the cleanliness of the room. Additionally, the time of day can be considered an external factor because any given place may be relatively distraction free and quite suitable for focused learning at one time of day but full of interruptions and unsuitable for focused learning at another time of day. External factors may contribute to or detract from an individual's ability to learn effectively. Minimizing external distractions is key when choosing a physical environment for effective learning (Dembo & Seli, 2008; Zimmerman, Bonner, & Kovach, 1996).

Internal factors are generally abstract, intangible, affective elements. They include distress (physiological and emotional), anxiety, and attitude (Dembo & Seli, 2008; Richard-Amato, 2010). Trying to study when emotional is a difficult task. Worries about an upcoming exam or making a tuition payment on time can disrupt concentration. Physiological distress, including hunger, illness, and fatigue, also impedes concentration and limits learning productivity. The time of day can also be considered an internal factor because the learner may be weary and unable to concentrate after eating a heavy lunch or after a long day of work but ready and able to learn at other times of the day. Other internal factors such as anxiety or attitude may be triggered by the learning environment.

Physical Environment and Language Learning

Language teachers have long maintained that learning context can improve second-language comprehension and acquisition (Brown, 2007; Cummins, 1981; Kelly, 1969; Omaggio Hadley, 2000). Typically language-learning context refers to linguistic (texts) and social (people and interactions) components, but physical elements such as sights, sounds, temperature, and lighting also factor into the language-learning context. Particularly relevant to language learning are internal factors, such as the affective factors attitude and anxiety, which may be triggered by the physical surroundings (Brown, 2007; Omaggio Hadley, 2000; Richard-Amato, 2010).

Research shows that attitude affects second-language learning success (Gardner & Lambert, 1972; Masgoret & Gardner, 2003; Murray & Christison, 2011). Learners' attitudes are generally directed toward the learners themselves, the target language, and speakers of the target language (Gardner & MacIntyre, 1993; Masgoret & Gardner, 2003; Oller, Hudson, & Liu, 1977). Individuals with positive attitudes and high self-esteem are more successful as language learners than are those with self-doubt or low self-esteem (see Chapter 2; Brown, 2007). Moreover, a learner's attitude toward the target language or the culture associated with that language may impact language learning (Harklau, 2000). For example, a person's negative attitude toward a foreign language can make being in a setting (physical/social) where that language is dominant so uncomfortable that language learning is adversely affected. This is a common phenomenon among some immigrants who have been forced to flee their homeland and relocate to countries where they feel out of place or unaccepted (Ogbu & Simons, 1998). Conversely, language learners who hold the language culture and host country in high regard usually have positive language-learning experiences (Brown, 2007; Gardner & Lambert, 1972; Oller, Baca, & Vigil, 1978).

Anxiety, which has also been found to impact the ability to learn language, is attributed to conditions of trait and state (Richard-Amato, 2010; Brown, 2007). Trait anxiety refers to people's predisposition to feeling anxious. Everyone feels a certain degree of anxiety but some have higher anxiety levels than others do. State anxiety, which is directly related to the internal aspect of the physical environment, results from being in uncomfortable situations, such as taking a test or speaking in public. Anxiety may be either facilitative or debilitative; the level of anxiety determines whether the anxiety helps or hinders learning (Brown, 2007).

One factor that may trigger debilitative levels of anxiety is the degree of challenge a learner experiences in a given environment. For example, a language learner who has been placed in a level that is too difficult will be frustrated and experience debilitating anxiety—such a learner would feel over challenged (Brown, 2007). Similarly, a language learner placed in a level that is too easy will be frustrated and lose interest—such a learner would feel under challenged. Research in language learning and learning theory suggests that learning is most productive in an appropriately challenging environment. While many aspects of Krashen's (1981, 1985) language-learning hypotheses are controversial and have come under much criticism, certain aspects, such as his input hypothesis ($i + 1$), are commonsensical and widely endorsed. According to the input hypothesis, learners must be exposed to "language that is just far enough beyond their current competence [+1] that they can understand most of it but still be challenged" in order to better acquire the language (Brown, 2007, p. 295). Few would argue with "the effectiveness of providing a reasonable challenge to students in a supportive, low-anxiety environment" (Brown, 2007, p. 296). Learners must be appropriately challenged in order to progress. Similarly, Sanford's (1966, 1968) concept of "optimal dissonance," or optimal anxiety, suggests that an appropriate balance of challenge and support is necessary for an optimal learning environment. If there is too much challenge (e.g., due to a student being placed at too high a level) and little or no support, learners can feel overwhelmed. If there is too little challenge (e.g., due to a student being placed at too low a level), an individual may feel safe but will not learn effectively. The amount of challenge a person can tolerate is a function of the amount of support that is available. An appropriate balance of challenge and support limits anxiety and maximizes learning capability.

Physical Environment and Writing

Finding a location with limited distractions is as important for effective writing as it is for any other academic activity. Understanding what constitutes a suitable writing environment for oneself is important when choosing a location. Not everyone has the same preferences. For example, the French novelist Marcel Proust (*In Search of Lost Time*) was so easily distracted by external noises that he had a cork-lined room built, in which he wrote from midnight to dawn. Novelist Margaret Drabble (*The Millstone, Jerusalem the Golden*) does her writing in a hotel room, where she can be undisturbed and write for days. British author J. K. Rowling, best known for the *Harry Potter* series, prefers to write in a café. Paul Matsuda, an accomplished scholar in second-language writing, once indicated that his most productive writing time is between midnight and 4 am because distractions are few and he is able to get more accomplished (P. K. Matsuda, personal communication, April 29, 2009). While these examples may be extreme, the point is that personal preferences matter when deciding when and where to write (see Zimmerman, 1998).

Experienced writers tend to have a good sense of what constitutes a suitable writing environment for them, but less experienced writers may not yet have a good sense of what constitutes a suitable writing environment for them. Novelist Stephen King (2000) offers some practical advice for inexperienced writers who have not yet determined their personal preferences: "If possible, there should be no telephone in your writing room, certainly no TV or videogames for you to fool around with. ... For the beginning writer in particular, it's wise to eliminate every possible distraction" (p. 156). Or as Boice put it, "Keep the writing context as simple and serene as possible" (Boice, 2000, p. 139).

The process of selecting a suitable physical environment for writing is illustrated by the second author of this book, who had three offices to choose from for working on this manuscript. Each location offers various advantages and disadvantages. One office is situated in a classroom building next to a vending machine station and has no external window. The building is removed from the distractions that are associated with other faculty and administrative offices; the computer in the office is connected to a reliable university Internet system, and there is a small resource library just across the hall. The second office is located on the top floor of a faculty office building, on the same floor as all the faculty and administrative offices. The office has a big picture window that frames a central courtyard with a fountain and garden and a panoramic view of a majestic mountain. Resources are extensive, including the author's professional library and the same university-supported Internet connection available in the classroom office. The third option is an office in the basement of the author's home. The Internet connection is inconsistent, and limited external light leaks in through a single window well, but noise levels are minimal and interruptions from faculty and students are nonexistent. After conducting a physical environment inventory (see "Activities and Approaches" later in this chapter), the author decided that the second office was the most conducive to writing.

It is important for writers to select writing locations that are relatively free of external distracters. In addition, writers needs to stay focused and free from distracting thoughts, emotions, and physical conditions. Ideal writing locations are seldom available, particularly for students with hectic lives on busy campuses. Self-regulated learners must find the best location possible for writing, modify the location as necessary and possible, and use adaptive strategies to control internal factors (Dembo & Seli, 2008).

Guiding Classroom Practices

The following classroom practices are designed to help teachers provide helpful feedback for learners in order to facilitate their abilities as writers by an understanding of how the physical environment contributes to self-regulated learning and effective L2 writing.

Provide Explicit Instruction About Physical Environment

Few, if any, writing texts teach learners explicitly about the importance of finding or establishing an appropriate physical environment for writing. This is no surprise since self-regulated learning theory and research have not been introduced in an L2 writing context until now (see Chapter 1). Because research suggests that physical environment makes a difference in performance (Dembo & Seli, 2008; Zimmerman, 1998; Zimmerman & Martinez-Pons, 1986), it is important to teach learners about the impact of location on writing.

The are several ways to help learners understand the importance of a supportive physical environment. The first step is to give a short presentation at the beginning of the course about what constitutes an appropriate physical environment. The presentation could include an overview of common distracters from and contributors to effective writing and a discussion of the "best" places to write. The presentation could be followed by activities, such as the ones in the following section, which reinforce the principles taught.

Create a Context-Rich Learning Environment

Kindergarten teachers are especially experienced with creating effective learning environments since they teach five-year-old children, who have remarkably short attention spans. Seasoned teachers know the children have short attention spans and structure the learning environment in their classes accordingly. Their classrooms feature multiple learning stations, and posters of the alphabet and key sight words with images depicting those words hang on every wall. Such an environment draws the students' attention to new learning opportunities when their minds start to wander from an assigned task. Insightful language teachers use similar strategies in creating engaging learning environments, not because their learners' attention spans are lacking, but because they know that context-rich environments contribute to language learning (Brown, 2007; Omaggio Hadley, 2000).

Insofar as possible, a classroom setting should encourage creativity and productive learning. Posters outlining key steps in writing or a sequence of images related to a current writing task may be displayed in the classroom. Something as simple as an inspiring scenic view can help enliven what may otherwise be a drab, lifeless classroom. Quotes that inspire good writing practices can be helpful if they are replaced frequently and referred to during lessons used for teaching purposes (see the "Great Quotes Wall" in "Activities and Approaches" later). Just as learners must modify their learning environments to promote effective learning, teachers must modify classrooms for the same reasons.

Provide Appropriate Physical Facilities

Some years ago a TESOL faculty member was asked to establish and direct a new writing center on campus that would be open to all students. When asked by the Physical Facilities office what kind of desks would be needed—fixed or movable—the newly appointed director replied that no desks would be needed. The writing center required round conferencing tables, movable chairs, a wall of study carrels that allowed for some degree of isolation, and several extra rooms for quiet study space. He also requested that large bookshelves be installed for writing reference materials. His aim was to create a writing center as favorable as possible to writing.

Few teachers have the luxury of requesting classroom furniture and shelves filled with reference books. However, teachers should make their classrooms as conducive as possible to student learning—for example, by moving desks into small circles for writing-group discussions. Teachers may also be able to request a specific room in advance when courses are being scheduled or ask a colleague to trade rooms. Physical facilities make a difference; make them conducive to the craft of writing.

Activities and Approaches

With a better understanding of the various elements that make up a physical environment and how location impacts learning, activities are now presented that can help learners evaluate the appropriateness of their learning and writing environments. Each activity was selected for its applicability to one of the chapter objectives, but some are applicable to multiple objectives, further reinforcing the importance of selecting appropriate physical environments for writing.

Understand How Physical Environment Impacts Writing Performance

Most learners realize that some places are just not conducive to study. However, they may have a favorite place to work but not be fully aware of how the location impacts their ability as a writer. Few, if any, textbooks teach this principle of location, but learners can easily be taught how to evaluate a possible study site.

A Tale of Two Sites

This activity is designed to help learners understand how locations with different physical characteristics impact writing performance. The teacher assigns learners two similar writing assignments to be completed in two noticeably different locations. The first site, selected by the teacher, is chosen for its busy, extreme conditions. It may be the center hall in the student union building at lunchtime or a train station at rush hour. Once at the site, the learner must write for 20 minutes on an assigned topic, usually something related to school, such as "Technology" or the "Value of Science." After writing for 20 minutes, the learner should spend 10 minutes writing a reflection on how easy or difficult it was to write under those conditions. The following questions can be used as a guide for this reflective writing: Were you able to focus on your writing? Does this writing reflect your real ability as a writer? What was most distracting about this site? How was your writing affected by the location? Was there anything about the location that helped you as a writer?

For the second writing assignment, learners should go to another designated site that is more conducive to study and writing, such as the library or a monitored study hall. As with the first assignment, students write for 20 minutes on an academic topic selected by the teacher, followed by 10 minutes of reflective writing using the same guiding questions.

These writing assignments should be followed by a class discussion of the experiences students had and the insights they gained. Following the discussion, the learners could write a brief, one- or two-page paper or journal entry comparing and contrasting the two sites in terms of their suitability as writing environments and reflecting on what they learned about the impact of location on writing performance.

Ask an Expert

Since many language teachers have had experience writing papers as university students, they understand how a physical environment can impact writing performance. For this activity, the teacher could assign learners to interview other teachers about the locations they typically used for writing when they were students as well as where they now write.

Some planning and arrangements will need to precede the activity. For instance, specific teachers could be contacted and informed about the activity and its purpose before learners start interviewing. Depending on the availability of other teachers, it may be necessary to ask one teacher to do multiple individual interviews. Alternatively, several learners could interview one teacher if necessary. Figure 5.1 includes directions for this activity and possible interview questions.

Ask an Expert

Directions: The purpose of this activity is to help you understand how experienced writers use their physical environment to help them be more productive writers. You will interview a teacher in your school about his or her writing-location preferences. Li sted below are the instructions and possible interview questions. Take good notes during the interview.

Step 1: Contact the teacher to set an appointment in advance.
Step 2: Give the teacher a copy of your questions at least two days before your visit.
Step 3: Arrive early for your appointment.
Step 4: Interview the teacher using the questions below as guidelines (take good notes).
Step 5: Write a thank-you note and send it to the teacher.

Introduction:
We have been studying how writing environments impact writers' performance. I would like to know what you have learned from your experiences about what makes a space conducive to writing.
1. Please describe what your ideal writing space would look like and why.
2. If you cannot have the ideal writing space, how would you modify a space to make it as good as possible?
3. When you were a college student, where did you do most of your writing?
4. Did you ever have to modify your space to help you focus? Please explain.
5. Does the time of day make a difference in how well you write? Please explain.
6. What distracts you most when you are writing, and how do you avoid that distraction?
7. Do you have any suggestions about how to avoid distractions while writing?
8. What advice can you give me about selecting or adapting a suitable writing space, that we have not already discussed?
9. Thank you very much for your time and help.

Figure 5.1 Ask an Expert Assignment Guidelines

After the interview, assign learners to write a short summary of the insights they gained from the "experts" about how physical environment impacts writing performance. As always, much can be gained from a focused follow-up discussion in pairs, in groups, or as a class.

Distinguish Among Factors that Contribute to or Distract from Writing Performance

As learners become aware of their options, they will be able to find suitable locations for writing. But until learners become consciously aware of their current writing location's strengths and weaknesses, they may not consider change necessary. These activities help learners understand how physical environments impact their writing performance.

Physical Environment Inventory

The purpose of the physical environment inventory is to draw the learners' attention to what their writing space is like as they consider the external environmental elements at the site. Because internal (affective) elements vary from one writing context to another, a physical environment inventory cannot adequately evaluate internal factors.

The inventory is conducted on a single sheet of paper (see Figure 5.2) that lists, in table format, some of the most common external environmental elements. The first column lists the elements, the second column gives a description of each element, and the third column is where the learners record their rating for each element. The instructions direct the learner to go to the site rather than simply visualize it, and then conduct an evaluation based on the descriptions on the form. The learner should consider each element and assign a rating of 1–5. The higher the score, the more suitable the site is for writing. A score of 40 is perfect, and 8 is the lowest possible score.

Once learners have completed a site inventory, a class discussion would allow learners to see how physical environments differ and recognize the importance of carefully and objectively selecting an appropriate writing space.

Case Study

Using the Three Offices case study in Figure 5.3, a teacher could ask learners to rate the appropriateness of each office as a writing space, using the Physical environment inventory (Figure 5.2). The learners could then be asked to answer four questions: Which site do you think the author selected and why? If you had to choose one of these three offices as your personal writing space, which would you select and why? This should be followed up with a pair, group, or class discussion.

Physical Environment Inventory

Directions: Take this handout with you to the location where you typically do your writing. Rate each external element according to the definition listed in the second column and the rating scale found below the table. Total your ratings for the external elements, and write your total in the last row. The closer your total is to 40, the more suitable it is for quiet, uninterrupted writing.

Element	Description	Rating
View/sight	Some locations have views that are beautiful but distracting. Others have views onto busy streets or public spaces that can also be distracting. A writing location should not be overwhelmed by views out of windows or onto busy distracting walls or spaces.	
Sound/noise	Sound or noise levels are a common distraction. Things to consider are music, email, cell phones, and other people who use the same or a nearby space. Noise levels should be minimal. How quiet is your space?	
Lighting	Adequate lighting is a must. Some places can be poorly lit making it hard to see. Other concerns may be flickering lights, or even glaring lights. How suitable is the lighting in your writing location?	
Furniture	A good writing location should have comfortable appropriate furniture on which to study and write. At the least, you should have a comfortable chair and desk or table with adequate space for your work. How suitable is the furniture in your writing location?	
Cleanliness	Messy, untidy, dirty conditions can be very distracting to writing and concentration on learning tasks. How clean, organized, and tidy is your site?	
Materials	Being able to write without interruptions requires that you have all the needed materials with you such as paper, pencils, dictionaries, etc. Does your space have the necessary materials?	
Temperature	Extreme temperatures can be very distracting. In some instances the temperature can be controlled, in others it is fixed. How suitable is the temperature in your location for writing and learning tasks?	
Time of day	Any room can be quiet and free from distraction at one hour and noisy, busy and full of commotion at another hour. During the time of day when you typically use this location to write, how suitable is it for writing and concentrating on learning tasks?	
Comments:		
	Total	

*Rating scale:

1	2	3	4	5
very poor for writing performance		neither poor nor excellent, just acceptable		excellent for writing performance

Figure 5.2 Physical Environment Inventory

Following this case-study analysis, the learners could write a similar case study based on their own experiences. They could describe their current writing space or a particularly good or bad writing environment they have used in the past. Since case studies are likely to be an unfamiliar genre to the students, a short assignment cover sheet with guidelines and a few examples would be helpful (see Messerschmitt & Johnson Hafernik, 2009, for sample case studies). Learners could be asked to leave out any information that would identify them as the author and to give their case study a title that is both descriptive and creative, such as "Simple and Serene" or "The Saturday Market."

Three Offices Case Study

A writer has a large writing task to complete over the course of several weeks. He has several office spaces to choose from in which to do this writing. Read the descriptions of each office below; then using the Physical Environment Inventory, rate how good the site would be for writing.

Classroom Building	Faculty Office Building	Home Office
This office is situated in a classroom building next to a vending machine station and has no external window. The fluorescent lighting is good. The walls are quite thin, and during the day muffled sounds from adjacent offices are almost constant. A loud bell rings every hour signaling class breaks. The building is, however, removed from other faculty and administrative offices; the computer is connected to the university internet system, and there is a very good resource library just across the hall. The office is generally well organized and has ample desk and table space. Custodial crews keep the office well cleaned.	This office is located on the top floor of a faculty office building. All the faculty and administrative offices are on the same floor. The office has a big picture window which frames a central courtyard with a fountain and surrounding gardens and a panoramic view of a prominent, majestic mountain. Resources are extensive; the author's professional library, a robust, university-supported internet connection and library delivery service all available in this office. The office is generally well organized and has ample desk and table space. Custodial crews keep the office well cleaned.	This office is located in the basement of the author's home. As such, temperatures are generally quite moderate all year. The internet connection is patchy; limited external light leaks in through one window well; a floor lamp and ceiling light must be on when the office is in use. Noise levels are minimal, and interruptions from faculty and students are nonexistent. With the phone turned off, it is a very quiet location. Books must be brought home for use since most of the author's professional library is at school. All work must be done on limited desk space which contains the computer and printer.

Element	Rating
View/sight	
Sound/noise	
Lighting	
Furniture	
Cleanliness	
Materials	
Temperature	
Time of day	
Total	

Element	Rating
View/sight	
Sound/noise	
Lighting	
Furniture	
Cleanliness	
Materials	
Temperature	
Time of day	
Total	

Element	Rating
View/sight	
Sound/noise	
Lighting	
Furniture	
Cleanliness	
Materials	
Temperature	
Time of day	
Total	

*Rating scale:

1	2	3	4	5
very poor for writing performance		neither poor nor excellent, just acceptable		excellent for writing performance

Figure 5.3 Three Offices Case Study Worksheet

Once all the case studies have been submitted, the teacher could make copies with the authors' names removed. The studies could then be used for pair or group work in which learners further analyze sites by using the physical environment inventory to identify case studies that describe good and bad writing environments.

Establish Personal Preferences for a Positive Writing Environment

Once learners have a general sense of the factors in a physical environment that can contribute to productive writing, they should reinforce what they have learned by applying that knowledge. They can do this by designing an ideal writing venue or modifying an existing site to facilitate their writing.

Illustrate It

The aim of this activity is to encourage learners to use their imagination and creativity as they think about how features of a physical environment can impact writing. Learners are asked to illustrate their ideal writing space either by drawing or by cutting and pasting pictures onto a poster. The more flexibility they are given, the more creative the final results will be. Instructions should be kept simple while still giving enough information to complete the task (see Figure 5.4 for sample directions). A copy of the physical environment inventory handout (see Figure 5.3) will help learners decide which features to illustrate.

Once the illustrations are completed, the real learning and evaluation begins. An excellent way to assess if learners do indeed understand how a physical environment impacts learning is to have them explain to their classmates and teacher in a brief presentation what they have included in their illustrations and why.

Alternatives to the preceding activity include having learners illustrate an unsuitable writing location. Knowing what to avoid is another way of reinforcing

---

Illustrating the Ideal Writing Space

Directions: Now that you understand the importance of selecting a suitable location for writing, you will illustrate an ideal writing space. You may draw your own pictures or cut and paste pictures from various sources to illustrate what you think a perfect writing space should look like. It can be in color or black and white—use your imagination. The only restrictions you have are to make sure your illustration fits on a piece of paper that is (indicate dimension requirements here). The Physical Environment Inventory handout should give you a few ideas of elements that you may want to include in your illustration. Have fun!

Figure 5.4 Illustrate the Perfect Space Assignment Guidelines

what students have learned about an appropriate physical environment for writing. An alternative to a class presentation would be to have the learners write a description of the space they have designed. Finally, the illustrations could be hung on the walls of the classroom for a few weeks. Teachers may find it helpful to take photographs of the illustrations for a future review session or for use when teaching the principle of physical environment to other writing classes.

Great Quotes Wall

Since what writers see in a writing space can influence performance, a good way to enhance productivity is to surround their space with positive, non-distracting reminders of good writing practices. One way to achieve this is by creating a great quotes wall. The idea is for teachers to draw learners' attention to what good writers do. The teacher will need to start this process by informing the class that this space will be used to post quotes that help remind them of good writing principles. Learners are welcome and, in fact, encouraged to participate by bringing quotes they find.

There is no right or wrong way to create a quote wall, but several guidelines may help. First, use the space for teaching, and keep it fresh. When a new unit is introduced in the class, the teacher may want to post a few short quotes that highlight concepts that will be covered. Replace the quotes frequently. This gives the quote wall greater impact. It is also a good idea to encourage learners to look for and share quotes they might find in their studies. In addition, learners may find it useful to start hanging inspiring quotes in their own writing space if possible and appropriate. Also, the quote wall could be created around themes such as revision, brainstorming, or editing. Figure 5.5 illustrates how a quote wall on revision might be structured.

Writer at Work: Do Not Disturb

Since publication is a requirement for faculty promotions at many universities, Faculty Development offices on campuses often offer workshops to help junior faculty develop productive writing practices. One topic frequently discussed in such workshops is the importance of isolating oneself from interruptions while writing. One way of doing this is to hang a "do not disturb" sign on the door (see Boice, 1997; Gray, 2005). Any writer may use this technique, but it is particularly useful for inexperienced second-language writers. Students could be assigned to create a sign that informs others not to disturb them. The examples that follow show the kinds of things signs might say.

- Writer at work; do not disturb.
- Writing in progress; come back in an hour.
- Writing under investigation; do not cross this line.

English Writing 105

The Value of Revision

"Great writing is never right the first time."
Your teacher's philosophy

"I have never thought of myself as a good writer. Anyone who wants reassurance of that should read one of my first drafts. But I am one of the world's great rewriters."

James Michener (1964)

"Clear writers have accepted the grim reality that nine-tenths of all writing is rewriting."

John Trimble (1975)

"By the time I'm nearing the end of a story, the first part will have been reread and altered and corrected at least 150 times. . . Good writing is essentially rewriting. I am positive of this."

Roald Dahl (1986)

Interviewer: How much rewriting do you do?
Hemingway: It depends. I rewrote the ending of *A Farewell to Arms*, the last page of it, thirty-nine times before I was satisfied.
Interviewer: Was there some technical problem there? What was it that had stumped you?
Hemingway: Getting the words right.

Ernest Hemingway (1965)

Figure 5.5 Great Quotes Wall Poster for Writing Classroom

Learners should be encouraged to be creative and design their own sign. A class competition might also be held to vote for the most effective, attractive, and creative signs.

Develop Strategies that Help Avoid Internal Distractions

Until now, little has been said about how to manage internal (affective) factors in order to maximize learning and writing productivity. Internal factors generally vary from one context and time to another. On one day a learner may be distracted by a minor illness, but after some rest and medication, the distraction is gone; likewise, the preoccupation over paying rent usually passes once the rent is paid. Since internal factors vary, a good way to manage them is first to understand what factors influence the learner and how those factors impact learning. With that understanding, appropriate compensatory strategies can be applied (Dembo & Seli, 2008). The suggestions that follow are intended to: (1) help learners understand what internal factors impact them, and (2) offer various strategies that help counter these internal distractions.

What Distracts You?

This activity is based on a worksheet (see Figure 5.6) that can help learners identify common internal distractions, recognize how those distracters may affect them, and determine solutions for overcoming those distractions. The worksheet has five columns. The first column presents a brief description of a distracting situation. Columns two and three allow the learner to indicate whether the distracter is either external or internal. Column four is where a ranking of 1–5 is placed to indicate how distracting the situation is for the learner, and column five provides a space for the learner to write a possible solution to the distracting situation.

This worksheet can be used in various ways. First, learners could simply identify which distracters in the handout are external and which are internal. While the focus of the exercise is on internal distracters, a few external examples have been included in the list to help learners see the differences. Second, learners could rank each internal distracter based on how much they perceive such a situation would distract them; the rating scale included on the handout can be used for this purpose. A logical follow-up to this step would be to have pair, group, or class discussions of each situation and have learners explain why a situation may or may not be overly distracting to them. Finally, learners could write possible solutions for remedying the distracting situation.

Once the worksheet has been completed, a teacher could conduct a class discussion about the strategies suggested by the students. This could be coordinated with a presentation of the following remedies, or strategies for countering internal distractions.

What distracts you?

Directions: Each statement below describes some kind of a situation that possibly could distract you from your learning tasks. First, identify by checking the appropriate box which kind of distraction it is—external or internal. Then using the *rating scale below the table indicate (1–5) how distracting you think this situation would be for you. In the last box, write a possible solution to the problem.

	Description	Ex	Int	Rank	Possible solution
1.	I stayed up late last night to finish a paper that was due for class today, and I feel very sleepy right now.				
2.	It is Friday afternoon; my friends have invited me out to dinner and a dance.				
3.	I just ate a big lunch, and now I have to sit in this warm room to do my English assignments.				
4.	Someone walks into the room where I am studying.				
5.	My roommate and I had a heated discussion last night.				
6.	I don't understand what the teacher expects me to do with this assignment.				
7.	The Grounds crew starts mowing the lawns outside my window while I am studying.				
8.	I have a slight headache.				
9.	The work I am asked to do for this class is just like the work I did last year in my English class.				
10.	I have not eaten since this morning; it's now 4 pm.				
11.	I paid a lot of money for my tuition. I don't think the school if giving me what I paid for.				
12.	My email alert rings while I am writing a paper for one of my classes.				

*Rating scale

1	2	3	4	5
Not distracting at all				Very distracting

Figure 5.6 What Distracts You Self-Check List

Remedies

A number of different strategies can be used to avoid internal distractions. The following are just a few examples of possible strategies for improving concentration on learning tasks. Many of these can be combined or modified to meet particular learning styles.

BE HERE NOW

Maintaining concentration is not any easy task because "writing is hard and distractions are easier" (Gray, 2005, p. 16). Furthermore, concentration requires practice. Unlike taking medication, which acts on the ailment without action on the part of the patient, concentration requires effort and practice on the part of the learner. One way to draw attention back to a task is by developing the "Be here now" concentration technique (Schuette, 1989). The idea is that each time you find yourself wandering mentally, you recite the line "Be here now" and bring your attention back where you want it. It may require repeating this phrase several hundred times over the course of a day, but practice will help, and the time between the "Be here now" utterances will increase. Practice will help.

A similar strategy to the "Be Here Now" technique is named after a piece of equipment used for horses. Blinders are small cups, usually made of leather, which are placed over the horse's eyes to keep the horse from being distracted or frightened by something to the side. The horse performs better when its vision is focused on its objective. While writers may not want to actually wear blinders, they can use this as a metaphor or a pneumonic device to keep reminding themselves to keep the blinders on, or to keep their focus on what needs to be done here and now.

THE SPIDER'S STRATEGY

Yet another strategy that is similar to "Be Here Now" and "Blinders" is a process of training yourself not to give in to distractions. For example, many people will automatically look up from what they are doing when someone walks into the room where they are studying, even if the person does not say a thing. The natural tendency is to find out who it is. The spider technique teaches that when a vibrating tuning fork is held next to a spider's web, the spider will come looking for the cause of the vibration. If this process is repeated several times, the spider will soon discover that it is a distraction not worth considering and stop responding. People can learn to ignore unimportant distractions as well. With effort and practice, this skill can be learned (Schuette, 1989).

WORRY/THINK TIME

Everyone has ideas or worries that pop into their heads from time to time; it's human nature. Often these ideas will require attention or action in the future. How a learner handles on-the-spot distractions is a measure of a self-regulated learner. A disciplined learner will stay focused on the present task and see it through to completion. A way to resolve these sudden ideas is to set time aside as worry or think time each day. Simply tell yourself that you will deal with this thought during your worry time. Keep a small note pad nearby; think of it as a worry note pad or a "data dump" (Gray, 2005 p. 16). Jot down in a word or two what the thought was: for example, "turn library book in by tomorrow," "call work," or "buy pizza for the party." Then, at the designated time each day, deal with the worries and tasks that have been noted.

PHYSICAL REMEDIES

Trying to work through a headache, many hours without food, or sleep deprivation will lower concentration, productivity, and writing quality. But most physiological conditions like the ones just mentioned can be remedied. If a learner is aware of the cause and its impact on writing productivity, appropriate action can be taken. Sleep, food, or proper attention to illness can cure the most common ailments that distract a learner from the tasks at hand. The strategy is to recognize the problem and take necessary steps to solve it.

Summary

This chapter has:

- defined the principle and elements of physical environment and how they positively impact self-regulated learning when appropriate modification and adaptation strategies are put into practice;
- identified key classroom guidelines that help learners understand how a physical setting may maximize their abilities as self-regulated writers; and
- provided a range of learner activities and approaches designed to help L2 writers recognize physical environmental factors that can contribute to or distract from effective learning and productive writing.

The next chapter:

- continues the discussion of environment, specifically social environment and how important environment is to self-regulated learning and improved writing performance;
- discusses pedagogical principles that help learners develop suitable social environment strategies; and
- illustrates activities and approaches for learner improvement in a social environment that lead to improvement in writing.

Chapter 6

Social Environment

Objectives

This chapter discusses the principle of social environment and its application to L2 writing, and outlines practices and activities to help learners:

- recognize when they are having difficulty learning or achieving goals;
- develop a positive attitude toward seeking help;
- learn social skills for effective interaction with peers, instructors, and learning support staff;
- develop strategies for seeking, finding, and evaluating help; and
- build a community of learning for writing improvement.

Definitions and Applications

The social environment principle of self-regulated learning focuses on the people *with whom* learners engage in relation to their studies (Zimmerman & Risemberg, 1997). It involves the interaction of learners with peers, teachers, tutors, and others to improve learning. Self-regulated learners recognize when they are having difficulty learning or achieving goals, and seek assistance. They see this as a useful strategy, and realize that they can change poor performance. Rather than attributing it to factors beyond their control—such as a lack of intelligence—or blaming it on someone else, they view their poor performance as a deficiency in knowledge or effort, both of which can be addressed with the application of relevant strategies. Learners who are focused on mastery of course material (rather than on getting good grades), have clear learning goals, and have confidence in their abilities, are likely to access social sources when they perceive the need for help (Dembo et al., 2006; Dweck, 2000). Low achievers, or those with low levels of self-efficacy (the belief in one's ability to be successful in a specific situation), may feel that asking for assistance reflects negatively on their understanding or ability.

Those who recognize that learning is an active rather than a passive process know that mastery of concepts and skills involves questioning, gathering information, analyzing, synthesizing, drawing conclusions, and practicing, not simply transferring information from teacher to learner. To encourage learners to take responsibility, instructors must help them acquire a positive attitude about seeking help, recognize when they need help, and identify appropriate sources of assistance. Learners may also need to acquire social skills so that they can effectively interact with peers, ask questions in and out of class, and get assistance from their professors and learning support centers. In other words, they need to know how to seek, find, and evaluate help.

Instruction and related exchanges between teacher and learner, and learner and learner, entail interaction within the social environment. This interaction supports language acquisition and aids the development of self-regulation. Applying the principle of social environment to language learning in general and to L2 writing specifically is discussed next.

Social Environment and Language Learning

Few factors are more important to language learning than social interaction. Language acquisition theories indicate the importance of risk-taking, or experimenting with language features such as grammatical structures and vocabulary, and getting feedback to determine communicative effectiveness (e.g., see Swain, 1995). Achieving communicative competence, or the ability to comprehend and use language to communicate accurately and effectively in a variety of situations, is a primary goal of most language instruction (e.g., see Canale & Swain, 1980; Hymes, 1971, 1972; Savignon, 1997, 2001), and includes both oral and written expression. To achieve this goal, learners must have opportunities to participate in meaningful and realistic language exchanges. Through these exchanges, they attempt to understand others and make themselves understood.

When applied to language learning, the social environment principle supports interaction. More specifically, it supports interacting for a realistic, communicative purpose—to get answers to questions and to help with learning. Seeking assistance gives learners a real purpose for communicating; they are not simply interacting with instructors and peers on possibly irrelevant topics in order to practice the language. Although a lack of proficiency on the part of learners may affect the effectiveness of the communication, and may thus compromise the accuracy and benefit of the help sought, the experience of formulating the request and asking follow-up questions to ensure comprehension is a worthwhile activity not only to develop self-regulation and receive needed learning assistance, but also to aid language acquisition. This process makes learners more responsible for communicating because they must clarify their responses and ask for clarification of their peers' and instructor's responses to ensure they get the help they need.

In pedagogical situations, instructors must be aware of learners' reluctance to participate and other anxieties. In the L2 classroom, these factors may be attributed to cultural variables. Learners may be accustomed to viewing teachers as authority figures and experts. Some cultural viewpoints do not support help-seeking behavior. Learners from such cultures may consider asking questions or requesting an instructor's help to be a criticism of their teacher's pedagogical skill and knowledge, which exhibits a lack of respect (e.g., see Beykont & Daiute, 2002). They may also feel that it is the instructor's role to tell them what they need to know, rather than being actively responsible for identifying and addressing their own learning needs. In such cases, teachers must approach these issues in a culturally sensitive way, helping learners understand the benefits of active learning, modeling appropriate behavior, and scaffolding classroom activities to assist learners in becoming comfortable with unfamiliar roles and responsibilities.

Social Environment and Writing

At first glance, the social environment may not appear critical to developing skill in writing. In many respects, writing is an independent activity—involving an individual in the act of formulating and expressing ideas. One can envision the solitary writer in a private retreat (office, cabin, loft, studio) isolated from family, friends, and civilization, composing laboriously or writing feverishly under the influence of inspiration. However, writing involves audience. Amateur writers must become aware that writing is the act of communicating with unseen persons. Visualizing these persons assists them in determining what to say and how to say it. Seeking feedback from a potential audience is beneficial to mastering written communication; the social environment dimension of self-regulated learning assists in this process.

Self-regulated writers recognize that receiving feedback throughout the various stages of writing (drafting, revision, and editing) is critical. They understand who to ask for help, how to ask, what to ask, and how to evaluate the information received. They feel comfortable sharing their writing, receiving constructive criticism, and providing feedback to others. Understanding that writing, and learning in general, are active processes in which success is strengthened by utilizing the social environment is central to becoming a self-regulated writer.

Guiding Classroom Practices

The following guiding classroom practices are designed to encourage learners to use the social environment for the purposes of language acquisition and the development of self-regulation. By following these guidelines, teachers can provide appropriate opportunities inside and outside the classroom to help learners achieve their goals and create an effective teaching and learning environment. The subsequent section identifies specific activities that use these practices as a foundation.

Establish a Communicative Classroom

For this to occur, the instructor must build a supportive environment in which learners feel comfortable taking risks and making errors. Instructors can reduce learners' anxiety when they try to understand meaning, are non-critical and non-judgmental, and paraphrase what the learner has said to ensure understanding (Gebhard, 2006). Instructors can also encourage and reward risk-taking by not overcorrecting learners' utterances, modeling correct language, and emphasizing fluency over form (although there is a time and place to focus on form). Learners' self-defense barriers, feelings of incompetence, and fear of using the language will decrease when they know they are accepted by instructors and peers, and that linguistic risk-taking builds proficiency (see the related discussion of internal factors in Chapter 5).

Reduce Teacher Centrality

Instructors need to relinquish their position of centrality in the classroom in favor of collaboration, including consistent use of pair and group work. Learners need opportunities to listen to each other, express their ideas, and share their writing (Gebhard, 2006). To be successful, peer activities must be carefully structured, with clear learner roles, tasks, and expectations. Through these means, learners will begin to recognize that they are responsible for the factors affecting their learning, and that support can come from multiple sources within their social environment. Their confidence will increase when they see that they are able to help others.

Respect Learning Preferences and Learner Needs

Learners have individual preferences for working independently or collaboratively, and need to determine when these modes of learning are most appropriate. They will also vary in their desire to participate in discussions and the degree to which they access and leverage the social environment of the classroom without encouragement. This variation depends on individual characteristics and cultural background. Some L2 learners hesitate to interrupt, are more comfortable reflecting prior to responding, and want to contribute to discussions only when they feel they have something of value to share (Beykont & Daiute, 2002).

To address these issues, teachers must give learners opportunities to experience different modes of learning (i.e., independent, collaborative) and to reflect on the advantages and disadvantages of each, depending on the learning task. They must also create an environment that supports effective participation and collaboration by ensuring that participation among learners is equal, that all voices are heard, and that diverse perspectives are valued (e.g., see Beykont & Daiute, 2002). Instructors must allow the response time learners need to process the language, reflect on what they want to say, and formulate their answers.

Provide Training, Modeling, and Scaffolding

As with all new learning tasks and behaviors, learners need appropriate training and opportunities to practice and develop related strategies. For instance, although self-reflection on performance is an important aspect of becoming a self-regulated learner, it may not prove useful unless it is accompanied by feedback or co-reflection, but peers often fail to provide this reflective dialogue as expected (van den Boom, Paas, & van Merrienboer, 2007). In other words, learners may not take full advantage of the social environment or may not know how to do so, and consequently do not realize its benefits.

Using the social environment to its full potential will likely not occur on its own. Instructors must prepare students to use their social environment by communicating a clear rationale for these kinds of activities, introduce the activities in incremental steps, and allow autonomy for how learners approach and accomplish them. Additionally, reflecting on an activity both individually and collectively helps learners understand benefits and identify areas for adjustment. The following story illustrates the results of not following these guidelines.

When one of the authors was an undergraduate student enrolled in a first-year university-level writing course, her professor asked students in the class to exchange their papers with a classmate. This occurred on the day the papers were due, just minutes before submitting them. No previous pair or group work or interaction of any type had transpired among students in the class. Thus, it was with trepidation and feelings of discomfort that students shared their papers with each other (essentially with total strangers) for a final "proof-reading." Furthermore, no instructions were provided as to what type of feedback was to be given as a result of this activity, nor was the opportunity available to make any substantive changes in the papers once feedback was received. Most of the students returned the papers to their partners with a polite, "That was really good. I enjoyed reading it."

Although well-meaning, the activity failed to effectively use the peer-level social environment to improve writing. The feelings of reluctance the students had about sharing their work with each other had a negative effect because they were not prepared for this, nor did they understand the advantages of using peer feedback or having an actual audience. No training or modeling had occurred prior to the activity nor were the expectations clear. In this case, not only was the activity *not* beneficial, but also it was even somewhat harmful to learner morale.

This activity would have been more effective had the students been accustomed to working with each other, had they understood the purpose and benefits of peer review, and had students had some autonomy in deciding what aspect of their writing they wished to receive feedback on. To accomplish this, the instructor needed to establish a supportive classroom environment by providing regular opportunities for learners to get acquainted with each other and to work in pairs and groups prior to the assignment's due date. They needed to have collaborated on various aspects of the writing process, such as brainstorming ideas on a topic, organizing these ideas, composing a thesis statement, giving feedback on drafts, and editing. Each of these activities should have been accompanied by clear instructions, modeling, feedback, reflection, sharing of reflections, and self-identification of ways to improve, thereby increasing autonomy. This training, modeling, and scaffolding would have increased the value of the activity and supported the learners in using the social environment to become self-regulated writers.

Negotiate Meaning

Building communicative competence and the ability to seek and provide assistance within a community of learners involves opportunities to negotiate meaning. This entails expressing oneself, clarifying meaning, seeking to understand other interlocutors, and ensuring that ideas have been effectively communicated. In an L2 context, learners negotiate meaning when they collaborate to explore topics for writing, provide feedback, ask for clarification, and react to responses. Negotiating meaning builds language skills and enhances self-regulated learning through interactions within the social environment with the purpose of improving learning, and, specifically, writing skill.

Consider Interpersonal Factors

When teachers and peers make verbal or written comments on learners' written work, emphasis should be on creating a collaborative environment that fosters learning. Teachers are generally aware that their comments can facilitate or hinder the development of learners' writing, and thus try to enhance their relationships with learners by minimizing comments focused on judging, evaluating, and criticizing (e.g., see Hyland & Hyland, 2006a).

Comments must be appropriate to the individual learner and focus on what will be most beneficial to that person. For instance, some learners prefer to get feedback regarding all improvements needed in a piece of writing, while others may be devastated by such an approach. The degree of directness or indirectness of the feedback may also be a factor for individual learners. In some cases, imperative comments on papers are more effective than teacher response that involves asking questions or making suggestions (Sugita, 2006). Suggestions and questions are often misinterpreted by learners, who feel that teachers should take a more authoritative stance (e.g., see Ferris & Hedgcock, 2005). While the teacher's goal is to encourage the learner to take responsibility for the writing and changes made, learners may expect specific direction. Additionally, peers are often reticent to give feedback that may be viewed as negative because they are uncertain of their expertise and desire to maintain social harmony.

To address these issues, teachers must monitor their feedback and how they express it. They must also help learners consider the best ways to give helpful feedback to each other. This can be accomplished with structured peer response activities and modeling. Teachers may need to help learners understand cultural differences in behavior and expectations. As teachers become more familiar with the personalities of individual learners and observe learner response to feedback, they can appropriately modify their comments and guide peers to do the same. The objective for the assignment must also be considered as response may be focused on content development, appropriateness of organizational patterns, or a grammatical feature; thus instructors must communicate to learners their strategies and philosophies for the response while considering interpersonal factors and learner expectations. Feedback may come across as harsh or confusing if too direct, but can be ignored if too indirect, even though feedback in that form is meant to encourage. Similarly, too little feedback may be viewed as laziness on the part of the teacher and too much positive feedback may falsely convey that the learner is performing well.

Activities and Approaches

The following activities suggest ways instructors can help learners recognize the benefits of the social environment and understand its role as one of the six dimensions enabling them to become self-regulated writers. These activities are based on the learning objectives introduced at the beginning of the chapter and support the guiding practices presented in the previous section. Some overlap of activity types and purposes exist within and across chapters. This repetition can be an effective learning tool. As learners become familiar with a strategy or an activity and have the opportunity to practice it for a variety of purposes, it becomes more easily applied and meaningful.

Also, by exploring different applications, learners can identify strategies most effective for them personally and for specific tasks.

Recognize Difficulties in Learning or Achieving Goals

This objective relates to some of the guiding practices and activities discussed in Chapter 2 on the principle of motive in that it involves self-assessment on the part of the learner and a needs analysis on the part of the instructor. It also has some relationship to the performance dimension of self-regulated learning as learners examine their performance, determine the degree to which they have met their goals, and revise or set new goals accordingly. This chapter focuses specifically on how the social environment can assist learners in identifying and overcoming challenges to reaching their goals.

Guiding Questions

Instructors can follow a number of procedures to teach students to use the social environment. These involve viewing the writing product, asking the learner questions, and observing the learner (Nation, 2009). This information gathering should focus on various aspects of the writing process including purpose, audience, content and organization, accuracy and fluency, drafting, and editing. Guiding questions for each of these stages can help learners analyze their strengths and weaknesses. The questions can be modeled in one-on-one teacher–learner conferences, used as the basis for peer review sessions, or considered independently by the learner. Through modeling and interaction with teacher and peers, learners incrementally move toward greater self-regulation. Questions help learners recognize areas in the writing process where they need assistance, and that needed support can be obtained through the social environment.

Guiding questions can be designed for each stage of the writing process. (For a useful list of questions, see Nation, 2009, p. 126.) A few possibilities follow in Figure 6.1. These can be adapted based on the level of the learner and specific teaching objectives. They can be used when reviewing a draft or be adjusted for use prior to writing. Each area could be examined separately over a number of class sessions so as not to be too overwhelming and to allow for more thorough discussion. A similar model could focus on a single stage of the writing process with multiple questions regarding that stage. To encourage self-regulation, teachers need to structure follow-up activities to see that learners have identified areas of difficulty and strategies for using the social environment to address them. This could involve a simple written reflection or oral report (even a brief sharing in front of the whole class) as to the outcomes of this activity.

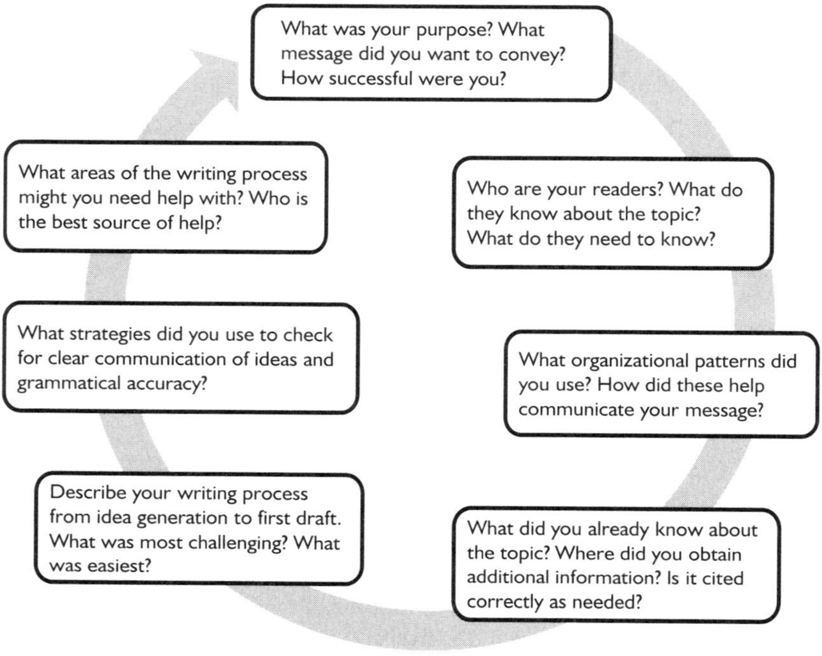

Figure 6.1 Guiding Questions

Dialogue Journals

As noted in the section on guiding classroom practices, effective journal prompts may not help learners become more self-regulated unless feedback or co-reflection is involved (e.g., see van den Boom, Paas, & van Merrienboer, 2007). Dialogue journal exchanges between the learner and the teacher on a regular basis, such as weekly, provide a way for teachers to get acquainted with learners and a safe means for learners to identify and express their feelings about difficulties. Teachers can structure journal assignments to collect information about learners' English language learning experiences, their goals and study habits, and especially, their strengths and weaknesses as L2 writers. Sample topics focused on the use of the social environment might include the following.

- When you write, what do you do best on your own—without help from classmates or your teacher?
- How can working with classmates help you become a better writer? In what ways have classmates assisted you in the writing process (e.g., brainstorming ideas, organization, commenting on content, editing or proofreading)? Give examples.

- How do you decide whether you should get help or simply continue to work on your own?
- How can your instructor best help you improve your writing skills?
- How have you successfully used writing resources available to you, such as the Writing Center or other learning assistance centers on campus or online?
- Describe a time you faced a challenge with your writing and sought help to solve it.
- Describe a time you faced a challenge with your writing and solved it successfully on your own.
- How effective do you find the feedback of others (e.g., roommates, family members, friends) on your written drafts? If effective, what makes it so? If not effective, what could you do to make it more effective?

Through these dialogue journals, instructors gain insights into learners' views regarding the social environment. As the dialogue evolves, teachers can encourage learners to try new strategies and monitor the success of these strategies. A nice feature of these journals is that learners are practicing their writing, acquiring language, building fluency, developing social skills (i.e., how to ask questions and respond to feedback), and communicating for a real purpose. In other words, they are improving their ability to seek help within the social environment and are becoming better writers in the process.

Certainly dialogue journals can also be effective between peers and even between peers in different sections of the same course if teachers structure and model these exchanges appropriately. This can be accomplished by providing examples of helpful exchanges, discussing appropriate language with which to express understanding and provide suggestions, identifying specific tasks and topics with which peers can be most helpful to each other, and designing the logistics for the exchange. (See Chapter 2 for further discussion about the use of peer dialogue journals for the purpose of providing learners with an authentic audience; see Chapter 3 for types of reflective notebooks.)

Muddiest Point

Similar to the one-minute paper idea described in Chapter 3, where learners reflect about what they learned at the end of the class session, the muddiest point technique involves asking learners to identify, possibly on a 3 × 5 index card, the muddiest point (i.e., the most unclear concept) that was discussed during the class session. The teacher collects the cards and examines them for themes or commonalities and addresses misconceptions in the next class period. This activity supports self-regulation in that learners are taking responsibility for noting what they do not understand.

To extend this activity and focus it more specifically on the development of self-regulation, teachers can have learners determine what they can do to get further information or increase their understanding on the topic they have identified. Learners could also be organized into groups to receive help from each other, thereby recognizing that the teacher is not the source of all knowledge, and that peers also have some expertise. A variation of the activity could be grouping learners with related questions together and having them seek answers from the textbook, the Internet, classmates, or other sources.

Additional ideas for the muddiest point activity include having learners read each other's writing drafts and identify the muddiest point; asking them to collect, categorize, and summarize the muddiest points identified in a class session; checking back in a later class period to determine if the muddiest points have been grasped; and including these points as exam questions (Angelo & Cross, 1993). The first activity lends itself well to an L2 writing classroom and is a good starting point for peer review, particularly as learners may have difficulty recognizing grammar errors or commenting on the technical aspects of writing. Almost every language learner, regardless of proficiency level, can identify an unclear idea. The experience of having to explain and clarify muddy points helps the writer to achieve clarity of expression. In our experience as L2 writing teachers, we have often asked learners to verbally clarify a sentence or section of their paper. Their verbal expression is often much clearer than what they have written. Our response is usually, "Put what you just told me in writing." Talking through the meaning of ideas with someone else is an excellent use of the social environment. To take this further, teachers should help learners recognize the value of verbally explaining their meaning to an audience and then recreating that explanation in writing.

Regarding the second activity—having learners collect, categorize, and summarize the muddiest points during a class session—learners could also be asked to find the answers to a set number of questions or to the question asked most frequently, explain the solutions to the class, and report on their strategy for finding the answer. In this way, they are becoming independent learners rather than relying on the teacher for explanations. This supports the practice of relinquishing teacher centrality.

Learners will need guidance and training to be able to express what they do not understand through training, modeling, and scaffolding. Providing examples may address this as well as teach learners to pay attention in class to identify what they understand and do not understand. Knowing that they will be asked to identify a muddy point at the end of class is incentive for learners to closely follow the class content and activities. For variety and to emphasize the positive, instructors might also ask learners to identify the clearest point and even to explain it to a classmate.

Team-Based Learning ™

The Team-Based Learning approach to teaching and learning has been written about extensively and applications have been identified for different disciplines (e.g., see Michaelsen, Knight, & Fink, 2004; Michaelsen, Parmelee, McMahon, & Levine, 2007; Michaelsen & Sweet, 2008; Michaelsen, Sweet, & Parmelee, 2008). It has also been successfully implemented across cultures and learner levels. As this movement is closely related to the social environment element of self-regulated learning, various aspects of it are addressed as applicable throughout the discussion of objectives for this chapter. Since the concept of Team-Based Learning cannot be treated in detail, however, readers may want to refer to the references cited and to the Internet (search the term "Team-Based Learning") to learn more.

Team-Based Learning involves assigning learners to teams that work together throughout the duration of a course of study. For each instructional unit in a course, learners prepare by doing assigned readings. Then they take an individual Readiness Assurance Test covering the material. These tests are administered and scored in class for immediate feedback. Teams next take the test together, determine their answers, and mark the answers on a scratch-off answer sheet (similar to a lottery ticket). If their first answer is incorrect, they confer and determine an alternative. Learners earn the most points for selecting the correct answer the first time. The group tests are scored in class. Invariably, group scores are higher than individual scores. Both individual and group test scores are part of the learners' grades. Learners can give input concerning how much these tests will count toward their final grades.

Teams have the opportunity to defend answers they think should be correct and point out questions or answers that appear ambiguous. They need to refer to textbook materials to support their views and present the case in writing to the instructor. In subsequent class sessions, the instructor has the opportunity to clarify materials that learners did not understand and address gaps in the learners' knowledge. Once learners understand the basic concepts of an instructional unit, the remainder of the time is focused on application activities.

The advantages of Team-Based Learning are that learners come prepared to class rather than needing the teacher to review what they should have studied. Learners work together to understand and learn the material. They are responsible for searching for answers. They use the social environment—each other, the instructor, and course materials—to grasp course content. In the process, they develop social skills, communication skills, and a desire to contribute to the group. Group dynamics change when assertive learners find that their answers are incorrect and reticent learners find that their knowledge is valued by the team. Learners are motivated and engaged.

Team-Based Learning focuses on the social environment and on learners taking responsibility for their learning. The instructor role is decentralized, and learners use language for communicative purposes, to negotiate meaning, and to consult with their peers and instructor in order to understand course materials. Learners recognize the advantages of the social environment in terms of improved learning outcomes. This approach has applicability for the various objectives associated with the social environment. In this case, it assists learners in finding strengths and weaknesses through individual preparation, assessment, collaboration, discussion, and negotiation.

Develop a Positive Attitude Toward Seeking Help

Willingness to seek help depends on "personal and environmental factors" (Dembo & Eaton, 2000). L2 learners may be unaccustomed to evaluating each other's academic performance or even their own performance, if they view this as the teacher's role. Similarly, they may not recognize their peers as valuable or reliable sources of help since peers are not authority figures. In addition, learners may feel threatened, lack confidence in their abilities, or have a performance rather than a mastery orientation to learning. Mastery learning entails "persistence, effort, and the use of more advanced learning strategies" (including help-seeking) (Dembo & Eaton, 2000, p. 481) as opposed to an emphasis on outperforming peers (e.g., see Dweck, 2000). As indicated by the pedagogical practices in this chapter, an open environment where teachers welcome questions, structure pair and group work, and invite collaboration (not competition), assists learners in developing help-seeking behaviors.

Readiness Assurance Tests

This component of Team-Based Learning can be applied to any element of the writing process. Taking individual and group tests helps learners experience first-hand the value of collaboration and help-seeking. Individual tests demonstrate to learners what they know on their own while group tests illustrate how an individual's level of knowledge can be expanded through collaboration. The following application demonstrates how this process works.

In a writing class, learners typically read about prewriting techniques, rhetorical patterns, composing thesis statements and topic sentences, types of introductions, unity and coherence, grammatical structures, and other topics. These are accompanied by examples and model writings as well as practice exercises. The Readiness Assurance Test is administered after the initial reading of a chapter or section of a chapter to determine how much learners understood about the writing concepts discussed therein. Once the individual and group tests are scored and instructors have responded to gaps in learner understanding, the majority of class time is focused on application, or actual writing activities and practice. Much of this is done in teams.

For instance, before examining the unity of their own or another student's essay (the concept of unity is taught through the assigned reading) the students are tested using the Readiness Assurance Test to ensure they understand the concept, and the teacher provides additional instruction to fill in any gaps in the learners' knowledge. Learners are then given a sample essay in which unity needs to be improved. The instructor provides background information about the essay topic and explanations of key vocabulary to aid comprehension (or has learners engage in a related warm-up activity aimed at building content schema). The learners' task is to identify sentences that are off the topic in each paragraph of the essay. To facilitate this, sentences are pre-numbered. Once the groups have reached a consensus, the instructor asks each group to write the number of the sentence(s) that are off topic on a card, and hold it up. (A variation might be to have teams put their answers on a sticky note and put the note on the chalkboard.) This procedure allows learners to see the answers of all teams simultaneously. Discussion then ensues among the teams regarding the rationale for their choices, making it necessary for answers to be well-supported.

Although this example describes only part of one class session, more extensive projects could be designed in which learners find solutions to problems and develop higher level cognitive skills by making and defending specific choices (e.g., see Michaelsen, Fink, & Knight, n.d.). This might involve selecting and defending the most appropriate choice for a thesis statement, introduction, or even a grammatical structure. In doing this, learners are going beyond simple identification of a type of introduction (e.g., funnel, dramatic story) or of the usage of a grammatical form (e.g., passive sentence, past perfect verb phrase), and are examining why it is the best choice in a particular context. In this way, learners are developing their cognitive abilities and processing the language at deeper levels. Most importantly, they understand that the social environment can be used to improve learning.

Performance Graphs

Because cultural background may affect L2 writers' views about seeking help, particularly from peers, learners need to know that those who get help are typically higher achievers than those who do not. Experiencing this first-hand through the Team-Based Learning group Readiness Assurance Test is one way to accomplish this. Throughout the course, instructors can periodically create a graph comparing individual and team scores. This is done by taking each team's cumulative test scores and the lowest, average, and highest scores for each team member, and showing the difference between the highest individual scores and the team scores. Research shows that over a 14-year period, teams outperformed the highest-scoring member by an average of close to 11%, and in most cases, even the lowest team score was higher than the top individual score in the class (e.g., see Michaelsen, Watson, & Black, 1989).

Learn Social Skills for Effective Interaction with Peers, Instructors, and Learning Support Staff

In order to effectively seek and obtain skills, learners need to possess appropriate social abilities. For L2 learners, this involves knowledge and practice with language forms and cultural interaction styles. For example, learners may be unaccustomed to working in groups and therefore lack associated abilities, such as stating an opinion, disagreeing respectfully, or finding an opening in the conversation. Learners need to be comfortable asking questions and seeking clarification in both social and academic contexts. Self-regulated learners are able to focus their requests for help to meet their learning needs (Dembo et al., 2006).

Modeling and Role-Play

Skills for effective interaction within the social environment can be developed through modeling appropriate behavior and role-play. Lower level learners may need familiarity with grammatical forms and vocabulary used for seeking help; teachers should introduce useful phrases, sentences, and practice dialogues as a way to scaffold and develop learner abilities. Higher-level learners may begin directly with a role-modeling task such as making an appointment with a student tutor or instructor, asking for help with a thesis statement, or disagreeing with a group member. An example role-play topic follows.

> Your teacher has assigned you to get help from a student tutor at the writing center. The tutor asks, "What can I help you with?"
> How do you respond?

As learners respond to the given situation, the teacher can guide them with appropriate vocabulary and grammatical structures and follow up with a discussion how this strategy will result in receiving appropriate help.

Communication Strategies

Suggestions for improving communication skills include ensuring that learners "own" their message by using personal pronouns and acknowledging their own views (e.g., "I think" vs. "some people think"), describe the behaviors of others rather than making personal judgments (e.g., "You are not letting others finish their comments" vs. "You are so rude"), and express how they feel as opposed to blaming others (e.g., "When you interrupt, I feel like my ideas are being ignored" vs. "You need to stop interrupting") (e.g., see Gordon, 2001; Johnson, 2003). They must also practice active listening skills that involve responding to the message in ways that acknowledge the content expressed and the feelings associated with it, and they must avoid a quick-fix solution (e.g., "I got a low score on my essay and I'm not sure why." Response: "You sound concerned about it" vs. "Go talk to the teacher") (e.g., see Gordon, 2001). Instructors should familiarize learners with these strategies and associated language structures.

Group Roles

A technique that may be beneficial for learners unaccustomed to group work is to assign specific roles to group members. These could include a discussion facilitator who ensures that all voices are heard and none dominates, a scribe to record key points in the discussion, a summarizer to reflect the main ideas back to the group, and a presenter who shares the group's ideas with the larger class. Groups must be accountable by having a specific task. The time provided for group work should be limited so that some pressure exists for completing a task. Those who finish early are ideally given additional tasks to prevent boredom and inattention.

Develop Strategies for Seeking, Finding, and Evaluating Help

Reminding learners that response to their learning processes and specifically to their writing can come from a variety of sources is important. They should understand that learning is based on interaction and that interaction requires interdependence (Little, 1995). They must also be able to discriminate among available sources of help. Instructors can help learners see the potential of help-seeking for language development, improved writing, and increased self-regulation, and how different sources of help are more appropriate than others depending on the specific need.

Flowchart Analysis

An important aspect of helping learners identify uses of the social environment is to consider when and why to seek help and from whom. This can be accomplished by creating a chart and having learners share their thoughts (see Figure 6.3). The flowchart activity can also be a follow-up to pair and group work to create learner awareness of the benefits of help-seeking, to aid reflection, and to evaluate outcomes.

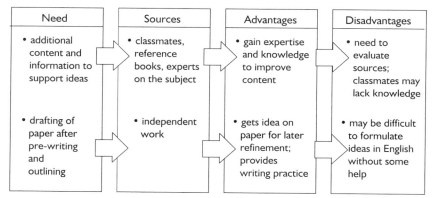

Figure 6.3 Help-Seeking Analysis

Steps for Seeking Help

Once learners have determined situations in which help-seeking is advantageous, and the most appropriate sources of help (i.e., peers, teachers, friends, study groups, writing center tutors), they need to identify what they want to know, prepare for the interaction, and anticipate possible challenges. Useful strategies include writing notes or lists of discussion points, identifying any needed new vocabulary, reviewing their request carefully, and ensuring it is specific (e.g., "I don't think I have enough support in this paragraph" rather than "Can you read this paragraph and tell me what is wrong with it?"). They should also consider having a back-up plan if a source of help is unavailable or they do not receive the help they expect.

Evaluation Logs

The section on Team-Based Learning explained how Readiness Assurance Test score comparisons make the advantages of collaboration apparent to learners. Additionally, team members should be asked to periodically evaluate the effectiveness of their team interactions. This procedure identifies positive social behaviors and behaviors that need to be changed.

Learners can keep a log with observations of how the team is functioning, create lists of incidences or changes that have affected the group positively or negatively, or write an analysis of barriers the group faced and how they were overcome (e.g., see Team-Based Learning: peer evaluation, n.d.). These documents can be shared and discussed with team members. Members can examine areas of miscommunication and make suggestions for how to resolve them. As learners work together over time, they become more comfortable providing and receiving honest feedback.

For evaluation purposes, team members can give each other an overall score (e.g., out of 10 or 100) accompanied by a brief comment (e.g., see Michaelsen & Fink, n.d.). The score is computed as part of the course grade—perhaps 5%. Instructors should provide enough criteria to encourage useful feedback and to discourage learners from simply giving each other high scores. (See Table 6.1 for a possible form.) They must illustrate types of helpful comments and explain how scores correlate to grades. Learners can be given a completed sample form as an example. An alternative is to have learners indicate what they appreciate about each team member and something they would like to request of each team member. Learners submit these evaluations to the instructor by e-mail. The instructor compiles them, removes the names of the evaluators, and gives them to each learner. Summative feedback on team work allows learners to determine the

Table 6.1 Team Evaluation Form

Your Name:	Group Member's Name:	Group Member's Name:	Group Member's Name:	Group Member's Name:
Evaluate your group members by assigning a score out of 10 for each of the following factors.				
Prepared for discussions				
Participated actively by sharing knowledge and ideas				
Respected the ideas, opinions, and feelings of others				
Balanced listening to others with contributing to the discussion				
Encouraged others to participate				
Showed flexibility and cooperation				
Gave and accepted useful feedback				
Explained ideas clearly				
Did an equal share of the work				
Give one commendation to this group member				
Give one suggestion to this group member				
Total Score				

effectiveness of their social skills. Similar types of evaluation processes could be applied to evaluate other sources of help—teachers, friends, or student tutors in learning assistance centers.

Build a Community of Learning for Writing Improvement

When learners work together as a community of both learners and writers to improve their writing skill, they become committed to helping each other, develop an appreciation for collaboration, and benefit from receiving feedback on their writing. Building a community can be accomplished through a variety of teacher-facilitated activities and approaches to response.

Appreciative Inquiry

Appreciative Inquiry is a technique that helps people emphasize the positive by looking for the best in themselves and their units (Hammond, 1996), rather than focusing on problems or what is not working. The process looks for what works by creating statements describing "where the organization wants to be, based on the high moments of where they have been" (Hammond, 1996, p. 7). The statements are based on actual events and periods of time in the organization's (or team's) history.

Participants in an Appreciative Inquiry workshop focus on questions such as the following: What are our greatest strengths? What do we do well? What circumstances allowed us to achieve our best work? What do we dream about doing? Answering these questions elicits stories and examples of times when the group or organization worked together particularly well, and leads to a discussion of what would happen if these circumstances were always present. Participants create "provocative propositions" (Hammond, 1996, p. 41) by applying the phrase "what if" to the themes elicited (e.g., What if we always met our deadlines? What if we divided the work load equally among us?). The derived questions remind group members of times when they were most effective and serve as guidelines for future accomplishments. They also become guiding statements that remind participants of their successes and their abilities to achieve their dreams by extending positive behaviors into future work.

This technique is most effective when communities of learners (or teams) have been working together on assignments and projects over a period of time, although the process could also be applied to a whole class to determine how the individuals in the class (not just the teacher) contribute to a positive learning environment. Examples of provocative propositions for an L2 writing class might involve having learners identify behaviors and events (e.g., coming to class on time and prepared, comments made by classmates, a specific activity, lesson, or writing concept) that contributed to greater understanding and improved skill.

The Appreciative Inquiry process might be implemented at midterm so that teams can determine how they can best build on their most effective work to make greater progress over the remainder of the course. The result of the Appreciative Inquiry process is that participants increase "commitment, confidence, and affirmation that they have been successful" (Hammond, 1996, p. 7). They have also identified how to create additional instances of success. Combining Team-Based Learning with Appreciative Inquiry has the potential to optimize positive use of the social environment and help learners become self-regulated writers.

Peer Review Groups

A peer review group meets with the instructor to review paper drafts. This process helps learners form a community and use their social environment to become better writers by allowing them to learn how to evaluate their own writing and other's writing in a small group setting. The instructor can model how to give feedback using one of the learner's drafts. Then as a group, the learners evaluate the next paper with guidance from the teacher. A review sheet with three or four areas listed for the students to focus on based on the writing techniques for a particular instructional unit, accompanied by guiding questions, will aid this process. (See Chapter 2 for example feedback and scoring forms.) For instance, if the emphasis is on writing a strong thesis statement, the review sheet could identify features of a good thesis such as, identifies the topic; conveys an idea, attitude, or viewpoint about the topic; is a complete sentence; does not announce the topic; and does not convey more than one idea about the topic. These points will vary depending on what has been taught in class sessions.

This technique can be extended by having groups participate in a similar procedure with a trained peer tutor in a writing center. The peer tutor can be included in an initial session with the teacher and learners, or the teacher can meet with the tutor separately to explain the procedure. Learners could either be grouped together by common areas of need (e.g., organizational patterns, grammatical forms, support and development of ideas) or organized into mixed groups to increase the likelihood that they can help each other.

Social Networking

The use of social networking for learning purposes expands the potential of the social environment and adds a different dimension to the creation of communities of learners. Providing extensive discussion about the applications of social networking for L2 writing is beyond the scope of this book; however, some general ideas follow. Instructors should be familiar with technology-based applications that support interaction such as blogs, discussion forums, and social networking sites. Most learning management systems have a component designed to facilitate discussions among peers and instructors. These systems often include the ability to share work and collaborate on assignments. Google Docs or Dropbox are other ways that learners can share information, revise and edit a group document, collaborate on presentation slides, engage in peer review, work on spreadsheets, exchange data, create and distribute surveys, and schedule group meetings and assignment deadlines.

Generally, learners will not use these forms of exchange unless required. Thus, to build an effective, technology-based learning community where learners assist each other, instructors need to establish guidelines for how learners can collaborate, ensure that systems are easily accessible, and provide relevant training. The key to success in this area is designing activities and assignments that are not just busy work, but that are meaningful and related to specific learning outcomes (and, more than likely, to course grades). Instructors should get ongoing feedback from learners and adapt requirements and assignments accordingly. Instructors will also need to help learners understand that the style of writing for exchanges on course-related social networks needs to be formal to support language learning, rather than the conversational style that learners may be accustomed to when using social networking for personal, social purposes. Instructors may also want to design rubrics to grade participation and the quality of exchanges; group or team evaluations are also appropriate.

An example we have used of this type of activity involves a component of an online L2 writing course for intermediate-level learners. The course is hosted on a learning management system. The learners are assigned to write an outline of a paragraph based on a given topic and then record and upload a video of themselves sharing their ideas. Learners are then asked to respond to the video posting of one other learner in the class. This process engages learners in the writing process steps of brainstorming and planning; it also provides the linguistic opportunities for output and input. The activity is structured with clear steps and an outline format is provided. Learners are given a rubric for how they will be evaluated. They receive points for their own video posting and for responding to their peers' postings. Learners have responded positively to the activity and have made encouraging and helpful comments on the proposed content of their peers' paragraphs. These comments assist learners in understanding that they have an audience and in recognizing that writing can be a social activity. At midterm, the learners post their best piece of writing, read the writing of the other learners, and create a video posting that gives feedback to one other learner in the class regarding that learner's writing. Social networking is particularly helpful in the distance learning environment because it creates connections among the learners and develops a community of writers as learners continue to post video clips discussing their ideas, and respond to others' postings throughout the course.

Writing Process Community Activities

Learning activities focused on getting maximum benefit from the social environment are numerous. Table 6.2 summarizes a few of these using the stages in the writing process as a framework. Teachers can use these as a starting point, adapt them, and generate related activities to build communities of writers. These activities will be most successful when accompanied by training, modeling, and scaffolding. Additionally, instructors can use these activities to help learners recognize the impact of the social environment in improving learning outcomes.

Although writing may not appear to be a social activity, it is an act of communication, a process that inevitably involves more than one party. The social environment principle and related activities help learners understand the significance and potential benefit of seeking help, collaboration, and community. This principle aids both language acquisition and the development of self-regulation.

Summary

This chapter has:

- defined and explored the concept of the social environment generally and as it relates to language learning and L2 writing specifically;
- identified key pedagogical practices involved in facilitating learners' use of the social environment to improve language acquisition and writing ability; and
- provided a range of learner activities and approaches designed to improve use of the social environment and help learners become self-regulated L2 writers.

The next chapter:

- explores the self-regulated learning principle of performance, specifically how performance is important to self-regulation and how it can benefit language learners generally and L2 writers specifically;
- discusses pedagogical practices that help learners effectively implement the dimension of performance and related strategies; and
- shares activities and approaches for learner improvement in the performance dimension that leads to improvement in writing.

Table 6.2 Writing Process Community Activities

Stage of the Writing Process	Purpose	Learner Community Activity
Pre-writing	Identify where and how learners do their best thinking and idea generation	Discuss strategies for generating ideas—for example, talk to themselves, talk to friends, jot down ideas as they occur, think of ideas while walking alone or in a quiet room (Snow, 2006); discuss pros and cons, try a new strategy and report back
Organizing	Provide adequate support for ideas and organize them effectively	Write a group outline—based on a brainstormed list of ideas, learners combine ideas with those of other groups, select and arrange them, and create an outline (Snow, 2006); outlines are shared among groups and checked for adequate and appropriate support for each main idea
Drafting	Allow for multiple sources of response (in addition to the teacher) to establish audience awareness	Arrange a round robin group paper exchange that includes the teacher; group members read drafts, write a specific comment/suggestion (teachers need to model and guide learners in giving appropriate comments and identify a focus for the response), and pass the draft on; learner reflects on how the comments influenced changes in the paper. An alternative is to have learners identify what they want feedback on, thereby placing greater emphasis on self-regulation
Revising	Encourage awareness of the features of good writing, the value of feedback, and the need for multiple drafts	Have learners identify criteria they feel are important in a piece of writing and put them in order; let them negotiate these items with those the instructor feels are important (e.g., see Hedge, 1988); learners consider their own and others' papers using the criteria and then revise accordingly
Editing	Build accuracy and ability to find and correct errors	Ask peers to identify sentences or sections of a paper that are difficult to understand; examine these closely for grammatical inaccuracies and reword; develop a personal checklist of common errors or weaknesses for self-evaluation purposes (e.g., see Harmer, 2004)

Chapter 7

Performance

Objectives

This chapter discusses the principle of performance and its application to L2 writing, and outlines practices and activities that help learners:

- develop self-observation and evaluation strategies;
- incorporate strategic planning with goal setting;
- implement and monitor learning strategies; and,
- strategically monitor performance outcomes.

Definitions and Applications

The principle of performance, the *what* aspect of self-regulated learning, is the practice of a learner monitoring the level of success on a task. Sometimes referred to as management skills (Zimmerman, Bonner, & Kovach, 1996), this principle focuses on a learner's ability to set realistic goals, evaluate progress, and make necessary changes in performance to achieve these goals (Dembo & Eaton, 2000). Zimmerman (1990) notes that "virtually all researchers assume that self-regulation depends on continuing feedback of learning effectiveness" (p. 5).

Performance monitoring is best accomplished when focus is directed to specific benchmarks. The five principles discussed in previous chapters—motive, methods, time, physical environment, and social environment—provide these benchmarks. Ideally, all of these principles should be monitored by the learner to ensure improvement and progress. For instance, if a learner receives a test score that is lower than expected, she can review the principles closely to determine what resulted in the lower score. Students can ask the following questions: Were appropriate study methods employed in a setting conducive to learning (physical environment)? Were proper goals (motive) established? Perhaps a misuse of time contributed to poor performance, or more assistance was needed from the teacher or tutor (social environment). This process of checking outcomes is central to self-regulated learning. The principles presented in this book contribute to helping leaners regulate their performance. They provide a means to an end—improved writing skill and improved academic performance.

The principle of performance by a self-regulated learner is manifested in many ways and in diverse contexts. In nonacademic settings, the practice of self-monitoring for performance improvement is common. Athletes, for example, often use video of themselves to refine their techniques. Musicians use recordings as a means of monitoring and improving their performance, and an essential aspect of airline safety for pilots is to constantly monitor and adjust their performance on key flight operations (Dembo & Eaton, 2000; Dembo & Seli, 2008). The same is true in academic settings. Successful students monitor their performance (Zimmerman, 1990). For instance, these students are often aware of how well they performed on a test even before they receive the results because they monitor themselves as they take the test. They recognize when certain questions are problematic for them (Zimmerman & Martinez-Pons, 1986). Statements such as "I always check my work before submitting it for a final grade," and "I keep a list of my most common errors marked by the teacher to improve my writing" suggest that self-regulated learning principles are in practice (Zimmerman & Martinez-Pons, 1986).

A significant point made in each of the preceding chapters bears repeating here: self-regulating skills can be learned, and typically lead to learning improvement. Such is also the case with performance (self-monitoring): "Self-monitoring training has been found to enhance performance across a wide variety of academic measures" (Zimmerman & Risemberg, 1997, p. 117).

Performance and Language Learning

Before considering how the principle of performance applies to the contexts of language learning and writing, a brief reminder of this principle's key elements may be helpful. Essentially, self-regulated learners who monitor performance assess their level of success on specific tasks, set realistic goals, evaluate progress, and make necessary changes in performance to achieve their goals. It is important to note how each of these steps is interrelated and how the steps build on each other.

The term *monitor* is significant here, yet it may be confusing, especially in a language learning context. If a trained language teacher were asked what comes to mind when the word *monitor* is mentioned, most likely the term will summon a response in reference to Krashen's monitor hypothesis (1981, 1985). Krashen maintains that a language learner can and does monitor language production, but this is not the same sense of monitoring associated with self-regulated learning theory. According to the monitor hypothesis, a language learner can employ learned knowledge (rules) to monitor (edit) language in certain situations, usually in writing, which is a language skill that lends itself well to careful review (monitoring) of what has been produced.

According to Krashen, this type of monitoring generally takes place only after high levels of fluency have been achieved. This form of monitoring is obviously not the same as setting goals, evaluating progress, and making necessary changes, which can be done from the beginning of the L2 learning process.

The term *monitor* may also prompt, among some language teachers, a reference to the noticing or awareness hypothesis (Schmidt, 1990). Schmidt (1990) posits that *noticing* means that learners intentionally control language input and output. Noticing occurs in a variety of ways and comes from multiple sources. Learners can intentionally observe language as it occurs around them, or they can receive feedback from others, such as a teacher, which also helps them be more aware of their language development. It has been suggested that noticing alone is not sufficient for acquisition to occur, nor is it the only way language is learned. Ellis, Sheen, Murakami, & Takashima (2008), for instance, suggest that a learner must notice and then understand before acquisition occurs. In this sense, noticing is a form of self-regulated monitoring in that language learners must notice their own and others' uses of language in order to recognize where they need to make improvements. In this sense, noticing is connected to the self-regulated learner aspects of goal setting, monitoring progress, and changing performance.

One theory of language learning that has considerable application to the self-regulated learning principle of performance is skill acquisition theory (DeKeyser, 2007). This theory, which has been studied in diverse domains ranging from academics to sports and industry, strives to explain the process a learner must go through to achieve automaticity in the use of skills such as language. Skill acquisition theory suggests that proficiency can be achieved through deliberate attention to and feedback on language features. Furthermore, it suggests that declarative knowledge precedes procedural knowledge, which leads to automaticity. Said another way, a learner must first be presented with the concept that is to be acquired and then be provided with meaningful and multiple opportunities to practice. This, then, leads to production. Language teachers may know this sequence best as *presentation, practice, production* (PPP) (Bryne, 1986; DeKeyser, 2007; Harmer, 2007). As noted in Chapter 4, skill acquisition theory aims to describe how learners develop "fluent, spontaneous, largely effortless, and highly skilled behavior" (DeKeyser, 2007, p. 97).

The parallels between the self-regulated learner principle of performance and skill acquisition theory are significant. Self-monitoring and feedback are essential elements of language learning when approached through a skill acquisition theory lens. Research suggests that explicit attention to language and the learners' progress are essential to improvement (see DeKeyser, 2001). This attention can come in the form of goal setting and monitoring progress, both by the learner and the teacher. Furthermore, skill acquisition theory suggests that monitoring performance involves making adjustments as features of the language are practiced and needed improvement is detected (see DeKeyser, 2007).

Performance and Writing

The self-regulated learning principle of performance is applicable to each of the major language learning skills: reading, writing, listening, and speaking. However, the productive skill of writing is particularly suitable for self-monitoring. This is due, in part, to the static, revisable nature of the language produced. Unlike speaking, where recordings and perhaps transcripts would have to be made to evaluate performance (e.g., see Lynch, 2001), a written product is always present, tangible, reviewable, and revisable. Thus, the very nature of writing makes it particularly possible to determine the level of success on a task, make necessary changes, and evaluate progress. Murray (2000) describes this dynamic nature of writing well:

> A piece of writing is never finished. It is delivered to a deadline, torn out of the typewriter on demand, sent off with a sense of accomplishment and shame and pride and frustration. If only there were a couple of more days, time for just another run at it, perhaps then. (p. 51)

A number of practices that are typically used to teach writing coincide with the principle of performance. For instance, learners use logs of various types to track their progress over time. Error logs are commonly used in writing to help writers focus on recurring grammatical errors with the aim of making necessary changes on future writing tasks (Evans, Hartshorn, & Strong-Krause, 2011; Ferris & Roberts, 2001; Roberts, 1999). An adaptation of the grammatical error log is a rhetorical correction log (Yi, 2010). As with grammar logs, rhetorical logs allow writers to keep track of rhetorical deficiencies that teachers note on a writing assignment, such as having a weak or missing thesis statement, poor coherence between sentences, or lack of unity.

Portfolio compilation, which has also become a common feature of writing courses, is another aspect of classroom writing production that has excellent potential to blend well with not only the principles of the process approach (Hamp-Lyons & Condon, 2000; Johns, 1997; White, 1994), but also with self-regulated learning. While portfolios have multiple purposes and formats, the basic idea is for learners to present their work as it has evolved over a designated period of time (semester or term). What makes portfolios a particularly helpful tool for developing self-regulated writers is that such an approach "when carefully planned and consistently implemented … engages both students and teachers in continual discussion, analysis, and evaluation of their processes as learners and writers" (Ferris & Hedgcock, 2005, p. 319). Furthermore, it is an excellent way for learners to reflect on what they have accomplished and where they wish to improve. Said succinctly, a portfolio can "foster student reflection and help them to self-monitor their own learning" (Nunes, 2004, p. 334).

Arguably, the aspect of second language writing pedagogy that is most related to the principle of performance is the process approach. While process writing is not a codified list of practices that must be slavishly adhered to (Liebeman-Klien, 1986), there are generally accepted practices that distinguish process writing. For instance, multidrafting, expert and peer feedback, and substantial revision and reflection are all important practices espoused by teachers of process writing (Ferris & Hedgcock, 2005). These practices blend nicely with the principles of performance: setting realistic goals, making necessary changes in performance to achieve goals, and evaluating progress. To illustrate, a colleague maintained that her most important task as a writing teacher was to help her students see what Murray (2000) suggests—that a piece of writing always has the potential to be improved, strengthened, clarified. Our colleague's mantra was "I don't give grades, I help students become writers." She does this by holding frequent progress conferences with students, allowing them to articulate ways they could improve an assignment. Furthermore, she always gives her students the opportunity to improve a paper even after a "final" grade has been assigned.

Guiding Classroom Practices

The six guidelines that follow have been selected for two primary reasons. First, they are intended to bolster learners' abilities to self-monitor for writing improvement. As has been noted, skill acquisition theory suggests that skills must be reinforced and repeated to have a lasting effect on performance (DeKeyser, 2001, 2007). Self-regulated learner research refers to this as "routinization" of a skill or strategy (Zimmerman, 1998, p. 83). Second, writing teachers carry heavy loads; therefore, these guidelines are structured in such a way that implementing them would not increase a teacher's load but perhaps reduce it in some ways. The more that classroom practices make efficient and effective use of a teacher's time, the better.

Provide Specific, Consistent Feedback Whenever Possible

The first step in self-monitoring is for learners to evaluate and monitor their strengths and weaknesses. To facilitate this process, teachers should provide specific, consistent feedback (see the 10 writing response principles listed in Chapter 1). When feedback is specific, it should be clear to the learner what has been done well and what needs to be modified in a future draft or assignment. Specific feedback can be given in such ways as quiz grades, homework scores, clear explanations, or rubrics.

Consistency is just as important as specificity. A teacher can help learners monitor their performance by being consistent with the form of feedback provided. For instance, using the same correction or feedback symbols for all assignments helps the leaner build on past feedback. If a teacher uses the symbol *awk* to indicate that the language used is likely caused by first language interference, and the learner has been told what this symbol means, then future uses of the symbol will help the learner in the revision process. The more objective the feedback, the more consistently learners will be able to apply it to goal setting and strategic planning. Rubrics are particularly useful in this regard (see "Rubrics" later).

Ensure that All Writing Tasks are Clearly Presented

A learner's ability to monitor performance during a task depends on a clear understanding of what the final product should look like. The clarity of expectations for any given task will determine how a learner envisions the final product. The clarity and level of detail that a teacher provides for a writer can make a writing task appear either manageable or seemingly insurmountable (Flower, 1990; Johns, 2009; Wolfersberger, 2008). Johns (2009) offers seven features that teachers should include in their writing prompts to help L2 writers. She presents these in the form of questions: 1. Who am I as a writer? 2. Who is my audience? 3. In what genre am I to write? 4. How do I organize my text? 5. What sources am I to draw from? 6. What don't I know about the assignment? 7. How will I be assessed? Ensuring that the information these seven questions ask for is embedded in a prompt, facilitates an L2 writer's task immensely.

In light of these guiding questions, consider the following prompts used in an advanced writing class. The first time the prompt was used, it was presented as follows: "Write a three-page, double-spaced comparison and contrast paper discussing the two leading fast-food restaurants in our city." In a subsequent use of the prompt, it was modified in the following way (numbers in brackets indicate which of the seven questions above are being answered):

> In this paper you are to assume the role of an employee who is working for a company that wants to invest in a fast-food restaurant in your city [1]. You are to gather information on the two leading restaurants in your city from information available online and in current business magazines [5]. I have listed a few links and titles of magazines at the bottom of this page that will get you started [5]. You will present your findings to the Chief Financial Officer in a three-page, double-spaced summary of the financial strengths and weaknesses of each restaurant [1, 2, 3, and 4].

Conclude your report with a recommendation as to which restaurant will be the best investment for your company [1, 3, and 4]. Please spend 30 minutes tonight thinking about this assignment. We will have group and class discussions tomorrow to clarify anything you may need help with [6]. As with previous writing assignments in this class, your paper will be graded using our class writing rubric [7].

While both prompts could be used in a class, the second version provides more structure and detail, which makes it easier for writers to monitor their progress and make necessary adjustments based on knowledge rather than assumptions. A good practice to follow is to always provide a handout with clear details of the writing task.

Include Scoring Rubrics

A central element to monitoring progress is to have a consistent metric against which progress can be measured. It is difficult for learners to measure their progress if they do not know specifically how their work has been graded. Rubrics are a relatively easy way to provide this metric. A number of rubrics can be found in professionally published materials, and class textbooks often include scoring guides. Our experience has taught us, however, that the best rubrics are those that are created by the teacher and even, in some cases, by the learners. A self-made rubric allows the teacher to incorporate and evaluate features that the local context demands and that the teacher deems important and appropriate to the learners.

The more specific feedback a rubric provides, the better the student is able to understand where improvement is needed (see Chapter 3). Consider these three examples.

- Student A gets an assignment back with a single grade at the top. Suggestions for improving the paper are marked throughout the text and in margins, with perhaps a brief note at the end suggesting that "more supporting examples would be helpful."
- Students B gets an assignment back with comments similar to those given to Student A, but her paper has two grades marked at the top— one for content and ideas and one for linguistic accuracy.
- Student C gets his paper back with a score marked at the top and a few notes in the margins and in the text on specific ways the paper could be improved. In addition, this student receives a full-page rubric that contains points for individual categories reflecting various aspects of writing, with the total points from these categories written at the top of the paper. The categories include such aspects of writing as content, organization, grammar, vocabulary, mechanics, neatness, and clarity of

ideas. Each of these categories also has a definition of what a strong and weak score means.

It should be obvious that Student C will be in a better position to self-monitor, correct, and improve his work, given the detailed and specific feedback received.

Make Goal Setting Part of Your Class

As discussed in Chapter 2, goal setting is central to being a self-regulated learner (Zimmerman, 2002). Oxford and Shearin (1994) observe that "goal setting can have exceptional importance in stimulating L2 learning motivation, and it is therefore shocking that so little time and energy are spent in the L2 classroom on goal setting" (p. 19). The more that goal setting can be incorporated into the classroom, the more likely it is that learners will develop the practice of self-monitoring. Giving learners opportunities to be proactive and set goals will give them a sense of control and structure (Dembo, Junge, & Lynch, 2006). Several key factors should be kept in mind when incorporating goals into the course:

- goals should be set by the learner goals;
- should be concrete, current, and challenging; and
- accountability needs to be built into the class structure to ensure that learners are working toward their goals.

Several activities have been included in the Activities and Approaches section to illustrate these goal-setting guidelines.

Allow for Revisions and Resubmissions

As noted earlier, several aspects of the process approach align well with the self-regulated learning principle of performance. Specifically, multidrafting allows learners to work through their ideas as they clarify their thinking and expression. Each time learners share drafts with classmates, peers, or a tutor, they are able to monitor progress and make necessary adjustments to the next version. Such a practice need not be an added burden to a writing teacher. In fact, it can lighten a teacher's load by ensuring that the final draft submitted is much cleaner and more concise because of the refining, revising process the paper has gone through.

Integrate Self-Monitoring into the Class Structure

Regardless of the level of writing that is being taught, it is possible to include techniques that require learners to monitor their own progress. Grading is a fact of nearly every classroom, and learners frequently ask, "How am I doing in class?" or "What's my grade?" Teachers quickly learn that keeping good records is essential to helping learners see their own progress. While recordkeeping is a teacher's responsibility, learners can learn much about self-monitoring if a teacher shifts some of this responsibility to the learners. For instance, the teacher can provide students with individual blank copies of the grade book and require them to record their score for each assignment as it is handed back. The teacher can then review this sheet with each learner in writing conferences to ensure it is being kept current and to discuss progress. Even though learning management systems are increasingly common and make grades and scores readily available to learners, asking them to manually record their scores reinforces self-monitoring skills. Various other activities are included in "Activities and Approaches" below to reinforce this guideline.

Activities and Approaches

As in previous chapters, the activities that follow are intended to be tools for teachers to help learners develop self-regulated learner skills. Unlike other chapters, however, activities in this chapter were drawn from the activities introduced earlier in the book that are closely aligned with the four objectives in this chapter. It should be noted that many activities in other chapters that were designed with one principle in mind can be used to reinforce various self-regulated learner principles. The Appendix lists a summary of all the activities suggested in this book, and indicates which self-regulated learner principles each activity develops and reinforces.

An important aspect of the four objectives for this chapter is that they are structured in such a way as to lead the learner through a cyclical, self-monitoring process. A learner first develops self-observation and evaluation strategies (objective 1), which can then lead to strategic planning with specific goals in mind (objective 2). Once this preplanning is completed, the learner implements and monitors learning strategies that are related to the plan and its goals (objective 3). Throughout the process, the learner monitors performance outcomes (objective 4). This interconnected approach to self-regulation, which was developed by Zimmerman et al. (1996), allows for "self-monitoring on each learning trial [and] provides information that can change subsequent goals, strategies, or performance efforts" (Zimmerman, 1998, p. 83). For example, the writer who follows this four-step process receives feedback from a teacher on a given assignment and uses the feedback to better understand deficiencies. This insight helps her set suitable goals and identify appropriate strategies for achieving those goals. She then monitors progress based on the set goals. This four-step cycle continues as she uses insights gained on one assignment to plan strategically for success on the next.

Additionally, since each of the four chapter objectives includes some form of the word *strategy*, it may be helpful to review the definition of this term prior to considering activities intended to help learners be strategic (see Chapter 3). Griffiths (2008) defines *strategy* as "activities consciously chosen by learners for the purpose of regulating their own language learning" (p. 87). The use of the word *consciously* is significant. To be strategic, an action must be intentionally taken. Furthermore, there must be choices—strategies from which to choose. Grabe and Stoller (2006) define strategic readers as those who "make use of a wide repertoire of strategies in combination rather than in isolated applications" (p. 195). Here it is important to note that a learner must have a variety of strategies from which to make conscious choices. Accordingly, the following activities are based on the assumption that strategic leaners are those whose learning behaviors are consciously selected from a repertoire of possibilities, with the purpose of achieving a desired outcome.

Finally, since the purpose of the activities is to help learners improve, the hypothetical student, Marinoa, who was introduced in Chapter 4, will be used to exemplify how individuals can monitor their performance. While she is a hypothetical student, many of the examples she illustrates come from our experience working with similar students. The intent is to give an example from which other learners can benefit as they develop self-monitoring skills and strategies. With an understanding of chapter objectives being cyclical in nature, of the definition of *strategy*, and of how Marinoa's behaviors will be used as an example, specific activities are presented that can be used to achieve the four chapter objectives.

Develop Self-Observation and Evaluation Strategies

The ability to monitor performance is essential to becoming a self-regulated writer. A key point to remember is that "behavior cannot be managed unless individuals are aware of it" (Dembo & Eaton, 2000, p. 484). The essence of this objective is for learners to be aware of their effectiveness as writers. Said another way, "self-evaluation and monitoring occurs when students determine the effectiveness of their current study methods" (Zimmerman, 1998, p. 82).

Feedback Loop Binder

A colleague once expressed a concern common among writing teachers this way: "I spend a great deal of time providing feedback to help my students improve their writing only to see it go unheeded in subsequent assignments." Learners' seeming lack of attention to feedback may be attributed to various factors, one of which is that they may be unsure of what the many forms of feedback mean and what teachers expect them to do with it (Ferris, 2003). One way to help learners and teachers make sure feedback achieves the desired aim of helping writers improve their writing skills is to create a feedback loop binder.

A feedback loop binder can be an excellent way to help learners take responsibility for their own learning by systematically tracking and appropriately responding to feedback. It is also an efficient way for teachers to monitor how their feedback is being perceived and applied. The binder can be designed and modified in any number of ways to meet individual teachers' preferences. However, it should be simple and inexpensive. To do this the contents should be limited to two forms: Strengths and weaknesses analysis, and Monitoring performance. These forms are discussed next.

STRENGTHS AND WEAKNESSES ANALYSIS

The first element that a feedback binder ought to have is some type of log that can be used to analyze feedback patterns. Any number of error analysis forms can be developed to help learners monitor their own work. These are usually most effective when the teacher and learners collaborate in designing the form. The strengths and weaknesses form illustrated in Figure 7.1, which is a type of categorization activity discussed in Chapter 3, helps learners summarize the feedback that teachers provide in categories that are consistent across various assignments. By the time learners have completed several assignments, they will start to see patterns of strengths and weaknesses that they can build on and correct in subsequent assignments. While copying and summarizing feedback from the margins of papers and rubrics to an analysis form like this may seem like busy work for learners, in reality it is an effective way to help them become aware of recurring problems in their writing that they may otherwise overlook, and regulate their own writing progress.

Using a form like this will require that teachers carefully select what they mark on papers. Too much feedback can be both overwhelming to the learner and difficult to manage on a feedback form such as this. The key is to focus on aspects of the learner's writing that need the most attention. While this example form uses categories of content, organization, vocabulary, grammar, mechanics, and neatness, these can be modified to reflect the goals of the writing assignment, specific aspects of the writing task, or a teacher's preference for feedback. Whatever categories are used, it is important to be consistent across assignments; otherwise, learners will not be able to clearly see where they have consistent difficulty.

In the strengths and weaknesses analysis form in Figure 7.1, Marinoa has taken feedback from her first assignment and a recent writing conference with her teacher, and summarized it in the appropriate spaces. With this, she is now building on past feedback as she looks forward to her next writing task. She can also apply the insights gained in completing this analysis to the self-regulated learner principles in the monitoring performance form that is discussed next (see Figure 7.2).

Strengths and Weaknesses Analysis

Name: Marinoa

Directions: Each time you receive feedback from your teacher on a writing assignment, you should write the comments and suggestions in the appropriate category boxes. This information should then be used to help you improve your writing on subsequent tasks in this course.

Category/ Assignment	Assignment 1	Assignment 2	Assignment 3
Content	My ideas seem to be best when I have a personal connection to the topic. I certainly am interested in this first topic. I need to be sure to do the pre readings this helped me get connected to the topic.		
Organization	In class, we talked about an introduction having 3 purposes: introduce the topic, catch the reader's attention, and present my thesis. I am not sure why the teacher thinks I did not do this. I need to get clarification.		
Vocabulary	I know my words are simple. Sometimes I feel like I am writing "baby language." My English vocabulary does not match what I am thinking.		
Grammar	Two areas of grammar stand out that need my attention: Sentences run on rampantly in nearly every paragraph Sentences without subjects.		
Mechanics	I need to be more careful with spelling. And I know all final papers must be double spaced. I think I was too rushed finishing the paper.		
Neatness	The teacher is right. I rushed my paper. I had to write in by hand several last minute changes.		

Figure 7.1 Strengths and Weaknesses Analysis Form

Monitoring Performance—Part I

The second part of a feedback binder should be a form on which learners measure their progress on the self-regulated learner principles introduced in this book. Leaners need to strategically plan how to build on their identified strengths and overcome weaknesses. The monitoring performance form (Figure 7.2) provides a systematic approach for applying each of the self-regulated learning principles. Each column in the form focuses on one principle (motive, method, time, physical environment, and social environment). Each row develops the four objectives (Parts 1, 2, 3, 4) for the principle of performance. Part 1 provides a space for the learner to write identified strengths and weaknesses. Part 2 is used to strategically plan and set goals based on the information included in Part 1. Part 3 allows the learner to identify learning strategies that will lead to goal achievement, and Part 4 asks the learner to systematically monitor performance outcomes. Each part will be discussed in order of application.

Monitoring Performance
Name: Marinoa
Assignment: Essay #2 "A Serious Social Problem"
Part I
Directions: Using the feedback you have received on the previous assignments, fill in the spaces in Part I with the strengths and weaknesses related to the various principles of motive, method, time, physical environment, and social environment. Information you have on your strengths and weaknesses analysis form will be helpful here.

Motive	Method	Time	Physical Environment	Social Environment
Why	**How**	**When**	**Where**	**With whom**
1.	What are my strengths and weaknesses ?			
I am not happy with the grade I earned on the last assignment. I want to study international business. I know good writing will be important.	I usually draft in my first language. Perhaps this is causing my grammar problems; my teacher thinks so. I keep getting comments about run-on sentences, & non-academic vocabulary.	I have got to do something about starting early on an assignment. The teacher was right. I rushed the last assignment.	I think my writing space is fine. I am not distracted.	I have never talked to a tutor or asked for feedback from my peers; perhaps I should.
2.	What are my goals?			
3.	What will I do to accomplish this?			
4.	How did I do?			

Figure 7.2 Part I Monitoring Performance Form

As Marinoa prepares for her second paper, she uses the feedback she received on the first assignment (see the strengths and weaknesses analysis form, Figure 7.1) and her first writing conference to fill in the spaces in Part 1.

Several aspects of the form Marinoa has completed so far are worth noting. She does not try to address all areas of concern identified in the strengths and weaknesses analysis form. Trying to attend to everything at once can be both overwhelming and self-defeating. Making incremental changes based on priorities is a far more productive way to improve (Evans & Henrichsen, 2008). Also, note how she has identified a positive aspect of her learning—her physical environment seems to be working. Building on the positive is also an important aspect of becoming a self-regulated writer.

Previous Chapter Activities

With the four chapter objectives in mind, activities from Chapters 2–6 were selected that have a strong connection to the objective being discussed. The activities listed in Table 7.1 are intended to help learners develop self-observation and evaluation strategies. While many other activities from previous chapters can also be used (see the Appendix for a summary of this book's activities), those presented here should serve as good examples. These activities can be used in any number of ways. For instance, since strategy use is very much a matter of preference, learners could be given a list from which to select strategies that match their preferences, or a teacher may choose several activities that meet the general needs of the class.

Incorporate Strategic Planning with Goal Setting

The following activities build on the concept that strategic planning and goal setting are best achieved when based on reliable information. Such information can be taken from the activities for objective 1 (self-observation and evaluation).

Monitoring Performance—Part 2

Once learners begin to understand their weaknesses and strengths through such activities as completing the strengths and weaknesses analysis form, they can begin to strategically plan how to build on their strengths and overcome weaknesses. Part 2 of the monitoring performance form below (Figure 7.3) is designed with this goal setting and planning in mind.

With Part 1 completed, Marinoa sets specific goals in Part 2 on aspects of her writing that she sees need to be improved. Note that she does not set a goal for each principle. It is certainly reasonable to expect that not every aspect of a learner's performance will need attention. However, it is always possible for a learner to try new strategies even in areas where performance may be strong.

Table 7.1 Objective 1 Supporting Activities

Objective: Develop self-observation and evaluation strategies

Activity (chapter/page)	Description In this activity, learners
Beliefs and experiences (2/*)	respond in discussion and/or writing to questions that explore their beliefs, experiences, and attitudes about writing.
Diagnostic tools to focus on form and meaning (2/*)	use various forms, such as tally sheets, to identify areas that need attention.
Record of achievement (3/ *)	complete a record of achievement (ROA) (Harmer, 2007) that contains comments that focus on self-assessment of successes and challenges, and outline plans for future progress.
Important or urgent (4/ *)	prioritize their writing activities by identifying what is important and urgent.
Procrastination survey (4/ *)	identify their personal strengths and weaknesses as time managers.
Physical environment inventory (5/ *)	take an inventory that illustrates how well they select sites conducive to productive writing.
What distracts you (5/ *)	complete a worksheet that helps them identify common internal distractions and recognize how those distractions likely affect their performance.
Guiding questions (6/ *)	ask questions of themselves about various aspects of writing—process, form, mechanics, and so on. These questions focus on the stages of writing to help learners analyze their strengths and weaknesses.
Muddiest point (6/ *)	identify topics discussed in class that they do not understand well; they can also be asked to determine what they can do to get further information or increase their understanding on the topic they have identified.

Monitoring Performance

Name: Marinoa

Assignment: Essay #2 "A Serious Social Problem"

Part 2

Directions: Based on the strengths and weaknesses you listed in Part 1, write specific goals for improvement in Part 2. You do not have to write a goal for each column—just those that need the most attention.

2.	What are my goals?			
I will raise my grade one full mark over the last paper.	Stop translating when I write. Understand what a run-on sentence is.	Meet each deadline on this paper.		Get more comfortable sharing my writing with others

Figure 7.3 Part 2 Monitoring Performance Form

Table 7.2 Objective 2 Supporting Activities

Objective: Incorporate strategic planning with goal setting	
Activity (chapter/page)	*Description In this activity, learners*
Accuracy goals(2/ *)	use tally sheets and other forms of grammatical feedback to set specific goals related to the common errors that have been identified.
Process goals(2/ *)	set goals on various parts of the writing process or components of good writing that they may be neglecting.
Language learning plan(2/ *)	set narrow and specific goals based on past performances. Learners share information with the teacher about the goal, their reasons for choosing it, and a method for how they will accomplish it (Snow, 2006).
Survey or reflection paper(2/ *)	complete a teacher-generated survey that measures the learner's motives for learning how to write in English. This survey can then be used as source for a reflection paper that helps the learner understand self-motivation and goal setting.
Class and small group scoring (3/ *)	review and score an example composition together as a class with a checklist or rubric to help them understand the criteria used for grading.
80/20 Rule (4/ *)	identify 20% of the writing tasks that they deem to be most important and then focus their attention on completing those tasks first.
Timeline cover sheet (4/ *)	complete a coversheet that divides an assignment into manageable parts and identifies deadlines for each.
Ask an expert (5/ *)	interview teachers (their own and others) about the locations they typically used for writing when they were students, as well as where they now write, in order to improve writing productivity.
Flowchart analysis (6/ *)	identify when and why to seek help and from whom. This is done by sharing their thoughts either in discussions or by writing about a teacher-created flowchart that outlines the need for social support in the writing process.

The more strategies a learner has, the better his or her performance typically will be.

Previous Chapter Activities

Activities for this objective come predominantly from Chapter 2, where motive and goal setting are the primary focus. Table 7.2 summarizes these activities.

Implement and Monitor Learning Strategies

Once learners have carefully analyzed a paper's strengths and weaknesses, identified aspects of their writing that need improvement, and set realistic goals using the monitoring performance form, they can then identify learning strategies to accomplish these goals. Since strategic learners consciously selected from a repertoire of possibilities with the purpose of achieving a desired outcome, it may be helpful to provide the learner with a summary of possible activities that can be used to develop learning strategies (see the Appendix for a summary of activities).

Monitoring Performance—Part 3

Marinoa's completed monitoring performance form (Figure 7.4) illustrates how she has incorporated strategies to improve her writing.

Monitoring performance

Name: Marinoa

Assignment: Essay #2 "A Serious Social Problem"

Part 3

Directions:

Once you have set goals in Part 2, you should select specific strategies you will use to accomplish these goals.

3.	What will I do to accomplish this?			
I will follow through on each of the goals listed in part 2 of this worksheet.	Work with a tutor to understand run-on sentences. Memorize one half of the Academic Word List in the next 10 weeks using spaced retrieval techniques. Work with my writing team in class on first draft to avoid translating.	I will use the Time-line coversheet the teacher gave us. Start using a 1,2,3;A,B,C system for my homework.		I will make an appointment with the tutor to discuss my 2nd draft. Attend the writing group I have been assigned to.

Figure 7.4 Part 3 Monitoring Performance Form

Table 7.3 Objective 3 Supporting Activities

Objective: Implement and monitor learning strategies	
Activity (chapter/page)	Description In this activity, learners
Reflective notebooks (3/ *)	use notebooks to record thoughts about the learning process. The format and content of these can include reflections on the learning process and on the strategies that are working best to achieve goals.
Record of achievement (3/ *)	complete a record of achievement (ROA) (Harmer, 2007) that contains comments focusing on self-assessment of successes and challenges, and that outlines plans for future progress.
Twenty-four hour evaluation (4/ *)	use a three-column log to record tasks they performed in the past 24 hours. Used in conjunction with the Important or urgent matrix (see Chapter 4). Learners determine how they might have prioritized their activities differently to make better use of time.
Be here now (5/ *)	recite the line "Be here now" each time they find themselves being distracted. It may require repeating this phrase several hundred times over the course of a day, but practice will help.
Worry/think time (5/ *)	set time-aside time each day that is worry or think time to tend to the distractions that need attention. While writing, learners have a small worry note pad or data dump pad nearby to jot down tasks that need attention after the writing task is complete.
Writer at work; do not disturb (5/ *)	identify their prefered writing space where distractions will be minimal. They then hang a creative "do not disturb" sign on the door to ensure undistubed writing time.
Peer review groups (6/ *)	meet with the instructor to review paper drafts. This process helps learners form a community and use their social environment to become better writers by allowing them to learn how to evaluate their own writing and others' writing in a small group setting.

Previous Chapter Activities

The activities listed in Table 7.3 are selected from previous chapters specifically to help learners implement and monitor learning strategies.

Strategically Monitor Performance Outcomes

With strategies selected to help them achieve writing goals, learners should begin monitoring how well each strategy is working. This monitoring can be done while a task is in progress as well as when it is finished. Monitoring during and after a task leads to improved writing.

Monitoring Performance
Name: Marinoa
Assignment: Essay #2 "A Serious Social Problem"
Part 4
As you start applying the strategies identified in Part 3, keep track of how well each is working for you. You should have all sections in Part 4 filled in after you receive your assignment back from your teacher. What you learned on this assignment can then be used to improve on the next assignments.

Motive Why	Method How	Time When	Physical Environment Where	Social Environment With whom
1.		What are my strengths and weaknesses?		
I am not happy with the grade I earned on the last assignment. I want to study international business. I know good writing will be important.	I usually draft in my first language. Perhaps this is causing my grammar problems; my teacher thinks so. I keep getting comments about run-on sentences, & nonacademic vocabulary.	I have got to do something about starting early on an assignment. The teacher was right. I rushed the last assignment.	I think my writing space is fine. I am not distracted.	I have never talked to a tutor or asked for feedback from my peers; perhaps I should.
2.		What are my goals?		
I will raise my grade one full mark over the last paper.	Stop translating when I write. Understand what a run-on sentence is	Meet each deadline on this paper.		Get more comfortable sharing my writing with others
3.		What will I do to accomplish this?		
I will follow through on each of the goals listed in part 2 of this worksheet.	Work with a tutor to understand run-on sentences Memorize one half of the Academic Word List in the next 10 weeks using spaced retrieval techniques Work with my writing team in class on first draft to avoid translating.	I will use the Time-line coversheet the teacher gave us. Start using a 1, 2,3 ;A, B, C system for my homework.		I will make an appointment with the tutor to discuss my 2nd draft Attend the writing group I have been assigned to.
4.		How did I do?		
Success! I earned a "B" on this paper.	Working with my writing team really helped me not to translate my early drafts. I have a good understanding of what a run-on sentence is; but I still have some in paper # 2—not as many. Still work to do here. I am on schedule with the AWL. I now need to think about how to use them in writing.	I really like the Time-line coversheet. I was able to meet all the deadlines. It is helpful to break big projects into small parts. 1, 2, 3; A, B, C system still feels strange to me. Perhaps I need to modify it to my learning style. I will give it one more try before I change anything.		The tutor was very nice and helped a lot with run-on sentences. Also I now have a friend I can call on in the future. The writing group in class also was helpful. I got several good ideas on my introduction.

Figure 7.5 Completed Monitoring Performance Form

Monitoring Performance—Part 4

At this point Marinoa's work is illustrated from beginning (Part 1) to end (Part 4) with each section of the monitoring performance form completed in Figure 7.5.

With these two simple forms—strengths and weaknesses analysis and monitoring performance (see Figures 7.1 and 7.2)—a learner has the essential elements for a feedback loop binder. Implementing the use of such a binder addresses the common concern writing teachers have that feedback is going unnoticed, and it helps the learner systematically monitor performance on each of the self-regulated learner principles as they relate to writing performance.

Previous Chapter Activities

As with previous objectives, the activities listed in Table 7.4 are selected from previous chapters in this book that help learners focus on their performance. In this case, these activities support learners as they strategically monitor performance outcomes.

Summary

This chapter has:

- defined and explored the principle of performance generally and as it relates to language learning and L2 writing specifically;
- identified key pedagogical practices involved in facilitating learners' use of performance to improve language acquisition and writing ability; and
- illustrated how the principle of performance, or self-monitoring, is inherently connected with the five other self-regulated learner principles that have been presented in this book to help learners become self-regulated L2 writers.

The next chapter:

- explains three approaches that can be used to implement SRL into a writing course curriculum;
- shares activities to introduce the concept of SRL;
- discusses a variety of ongoing course requirements related to SRL and how to implement them;
- explains the critical nature of the principles of motive and performance and how to weave these principles throughout a course; and
- addresses how teachers can provide learners with opportunities to select activities and develop strategies related to the SRL principles of method, time, physical environment, and social environment.

Table 7.4 Objective 4 Supporting Activities

Objective: Strategically monitor performance outcomes

Activity (chapter/page)	Description In this activity, learners
Rewards and punishments (2/ *)	become responsible for their own learning outcomes by foregoing a leisure activity in order to study when performance has fallen below expectations. When they do make progress, they may want to treat themselves in some way, such as having an ice cream cone or going to a movie.
Strategic questions (2/ *)	evaluate their own performance with a set of questions that probe how well or poorly they performed and why. This is typically done when the teacher returns the assignment, complete with feedback.
Whole class reflection (3/ *)	engage in a class discussion of a handout prepared by the teacher that summarizes what was done well by the entire class on a particular assignment, their common errors and weaknesses, and suggestions for improvement (Nation, 2009). During this discussion learners identify what they feel comfortable with and what is still unclear to them related to their own writing assignment.
Timeline cover sheet (4/ *)	complete a coversheet that divides an assignment into manageable parts and identifies deadlines for each one. This coversheet can be used as a metric to determine if an assignment was completed in a timely manner.
Assignment time log (4/ *)	record in a three-column log the assignment description or title, the approximate time that it took to complete the assignment, and brief comments and reflections on the time required for the task, such as why it took more or less time than expected, or why it was on time.
Physical environment inventory (5/ *)	take an inventory that illustrates how well they select sites conducive to productive writing. This can be used as a follow up after an assignment is completed.
Peer review groups (6/ *)	meet with the instructor to review paper drafts. This process helps learners form a community and use their social environment to become better writers by allowing them to learn how to evaluate their own writing and others' writing in a small group setting.
Evaluation logs (6/ *)	keep a log with observations of how the team is functioning, create lists of incidences or changes that have affected the group positively or negatively, or write an analysis of barriers the group faced and how they were overcome (e.g., see Team-based learning: peer evaluation, n.d.).

Chapter 8

Implementing the Self-Regulated Learning Approach in the L2 Writing Classroom

Objectives

This chapter discusses how to implement self-regulated learning (SRL) into an L2 writing classroom. It focuses on helping teachers:

- determine an overall implementation approach;
- introduce the concept of SRL;
- determine ongoing SRL course requirements;
- integrate the principles of motive and performance into a course; and
- provide learners with opportunities to select activities and develop strategies related to the principles of methods, time, physical environment, and social environment.

Previous chapters presented guiding classroom practices, as well as activities and approaches related to the six SRL principles. To help teachers create an SRL-focused classroom, this chapter demonstrates how these activities can be integrated in a holistic way to achieve desired outcomes. The chapter presents a curriculum plan for implementing the six principles throughout an entire course of study with periodic learner performance self-evaluations that involve monitoring, reassessment of strengths and weaknesses, and goal modifications. It illustrates the iterative approach required for SRL to be effectively realized in the lives of learners. Learners cannot develop self-regulation behaviors with only periodic exposure or superficial reflections on their learning. Thus, those using this approach must provide extensive practice, reinforcement, feedback, and guidance. To do this, a comprehensive plan, such as the one proposed in this chapter, is needed.

The first section in the chapter provides implementation options and ideas for activities that can be used to introduce the concept of SRL. Then, ongoing course requirements to help learners set goals and monitor their learning are shared. Because motive and performance are central to SRL, the discussion emphasizes how to weave learning related to these principles throughout a course. Then, ways in which teachers can provide learners with opportunities for autonomy in selecting activities and developing strategies related to the principles of methods, time, physical environment, and social environment are presented. These discussions are illustrated with selected activities from Chapters 2–7. Alternate activities can be used based on teacher and learner preferences. General caveats and adaptations for the selected activities based on teaching and learning variables are also provided; a more detailed discussion of curricular and contextual variables and related adaptations of activities can be found in Chapter 9.

Ultimately, learners need to acknowledge that they are responsible for controlling the factors and conditions that affect their learning experiences. This chapter demonstrates a coherent way for teachers to assist in this process.

Implementation Options

The concept of SRL will be new to most learners, so it must be introduced at the beginning of a course. Teachers will need to decide whether to present SRL and its principles all at once, gradually, or by combining both methods. Each possibility is briefly explored. These approaches are identified as concentrated, gradual, and selected reinforcement.

Option 1: Concentrated

A concentrated approach involves the teacher introducing the general concept of SRL in one class period, with a focus on each of the principles in the next few class periods. Learners form a plan of study based on their self-evaluations and teacher feedback on initial writing assignments (the topic of which could be SRL). They also create a time line for implementing this plan, which includes regular performance checks.

A concentrated approach to introducing SRL in the first few class periods allows learners to understand the various aspects of SRL, determine their strengths and weaknesses, and identify areas of individual focus for the remainder of the course. This implementation strategy is appropriate in situations where teachers have the flexibility to dedicate an initial block of time to SRL. Before adopting the concentrated approach, however, teachers need to determine the likelihood of learners being able to create and follow through on a personalized learning plan. This approach is most appropriate for advanced learners who can grasp the concepts easily and who may already possess some ability to be independent due to their L2 proficiency level.

The concentrated approach supports learner autonomy and control although teachers must facilitate and provide structure. They must identify how much and what type of structure learners need. Structure includes regular learner reports on progress, periodic teacher–learner conferences, goal and achievement sharing with peers in class, review of principles and strategies at various times throughout the course, and so forth. Few activities would likely be done in class as learners are working on individualized plans; however, teachers should provide learners with access to possible activities and introduce some of these in class.

Option 2: Gradual

A gradual approach involves an initial overview of SRL and its principles, perhaps in one or two class periods, followed by each principle being the focus of study for a two- to three-week period, depending on the length of the course. As learners practice each principle, they self-evaluate and set related goals and reflect on their performance at the end of the unit.

Introducing SRL gradually gives learners time to understand the principles, assess their learning behaviors, and practice associated strategies. One disadvantage is that learners may be focusing on areas in which they are already strong although it is likely they would still learn additional strategies. This approach favors high-beginning and intermediate-level learners who find it difficult to manage a large amount of information, and it does not require a block of class time upfront.

The gradual approach may also be more manageable for the teacher than the concentrated option because it is more structured and all learners focus on the same principle at the same time. Class time must be available for non-SRL course material to be spaced throughout the course. However, the amount of time spent introducing SRL and the number of activities incorporated for each principle can vary. Teachers can determine if they want to do one activity in class for each principle and assign additional activities for homework, or if students will practice multiple activities and strategies in class.

Option 3: Selected Reinforcement

A third possibility for SRL implementation in an L2 writing course is to introduce SRL briefly in one or two class periods (similar to the gradual approach) and have learners develop personalized SRL plans based on their self-assessment of strengths and weaknesses and on feedback on initial writing assignments (similar to the concentrated and gradual approaches). Teachers then reinforce various principles in greater depth at intervals during the course based on learner need. The latter component is the key difference between this approach and the concentrated and gradual approaches because it emphasizes the customization of learning activities to the needs of a specific group of learners.

With selected reinforcement, teachers choose principles of focus and related strategies based on their observations of learner needs in the classroom and through assignments. For example, one of the authors taught a class where learners did not understand the expectation to come to class prepared. They rarely did required homework in the course textbook or came with drafts of writing assignments completed. As a result, she designed materials related to the principles of motive and time to help learners examine their purposes for learning to write in English and how their lack of time management may be preventing them from achieving their goals.

The periodic in-depth sessions associated with this type of implementation do not need to cover a span of several weeks or constitute a unit of study (as with the gradual approach); thus overall, less class time is likely required than with the previous two approaches. The SRL activities interspersed throughout the course increase learner understanding of principles and strategies through review and practice. As with the other approaches, selected reinforcement supports the principle of performance in that regular monitoring occurs to encourage the development of SRL. The approach is appropriate at high-beginning to advanced proficiency levels. The primary drawback is that some principles might not be reviewed or reinforced, thus strategies that may be helpful to a few learners could be missed.

Summary

Table 8.1 provides a summation of SRL implementation approaches. These options allow learners to practice SRL strategies along with various aspects of writing—paragraph structure, rhetorical patterns, grammar and vocabulary items, revision strategies, and so forth. The SRL activities described in Chapters 2–7 support language development. Teachers can expand on any element of an activity to support not only writing skills, but also vocabulary, grammar, reading comprehension, listening, and speaking. In this way, SRL is not supplementary material but is integrated into the teaching and learning of writing skills.

Furthermore, the goals that learners form will be specifically related to language proficiency improvement; thus, teachers will find that the additional time it takes to learn about and focus on SRL will reap positive effects on the achievement of language learning objectives. Objectives for SRL and specific writing points can be identified for each class period or unit of study. An example of how this can be accomplished is provided later in the chapter in the section entitled "Autonomy and self-selection: Methods, time, physical environment, social environment".

Table 8.1 Summary of Implementation Options

Concentrated Plan: An in-depth introduction of self-regulated learning and principles during the first few days of the course. Curriculum must be flexible. Learners must have some ability to be independent. Teachers facilitate and provide structure as needed. Most appropriate for advanced-level learners.

Motive	Performance	Advantages	Disadvantages
• Plan created by learners. • Plan based on self-evaluation and feedback on writing assignments. • Continual analysis of learner strengths and weaknesses required.	• Time line for implementing plan. • Ongoing tracking of, reflection on, and adjustments to initial goals. • Changes based on assignment feedback. • Reports given to teacher regularly.	• Learner autonomy and control encouraged. • Little class time needed after initial introduction. • Learners self-select from a range of activities. • Activities done mostly as homework.	• Extensive time required up front.

Gradual Plan: Brief overview of SRL and principles in one or two class sessions. Each principle is focused on in-depth in designated units throughout the course. Curriculum must be flexible. Appropriate for high-beginning and intermediate-level learners.

Motive	Performance	Advantages	Disadvantages
• Plan created by learners. • Plan based on self-evaluation and feedback on writing assignments. • Continual analysis of learner strengths and weaknesses required.	• Ongoing tracking of, reflection on, and adjustments to initial goals. • Changes based on assignment feedback. • Reports given to teacher regularly.	• Learners gain an in-depth understanding of SRL. • Potential to increase number of strategies in areas in which they already have both strengths and weaknesses. • Learners focused on same principle. • Ongoing discussion of principles promotes goal analysis and revision. • Activities adjustable for work in class or homework.	• Learners may focus on strategies they do not need to work on. • Learner autonomy limited regarding principle of focus and choice of related activities.

Selected Reinforcement Plan: Brief overview of SRL and principles. Selected principles based on learner needs and performance. Some teacher autonomy over curriculum needed. Adjustable for all proficiency levels.

Motive	Performance	Advantages	Disadvantages
• Plan created by learners. • Based on self-evaluation and feedback on writing assignments. • Continual analysis of learner strengths and weaknesses required.	• Ongoing tracking of, reflection on, and adjustments to initial goals. • Changes based on assignment feedback. • Reports given to teacher regularly.	• Customized approach based on teacher identification of learner needs. • Moderate class time required depending on learner strengths and weaknesses. • Activities adjustable for work in class or homework.	• A limited number of principles and strategies may be introduced and practiced. • Some needed principles and strategies may be missed.

Introductory Activities

All of the implementation approaches involve familiarizing learners with the definition of SRL, its principles, and some associated strategies within the first few classes. This can be accomplished in a variety of ways. Stories, case studies, a brief academic reading passage or lecture, a PowerPoint presentation, or a video clip can be used to introduce and define SRL and its principles.

One possibility is to provide learners with scenarios or high-interest stories that demonstrate situations in which learners need to be responsible for factors or conditions affecting their learning (e.g., the desire for a high grade due to parental expectations [motive], receiving a failing exam score [methods], failure to complete assignments by the due date [time], limited access to a computer due to family demand [physical environment], lack of understanding a teacher's correction symbols on an assignment [social environment], or continued poor performance on a particular type of assignment [performance]). The relevant SRL principles can be introduced and learners asked to match the principle with the related scenario. Associated strategies related to the various scenarios can then be identified and categorized to help learners understand how they can control factors that affect their learning.

A formal presentation or lecture about SRL with comprehension and discussion questions may also be appropriate. The length and complexity of the presentation or lecture, as well as needed vocabulary and grammatical constructions, must be adjusted for learner proficiency levels. Lectures could be highly structured with simplified language and pre-discussion of vocabulary for learners at high-beginning or intermediate levels who could complete an outline with gaps as they listen. Pair and small-group work may be useful for discussion, with learners checking answers to the matching exercise, and comparing lecture outlines and notes.

Learners can respond to the introductory activity through one of the on-going course requirements discussed next, such as a journal entry or 10-minute paragraph using the following prompts. The responses to these questions can be used to establish goals.

- What is SRL?
- What are the various principles?
- What are your strengths and weaknesses in each area?
- Which principle would you like to work on and what strategies can you use to improve in that area?

Ongoing Course Requirements

In addition to determining an implementation approach and introducing learners to the concept of SRL, teachers must decide which ongoing course requirements they will use to support learner goal identification (i.e., motive), and to help learners monitor their performance. Both motive and performance are integral to incorporating SRL into a course and are critical to all of the implementation approaches (see Table 8.1). This section identifies possible activities from previous chapters to illustrate how learners can set goals, and monitor and track performance based on self-evaluation and teacher feedback.

An SRL learner journal (Chapter 2), the 10-minute paragraph (Chapter 3), and 10 perfect sentences (Chapter 4) are possible activity choices through which learners not only practice writing skills, but reflect on their learning and monitor their performance. A feedback loop binder (Chapter 7) is an effective way for learners to process and use teacher feedback. These course components are next discussed as part of an overall curriculum plan for an SRL-based writing course.

SRL Learner Journals

One way to help learners reflect on their goals and performance is to have them keep and regularly submit an SRL journal in which they discuss one SRL activity per week, what they learned from it, and how it has affected their goals. The journal provides writing practice as learners apply the writing skills they are learning to their journal entries. This may include sentence-level work for learners with low proficiency levels, paragraph-level writing at the intermediate level, or essay writing for advanced learners.

Teachers must respond to the journal in a way that encourages learners to think deeply about their learning and set appropriate goals. Teachers can design a rubric for this purpose that combines expectations for content, organization, and grammatical accuracy. The primary focus should be on the learner's development of SRL and related goals. These rubrics will aid grading in large classes. Another approach for large classes is to grade only a random number of journals per week, ensuring that every student journal is responded to a certain number of times over the course without learners knowing when their journal will be graded. Class time can be set aside for learners to read and react to each other's SRL journals, thereby decreasing teacher control and increasing student SRL practices.

Guidelines for peer response should be provided by the teacher (e.g., "Write two or three sentences about what you learned from your classmate's journal," or "Write two or three sentences that show your understanding of your classmate's goal"). Teachers can spot check these peer comments in class periodically during the semester, and also give their own response to the journals from time to time. They should share examples of helpful peer comments. Learners need to understand that teachers are not avoiding their duties by requiring peer response, but are encouraging use of the social environment, helping learners understand that they can get useful feedback from a variety of sources, providing additional language practice, and supporting the development of SRL.

If an online course management system or blog is available, SRL journal entries can be posted. Learners can be given specific instructions about how to respond to the postings, such as to make one comment and ask one question about a post. This activity reinforces SRL by helping learners not rely on teacher feedback; it also provides communicative language practice. Reponses can be written or in the form of a video post. The teacher's role is to monitor and score the responses based on criteria for the assignment. Teachers can provide comments about overall strengths and weaknesses to the entire class in an announcement or e-mail. This is also appropriate if learners submit hard copies of journals—teachers provide a score followed by in-class feedback. These teacher response strategies provide a solution to workload concerns for large classes.

Unless entries for journals are properly introduced and modeled, they will tend to be brief and superficial. Teachers should provide guiding questions or prompts such as the example prompts for the SRL introduction activities that were provided previously in this chapter. The quality of SRL learner journal entries improves substantially when teachers have high expectations and give clear instructions and examples related to these expectations.

Reflective Notebooks

An alternative to an SRL journal is a reflective notebook in which learners record thoughts about the learning process and the strategies they are using to achieve their goals. The SRL journal and the reflective notebook have a similar purpose, with the primary difference being that notebook entries are typically less formal and organized. Learners jot down their thoughts periodically, such as after doing an assignment or receiving a scored test or assignment. Class time can be provided for learners to take a few moments to note how they did on the assignment and analyze reasons for their strong or weak performance (e.g., beginning the assignment early, application of a particular editing strategy, seeking help from a tutor or peer, failure to do the homework leading up to the assignment, etc.). They can then determine what they should keep doing or stop doing in order to master a particular writing skill.

These reflective notebooks are a particularly effective tool when learners carry them around and make notes of new vocabulary or grammar constructions they encounter in reading or listening situations, key ideas from textbook readings or class sessions, or ideas from their peers for improving their learning. The notebooks can be in electronic form, such as on a smart phone, iPad, or computer, if these are devices that learners regularly carry. However, the notebooks must be in a format that can be printed, submitted by e-mail, or transmitted in some other way to the teacher.

The evaluation of reflective notebooks is somewhat different from evaluation of an SRL journal. Prior to submitting them, the learner might write a couple of summary sentences of the entries for that week, or a paragraph about what was learned from the entries regarding writing skill progress and SRL development. These could be submitted for a grade, which would be based on content, organization, and language use, thereby reinforcing the writing skills practiced. The content of these summary assignments needs to be reviewed carefully by the teacher to determine the depth of reflection and specificity of goals. (This is discussed in more detail in the SRL journal and feedback loop journal sections in this chapter.)

The notebook summaries might occur only periodically throughout the course as part of a self-evaluation. In interim weeks, teachers might spot check the learner notebooks in class to see that they are being completed. This could be followed by a class discussion of what is working and what is not working related to SRL goals and monitoring performance. Teachers could indicate beneficial practices and non-beneficial practices. Peer sharing of how learners use their notebooks can also be planned into class sessions periodically so that learners can exchange ideas.

Spot checking and peer sharing work well in large classes. In fact, the reflective notebook lends itself well to this situation because it can be briefly reviewed in or out of class, and a quick written or verbal comment can be provided by the teacher or a peer. Learners should understand that the purpose of the notebook is to help them strengthen their ability to become better learners; they need to take ownership of it and use it in a way that is most useful to them. As such, it could take the form of a grammar notebook (Snow, 2006) with regular summary reports submitted to the teacher (Harmer, 2007). Other variations of reflective notebooks (e.g., reflections on strategy use, notes about effective class activities, ideas for how to improve performance on an assignment, one-minute papers about what was learned in a class session, corrected sentences with notes on grammar rules and errors, etc.) are provided in Table 3.5 (Chapter 3).

One disadvantage of a reflective notebook over the SRL journal is that it does not involve as much extended writing practice. The entries are typically in note form, rather than full sentences or paragraphs. However, requiring a written report from time to time based on the notes addresses this disadvantage. An advantage of the notebook is that it is not based on teacher-provided prompts, but is generated solely by the learner and documents what the learner feels is important—certainly a step toward becoming a self-regulated L2 writer.

10-Minute Paragraphs and 10 Perfect Sentences

10-minute paragraphs or, for learners at lower proficiency levels, 10 perfect sentences, can be written in class to respond to various SRL activities. These activities reinforce both the understanding of SRL principles and the ability to communicate about them. The paragraphs can be graded as explained in Chapters 3 and 4 respectively, or learners can respond to the content of each other's writing with appropriate teacher guidance, as explained in the learner journal section above. Learners can then revise their work, with teachers providing feedback on accuracy and other writing aspects in later drafts. Learners could select the final draft of one paragraph each week as a weekly journal submission. This would provide learners with a well-written record of their SRL journey throughout the course. Although teachers would have some expectation of learners composing a well-written paragraph or sentence according to course objectives, the primary purpose of the paragraphs is to reflect on the SRL activities and their efficacy.

Having learners post their paragraphs or sentences on a learning management system, as explained earlier in the chapter, and responding to the postings of other learners, may also be adopted. These practices not only decrease teacher grading time and increase SRL behaviors, but give learners a real audience for their writing, one of the concepts introduced in Chapter 2. Teachers need to consider the size of their class and be creative in maximizing learner practice in ways that do not create burdens for grading. By keeping the principle of learner responsibility in mind, rather than a teacher-centered focus, grading workloads can be addressed.

Feedback on Form and Meaning

As explained in Chapter 2, in order to set goals, learners need feedback on form and meaning in their writing. This is critical to each of the implementation approaches summarized in Table 8.1 and must be attended to in the first few class sessions. If possible, learners should receive teacher response on more than one assignment early in the course to inform their self-analysis. Teacher response to writing must be continual so that learners can monitor their performance and adjust their goals, but they need specific feedback upfront to consider during the self-evaluation process, along with their own views of their abilities.

To increase awareness of grammar weaknesses, encourage more responsibility for editing, and ultimately improve grammatical accuracy, a system of correction marks or symbols should be used. For an example of a system that has been tried and tested and proven effective, see Chapter 2. To help learners become more familiar with grammar correction marks (see Table 2.4, Chapter 2), teachers should review the symbols and example sentences. One way to do this is to have learners look at the example sentences in the table and correct the errors. Next, teachers can give learners selected sentences with similar types of errors from other learners' writing assignments and have them correct these as a class or in small groups or pairs. The goal is to ensure that students know what the symbols represent and have some idea about how to correct sentences with errors. Teachers may need to review grammar rules or give grammatical explanations as part of this process.

Additionally, some symbols may require specific explanation. For example, learners often do not recognize that the symbol "d" (determiner) includes articles. They also need to know that a "d" may indicate that the wrong determiner was used, a determiner was used but not needed, or a determiner was not used but is needed. This is true for other symbols such as "s/pl" and "pp." Reviewing examples will help learners to use these symbols independently to make corrections. This activity can be accomplished in a large class by showing examples on the board or a PowerPoint slide. Handouts can be prepared with example sentences, and students asked to work in groups and then come to the board or computer to provide corrections.

While learners will not be able to correct every sentence, having an error identified aids their ability to make appropriate changes. This technique for labeling and requiring correction of errors may not be efficacious for learners who are not well-versed in grammatical terminology, such as those who have learned the language informally. In this case, other strategies for providing feedback on grammar should be adopted, such as asking questions about the meaning of a sentence to prompt the writer to express the idea in a different way. In cases where learners are unlikely to be able to correct an error, as is often true for many preposition errors, or where the error is merely distracting rather than interfering with meaning, teachers can be selective in what they mark, or provide the correction directly.

Regarding feedback on meaning, teachers can develop rubrics (see Chapters 2 and 7). Ideally, teachers would introduce these to learners when assignments are explained so that learners understand expectations, but the rubrics should also be reinforced when assignments are returned. Example peer and teacher feedback forms are provided in Chapter 2 and can be adapted to fit specific needs. A rubric for the SRL journal, for example, should focus on learners identifying what they learned from an SRL activity, providing specific examples to support their ideas, and indicating action steps leading to goal accomplishment (see discussions about teacher response and student entries in the sections on SRL journals and the feedback loop binder in this chapter). Other writing features, such as organization and grammatical accuracy, may be included, depending on writing course objectives. Learners can help design rubrics to increase awareness of expectations and reinforce SRL behaviors.

Feedback Loop Journal

As explained in Chapter 7, when teachers return assignments with comments (e.g., in the form of correction marks, rubrics, margin or end comments, etc.), learners should complete two forms: (1) the strengths and weaknesses analysis in which they note their performance on various writing features, such as content, organization, vocabulary, grammar, mechanics, and neatness (alternative categories can be determined as desired); and (2) monitoring performance, which involves learners reviewing the findings of the strengths and weaknesses analysis and categorizing them according to the six SRL principles. This is followed by learners determining goals, action steps, and, at a later point, reflecting on goal achievement.

Teachers will likely need to guide learners through the process of completing these forms for initial writing assignments. Class time should be used for this and good models of completed forms shared. As with the SRL journal, the most common challenge for learners will be identifying specific weaknesses and developing specific goals for improvement. Typically, when asked to set goals, learners will say, "I need to study hard. I have to attend class and do what the teacher says." These comments demonstrate that learners are accustomed to a teacher-centered model of learning and that they believe that everything they need to know or do to improve their writing skills will be provided in class by the teacher.

The following examples demonstrate the difference between initial learner responses, which tend to be general, and more focused responses that learners have written as the result of teacher guidance:

- General identification of strengths and weaknesses related to editing strategies:
  "Peer-editing and self-editing worksheets are really helpful for me to understand what I need to focus on in each chapter. So, I can see very clearly, and I can check how much my skills were improved."
- Specific identification of strengths and weaknesses related to editing strategies:
  "In English, I find it difficult to write essays and writing without grammar errors. So, I need to improve them. I am quite good at editing my writing with teacher's comments. One error that I made several times in my first paragraph was use of the past tense. I made a list of these sentences. And I reviewed the rule for past tense."
- General identification of strategies and goals related to use of time:
  "I need to spend more time to do my assignments and every morning little by little and one by one to do it. I am now following my daily schedule."
- Specific identification of strategies and goals related to use of time:

"First I am looking at all assignments in this week and make a plan for every day. I will find out which part is easy and do that first like vocabulary. Some parts take long time to complete such as writing assignment because I must think about the content, write down, and if there are unfamiliar words, I have to find out how to use it. I will do this when I have long periods of time to study."

Learners quickly understand what is needed to make their responses and goals more specific. If learners do not grasp this from the examples shared, they usually do so after the teacher responds to their submission, whether it is an SRL journal, strengths and weaknesses analysis or monitoring performance form (see Figures 7.1 and 7.2 in Chapter 7), or other type of reflection.

Caveats

Because several of these tools have the same purpose and using multiple tools may be overwhelming, teachers should not use all of them. Those new to this approach may want to begin with the grammar correction marks and the error tally sheet (Tables 2.4 and 2.5, Chapter 2), or implement 10-minute paragraphs with these two tools. Similarly, an SRL journal, reflective notebook, or a feedback loop binder might be selected, but not more than one of these. With some experimentation, teachers will find what works best in their context and may be able to include additional SRL assignments that are appropriate. Teachers might also consider introducing various options to the learners and having them choose, either individually or as a class, which tool would be most effective. This supports SRL.

Two Central Components to SRL: Motive and Performance

The previous sections explained several components that must be considered when determining an overall curriculum plan for an SRL-based writing course. These include an implementation strategy, activities for introducing SRL to learners, and course requirement set up for monitoring goals. The latter are related to the two central aspects of SRL—motive and performance. These are also noted in Table 8.1, which illustrates how these principles apply across all implementation approaches. This section presents selected activities related to motive and performance, and explains how these can be incorporated into a course. It provides an in-depth discussion of possible adaptations for the activities, clarifies how they can be combined with the ongoing course components discussed previously, and illustrates how they support language learning. The purpose of this in-depth treatment is to help teachers visualize a holistic approach for assisting learners in becoming self-regulated L2 writers.

Motive should be the first principle introduced because it involves determining a purpose for learning, strengths and weaknesses, and goals for improvement. It is similar to conducting a needs analysis, which is often a component of an L2 writing course (e.g., see Ferris & Hedgcock, 2005). The other principles can be presented in any order, although the principle of performance must be woven throughout the course as learners monitor, reflect on, and modify their goals. This can be accommodated through the ongoing course requirements discussed in the last section.

Because learners have individual strengths and weaknesses, the other four principles may receive less or more emphasis as needed. The selected reinforcement implementation option suggests that these principles be addressed based only on class needs, while the gradual approach involves addressing all of them. The concentrated implementation approach also introduces all of the principles and some strategies. With all three approaches, however, learners form individual goals.

Motive and Goal-Setting

Initial class sessions are critical in helping learners increase awareness of their responsibility for learning. Rather than sitting passively in class and waiting to be instructed, learners must recognize that attendance and rote completion of homework is insufficient to help them make progress in the acquisition of L2 writing skills. They need to examine their own deeply held beliefs about learning to write in a second language. They must determine why and for whom they are learning—do they really understand how important writing skills are to future education and employment contexts? Do they believe they can get by with minimally developed writing skills and inaccurate grammatical constructions? Are they trying to please their parents and families who may be paying the cost of their education? Are grades more important than learning? Do they truly want to achieve the ability to communicate clearly and fluently in writing? Selected activities introduced in Chapter 2 and implementation factors are next discussed.

Determining Motivation for Writing

The determining motivation for writing survey (see Table 2.2, Chapter 2) is one activity teachers can use to help learners explore and identify their reasons for learning how to write in English. Teachers can develop additional questions that focus on helping learners gain increased understanding of their purposes for learning how to write, and to determine whether these purposes are internally or externally driven. After the survey is administered, class results can be tallied. If teachers have access to automated response system technology, learners could view the questions in a PowerPoint presentation and enter answers on their remote devices. The answers are automatically tallied and graphs appear showing the results for each question. If this type of system is not available, similar free online systems can be used, or teachers can quickly tally the results and put them on the board.

Following the activity, teachers should conduct a debriefing. This can be done in pairs or small groups by giving students a few guiding questions such as those used in the following SRL journal prompts. Learners could write a brief summary of the class results or a reflection on their own survey results. This could be in the form of an entry in an SRL journal or reflective notebook, or a 10-minute paragraph using the prompts that follow:

- What did you learn about your reasons for wanting to learn to write in English?
- In what future situations will you need to have good writing skills in English (if any)?
- What motivates you to improve your writing (e.g., the praise of others, a feeling of achievement)?
- What are your short-term goals for learning to write in English?
- What are your long-term goals for learning to write in English?

This activity can be modified for learners with lower or higher proficiency levels by adjusting the language in the questions and the number of questions learners are required to answer. Pictures could be used to illustrate different reasons for learning how to write; learners with lower proficiency levels can select pictures representing their motive for writing in English. Needed vocabulary and grammatical structures can be introduced prior to the activity and example sentences or fill-in-the-blank sentences provided. Learners with beginning or low-intermediate levels of proficiency can respond with sentences rather than full paragraphs for the follow-up activity. Learners with advanced levels of proficiency will need less structure, can respond to more complex survey questions, and can respond at greater length.

Familiarity with Writing Concepts

Teachers can also have learners complete the writing concepts familiarity survey (Table 2.8, Chapter 2). This survey can be adapted based on what will be taught in the course. It provides learners with an overview of key writing skills they will learn or strengthen. The survey serves as a type of needs analysis, which teachers can use to plan the course. For example, if most learners in the class indicate familiarity with the idea of a topic sentence, then teachers might review this concept briefly and confirm that learners know how to write a topic sentence by viewing a sample of their writing—perhaps in initial ten-minute paragraphs or the first SRL journal entry.

The primary purpose of the activity is to help learners become aware of their level of expertise related to various writing skills. Survey results can be discussed in pair, group, or whole class formats, and by using the tally methods discussed for the determining motivation for writing survey. Learners can report their findings in a reflective notebook or 10-minute paragraph and begin to identify learning goals that can be documented in an SRL journal and transferred to appropriate forms in the feedback loop binder after the first written assignment is returned. To prompt learners in identifying goals, the strategic questions activity from Chapter 2 (similar to the questions listed below) can be used related to the survey findings. Teachers will need to guide learners away from responses such as "I learned that I am unfamiliar with many of the writing skills listed in the survey," and help them identify specific strengths, weaknesses, and goals with responses such as "I am not familiar with the terms unity and coherence. I will review information in the textbook on these concepts and try to apply them in my next writing assignment." Possible journal prompts follow:

- In which of these areas of writing do you feel you need to practice?
- How will you improve your skill in this area?
- How can teachers, classmates, or others help?
- What do you still need to find out about your abilities as a learner and as a writer?
- How will you get this information?

Testimonials of Former Learners

Another way to help learners identify their motives for learning, and perhaps to provide some with greater incentive, is to invite former learners to class for an exchange with current learners (see Chapter 2). This can be accomplished in a single class period or spread out across several class periods. The activity supports a number of language learning and SRL objectives. It can be implemented in three class sessions of about 45 minutes to 1 hour in length as next described.

PREPARATION

A panel of two or three learners are invited to class. Panelists who have cultural and linguistic backgrounds similar to current learners should be selected, and should have the potential to act as role models. For instance, one of the authors of this book had two former students who were hired as faculty members at the institution where they had begun as English language learners. They had completed their bachelor's degrees at that institution, gone on to complete master's and PhD degrees elsewhere, and returned to the institution as faculty members. Teachers could also select former learners who are a year or two ahead of current learners.

The goal of the first class session is for learners to prepare for the visit by understanding appropriate styles for introductions and interview questions. To set the stage, teachers should explain to learners who the guests are and why they are coming to class. The teacher might also provide biographical data about the guests and have learners work in groups to write introductions. Different groups could write introductions for different guests, or the groups could focus on writing an introduction for all of the guests. Depending on the level of the learner, teachers should provide needed vocabulary, grammatical constructions, and examples of formal introductions. For beginning or low-intermediate level learners, teachers might provide a template and have learners fill in the blanks with biographical data about each guest. In cases where groups are working on introductions for the same person, these should be compared and final versions of the introductions negotiated among the groups. This would be appropriate for more advanced learners. The learners should select who they want to read the introductions when the visitors come to class.

Teachers should also explain their expectations about asking questions. Is everyone in the class responsible for asking a question? What types of questions are appropriate? How many questions should be asked? Learners can be given time in class to write questions. This portion of the activity might begin with the whole class or small groups brainstorming to identify categories or general topics. Teachers must make the purpose for the questions clear—to determine the former learners' purposes for learning to write, to understand how they maintained motivation, to show how subsequent writing tasks were similar to or different from those they were assigned in English language courses, to explain effective strategies for writing they have developed, and to demonstrate ways in which they currently use the writing skills they learned. Example questions are listed in the Activities and Approaches in Chapter 2. The questions listed in Chapter 2 could be provided to learners; however, learners will be more engaged in the activity if they write their own questions. This also provides more language practice.

A variety of methods for organizing the introduction and question writing activities are possible. These include having part of the class write introductions and others write questions, using two class periods to complete the assignment—one to write introductions and one to write questions, asking the class to write introductions but providing the questions, dividing up the categories or topics for questions among different groups, and so forth. This activity lends itself well to learners with different proficiency levels and varying class sizes. It also supports writing skill and grammar objectives, such as organizing paragraphs with a topic sentence and support, learning the genre of a formal introduction, understanding correct sentence structure for questions, or use of past tense verbs. Learners can use one of the ongoing course assignments, such as a reflective notebook, SRL journal, or 10-minute paragraph, to write about what they learned regarding speaker introductions, question writing, grammatical constructions, or about their experiences working in groups.

THE VISIT

Depending on the format for the testimonials, learners can participate by making introductions, facilitating the discussion, asking questions, and thanking the guests. The format and assignments must be determined ahead of time. Teachers will also need to provide guidance as to what these various roles entail and how learners can fulfill them. During the presentation and discussion portions of the class, lower-level learners might be asked to listen for specific ideas, such as one way a guest currently uses writing, one strategy a guest finds useful, or one way in which the English language course prepared the former learner for actual writing tasks. Advanced-level learners might have copies of the questions and make notes about the guests' responses to the questions.

In large classes, more emphasis would be focused on listening, since fewer learners would have the opportunity to ask questions. As such, the activity can be expanded to include listening and note-taking strategies (related to the SRL principle of methods). In addition, less time could be spent on the preparation stages related to writing introductions and questions, since these could be provided by the teacher. These decisions must be made by individual teachers, depending on curriculum parameters. However, the more language practice and responsibility learners are given, the greater the likelihood that they will develop SRL skills. In particular, their motivation will increase as they become involved in determining what and how they learn.

FOLLOW-UP

In the follow-up phase to the activity, learners should identify the main points of value from the testimonial activity. SRL journal or 10-minute paragraph prompts might be introduced as follows:

- What are the most important lessons you learned from the experiences of our class guests?
- How do these lessons change your motive for learning to write?
- How do they change the strategies you use?
- What new ideas do you have about how you might use writing in the future and its importance?

For learners with lower proficiency levels, selecting just one of these questions might be appropriate. Teachers can also provide example sentences, needed vocabulary, or sentence stems for completion (e.g., "One strategy I want to use is _____ ."). Learners could also be asked to write two sentences—what they found most interesting and what would they like to know more about—or to compare their classmates' responses to their own and find one similarity and one difference.

Performance

Regular performance self-evaluations that involve monitoring, continuing assessment of strengths and weaknesses, and modification of goals is critical to SRL. One means of achieving this is through ongoing course requirements such as SRL journals, reflective notebooks, or a feedback loop binder. This section focuses on two additional areas.

Reinforcing SRL Principles

Chapter 7 provides a list of activities from previous chapters that learners can use to develop self-observation and evaluation strategies, incorporate strategic planning with goal setting, and implement and monitor learning strategies. To support the principle of performance, teachers could review a few of these activities with learners or provide them with a descriptive handout. The list could be reduced to two or three options for each principle of performance objective (i.e., self-observation and evaluation, strategic planning and goal setting, implementing and monitoring strategies) to avoid overwhelming the learners.

Learners should choose activities that address their weak areas. This reinforces the development of SRL in that learners are making decisions about their own learning. As they explore various performance activities, they can reflect on their learning in a 10-minute paragraph (or 10 perfect sentences), SRL journal, or reflective notebook. When learners feel they have made progress in a particular area, they can select an additional activity.

Conferences

Along with ongoing assignments that must be introduced at the beginning of a course, teacher–learner conferences should be planned into the schedule as a means of focusing on performance. Chapters 2 and 4 provided some information about conferences. This section demonstrates how conferences can be designed to support SRL and the principle of performance, and suggest caveats and adaptations.

Typically, when learners meet with a teacher, they expect to be given direction. To encourage self-regulation, learners should be guided as to how to take control of their learning in this situation. This can be accomplished with a worksheet that guides learners through the following steps: preparation, participation, asking questions, and practicing (Andrade, in press).

These steps can also be followed for peer tutor appointments or other instances of help-seeking.

To prepare, learners write down questions they want to ask. The questions may be related to the writing assignment, performance in the class, or a point in the textbook. The questions should not be, "What are my weaknesses? How can I get a better grade? What can I do to improve? Can you check my paper for errors?" These are the questions that learners often ask, but they do not reflect taking responsibility for learning. Teachers need to make learners aware of this and illustrate appropriate questions. Examples include the following: "I notice that I have a lot of word form errors in my writing, but I can't quite understand what is wrong." "I thought I had a controlling idea in my topic sentence but you said that my topic sentence was a fact." "Can you help me review my use of verb tense in this paper and see if I'm on the right track?"

The next two steps—participating and asking questions—focus responsibility for the conference on the learner. They also provide communicative language practice in which learners are conversing with a specific need in mind. As part of this step, learners take notes and record the answers to their questions. The practice step involves learners using what they learned from the conference. They should identify one or two ideas and apply them to their current and future writing assignments. This can also be part of the reflection process as they monitor their performance and modify goals.

In the case of high-beginning or intermediate learners, this process needs to be simplified. Learners may not have the language to engage in an in-depth discussion of their writing. However, they could prepare a question or two by being provided with example sentences and a worksheet to complete in preparation for the conference. Alternatively, they can complete this worksheet in the conference itself. More advanced learners might take notes in the margin of their papers. In both cases, learners should reflect on the outcomes of the conference in their SRL journals or reflective notebooks. Role-playing a successful conference interaction or preparing a brief video clip of a conference would provide variety and reinforce the steps.

The two forms in the feedback loop journal (see earlier section on feedback loop journals or Chapter 7) are an excellent source of topics for writing conferences because learners have already reviewed their assignments, recorded the comments on those assignments and assigned them to specific areas related to writing features (content, organization, vocabulary, grammar, mechanics, and neatness), categorized the comments based on their relevance to the SRL principles, and determined goals and action steps. The conference serves as a mechanism for learners to receive guidance with this process, ask for clarification, or get help with specific writing features.

Progress conferences, mentioned in Chapter 4, are another type of performance activity. They focus on questions such as the following:

- What are your greatest strengths as a writer?
- What are your greatest weaknesses?
- What do you want to accomplish in this class to improve your writing?
- What are you going to do to improve yourself as a writer?
- What can your teacher do to help you achieve your goals?
- What is something you have written in your second language that you are particularly proud of?
- Why are you proud of it?

These questions serve as the basis for the conferences throughout the semester, help learners prepare, and emphasize SRL. In subsequent conferences, notes are reviewed and goal accomplishment discussed.

Conferences serve a myriad of purposes but can be time-consuming and may not be feasible in large classes. To address this, teachers can consult with learners briefly during class when other learners are working on their own or in groups. Similarly, teachers can meet with pairs or small groups in or out of class and model how to give feedback on a writing assignment (see discussion of peer review groups in Chapter 6).

Autonomy and Self-Selection: Methods, Time, Physical Environment, Social Environment

As learners begin to identify their strengths and weaknesses and expand their knowledge of possible strategies, teachers should encourage them to select from a variety of activities to reinforce self-regulation. This process can begin with any of the ongoing course requirements described in the chapter—SRL journals, reflective notebooks, feedback on form and meaning from rubrics and error correction marks, and the feedback loop journal. Similarly, the integration of the principle of performance throughout the course in the form of the activities summarized in Chapter 7, as well as teacher conferences, helps learners develop the ability for self-observation and evaluation, strategic planning and goal setting, and implementing and monitoring strategies.

Chapters 3–6 on the principles of methods, time, physical environment, and social environment contain a large number of activity options. Teachers new to SRL should select two or three activities from each area. Based on the three options for integrating SRL components into a course—concentrated, gradual, and selected reinforcement—teachers can determine to what extent all of the principles will be focused on, and the number of activities to be done in class or assigned to be completed outside of class. Each of the implementation strategies has advantages and disadvantages as described in Table 8.1. The next section explains how the four principles might be addressed within these three implementation options. These options assume that the principles of motive and performance are the backbone of any SRL-focused L2 writing course. This discussion will allow teachers to determine how to manage and coordinate activities over the period of study.

Option 1: Concentrated

In the concentrated approach, the concept of SRL and all of the principles are introduced in an intensive block at the beginning of the course—perhaps 6 or 7 class sessions of 45–60 minutes or the equivalent. Also during this timeframe, learners need to receive feedback on writing assignments to determine their strengths and weaknesses. The content of these writing assignments can be SRL, personal experiences with writing, or analyses of beliefs and behaviors about writing, language learning, and learning in general. During this concentrated block, learners are developing increased awareness of themselves as writers and learners.

By the end of this extensive introduction to SRL, learners can identify preliminary goals, understanding that these are flexible and will be adjusted over time as they reflect on performance. They will know which of the areas—methods, time, physical environment, or social environment—they should focus on. Teachers can provide learners with a resource guide containing selected activities in each of the areas. Learners can do one of the activities each week during the course in conjunction with some type of reporting mechanism, such as one of the journal options, the feedback binder forms, or conferences. Through this process, teachers can help learners monitor their performance, and learners can determine whether or not to continue with additional activities for one principle or move to another.

Other than the investment of time upfront, this approach can take little class time. Journals and other reflective pieces can be completed outside of class if desired. Additionally, these reporting activities involve writing practice and support writing course objectives. It is advantageous for learners to share their experiences with the activities and respond to each other's ideas. This could occur through a discussion forum in an online course management system rather than in class, if desired (see SRL journal discussion). The approach described, related to concentrated implementation and learner selection of activities, is the most autonomous of the three.

Option 2: Incremental

In contrast to the concentrated approach, the gradual option is the most structured. It involves an initial introduction to SRL that is sufficient for learners to understand the concept, followed by units of study on each of the principles. This allows learners to absorb and practice the concepts in a controlled and systematic way. Depending on the amount of class time available and the flexibility of the curriculum, teachers can spend as little as one class session on each principle (methods, time, physical environment, social environment) or plan an SRL-related activity or reflection in every class period for a unit. Motive involves an initial assessment of strengths and weaknesses and formation of goals. The principle of performance is an iterative process that occurs throughout the course.

An entire unit that focuses on content about the principle, introduced through readings, lectures, video clips, or other means, can be designed. In this case, SRL objectives and writing objectives would be identified for each class session. For example, below are sample objectives for a class session that addresses motive for learning to write in a second language and comparison/contrast paragraph structure. The objective is related to the activity on testimonials of former learners presented earlier in the chapter.

- SRL objective: Learners will examine their motive for learning to write in English by hearing about the experiences of learners similar to themselves who have benefited from the ability to write effectively.
- Writing skill objective: Learners will practice writing comparison/contrast paragraphs by selecting three points of comparison related to the writing experiences of two of the class guests (former learners in an L2 writing course).

Subsequent units would focus on other SRL principles and selected activities. As with the concentrated option, activities could be done in or out of class. Learners would report on the activities, their learning and goals, and other pertinent information using the methods described in this chapter, or alternative methods discussed in Chapters 2 and 7 (motive and performance).

With this implementation strategy, all learners would engage in activities related to all of the principles. They might be given autonomy to choose from a variety of activities within each principle, however. If so, a resource guide with options could be provided. Almost all learners would be able to extend their strategies this way even if they already have strengths related to a particular principle. An advantage of this approach is that learners are gradually receiving feedback on writing assignments and being introduced to new strategies that enable them to connect the findings from performance analyses with an appropriate principle-based strategy, such as time use, getting help, changing their study environment, or implementing a new vocabulary-learning skill.

Option 3: Selected Reinforcement

The third implementation option, selected reinforcement, combines aspects of the concentrated and gradual approaches. SRL and its principles are introduced briefly at the beginning of the course; learners form preliminary learning goals based on initial feedback on writing assignments and awareness of their strengths and weaknesses from motive-related activities as well as from previous experiences with writing; and teachers select principles and activities to focus on in greater depth throughout the course. These should be based on learner needs as determined by observations of learner behaviors and writing assignment performance. Thus, the course is tailored to teacher perceptions of learner needs, and principle-based strategies are introduced and practiced strategically. It should be pointed out, however, that teacher perceptions must also be informed by learners' motives, goals, and reflections on performance.

As with options 1 and 2, the principles of motive and performance are considered central to the course; learners can be given options for activities related to methods, time, physical environment, and social environment as they are introduced. In some cases, one or more of these principles may not even be addressed, or may be addressed only minimally if the teacher deems it is not critical based on the information derived about learners from their assignments and reflections. If only a few learners could benefit from help in an area, the teacher could suggest specific activities for those learners. As such, a resource guide to activities with 2–3 activities each for methods, time, physical environment, and social environment could be distributed.

This brief review of implementation strategies with an emphasis on teacher and learner selection of activities demonstrates a range of possibilities with varying levels of learner autonomy supported. All of the options allow for learners to select activities for areas where need is greatest. However, the concentrated option provides the most extensive autonomy for the learner, and the gradual option offers the least autonomy. All three approaches enhance autonomy when teachers provide learners with an activity resource guide or simple handout with a choice of activities in a given area. Any of the relevant activities from previous chapters can be selected.

Adaptations

The SRL approach must be iterative to be effectively realized in the lives of learners. Learners cannot develop self-regulation behaviors with only periodic exposure to the concepts or by writing only superficial reflections. Thus, teachers must provide extensive practice, reinforcement, and guidance. Teachers must understand that ultimately, learners need to acknowledge themselves as responsible for controlling the factors and conditions that affect their learning. This being said, teaching situations vary; thus, we provide a few concluding words about adaptations.

Depending on the length of class sessions, the number of class session per week, and other components of the curriculum, teachers may need to adjust the number of self-regulated learning activities per week. More than one activity can be implemented into a week of class sessions, or a single activity can be divided across several class sessions. Many of the activities reinforce other language learning areas, such as vocabulary, grammar, reading, listening, and speaking. With some modification, teachers can place a greater focus on these areas as desired.

Teachers should also be aware that they can build on the activities to reinforce both understanding and application of SRL as well as language proficiency and writing skill improvements gains. For instance, the learner testimonial activity, described in this chapter as a means of exploring motive, could be the basis of a comparison/contrast paper in which the learner compares or contrasts information from two of the guest speakers, or with one of the speakers and the learner's own experiences as a writer. Similarly, information presented about the definition of SRL could become a definition or classification paper when those patterns are introduced. In this way, content and vocabulary are recycled and learning is strengthened. The topic of SRL and its various components could be the basis for a content-based course if teachers have the autonomy to develop their own curriculum.

The selected approaches and activities presented in this chapter demonstrate how to introduce and integrate SRL into a writing course in a consistent and deliberate way. All of the activities in Chapters 2–7 are valuable and can be substituted for those selected. As discussed throughout the chapter, the content of the activities can and should be adapted based on course objectives, teacher or learner preferences, class size, and learner proficiency level. Similarly, teacher response methods can vary according to these factors. Chapter 9 provides greater detail about activity workarounds for environmental constraints based on variations in teachers, learners, and classrooms.

Summary

This chapter has:

- explained three implementation approaches;
- shared activities to introduce the concept of SRL;
- discussed a variety of ongoing course requirements related to SRL and how to implement them;
- shared the critical nature of the principles of motive and performance and how to weave these principles throughout a course; and

- addressed how teachers can provide learners with opportunities to select activities and develop strategies related to the principles of methods, time, physical environment, and social environment.

The next chapter:

- considers environmental constraints related to teachers, learners, and classrooms;
- examines how these constraints may affect implementation of an SRL approach; and
- provides strategies for adapting selected activities for each SRL principle that may prove problematic for the given constraints.

Chapter 9

Adapting to Environmental Factors

Objectives

This chapter discusses how self-regulated learning (SRL) activities selected from Chapters 2–7 can be modified for certain curricular constraints. Specifically, it focuses on how teachers can adapt these activities to:

- teachers' experiences;
- learners' expectations and abilities; and
- classroom variables.

One of the main objectives of this book was to provide teachers with a supply of activities that could be used to help their learners develop SRL skills and strategies. Chapters 2–7 contain 90 such activities (see Appendix A for a full list). While much thought went into creating these activities, not all of them will work equally well in every situation. Each learning context or environment is different and requires some adaptation (Harmer, 2007; Nation & Macalister, 2010). Consequently, this final chapter helps to create awareness of possible constraints that teachers may encounter while implementing the activities, and to identify corresponding teacher/learner strategies and activity adaptations.

Nation and Macalister (2010) note that the success of any curricular endeavor depends on a clear understanding of the teaching and learning environment. They identify three factors that must be carefully considered: teacher, learner, and the teaching and learning situation. Since SRL, to our knowledge, has never been introduced into an L2 writing curriculum with the objective of creating self-regulated writers, Chapter 8 focuses on how these principles might be incorporated into an existing curriculum. Even with that effort, there is a need to discuss ways that some of the suggested activities can be adapted to account for teacher, learner, and situational constraints.

A constraint can be either a positive or negative element in a curricular design (Nation & Macalister, 2010). For example, a common teacher constraint is level of training. Having teachers who are highly trained allows for much greater flexibility and adaptability in the learning activities that are used in a course. Equally impactful is having teachers who are less well trained and experienced. A common learner constraint is their proficiency level. Learners with high proficiency can be assigned far more complex tasks than can low proficiency learners. An example of a situational constraint is the availability of resources, such as computer technology. A program that has computer labs and Internet access has many more curricular options than does a program that has no such facilities. Understanding constraints, be they positive or negative, is essential to designing and implementing a quality curriculum. For this reason, the focus of this chapter is on understanding constraints that may limit or facilitate the implementation of SRL activities.

The chapter has six sections—one for each SRL principle. Each section presents various activities from Chapters 2–7 that may require modifications to account for teacher, learner, or situational variables. With the suggested modifications for these constraints, teachers should have a general understanding of how workarounds can be developed for other constraints not specifically mentioned in this chapter. Before considering the activities, it may be helpful to provide the general definitions for teacher, learner, and situational constraints that are used to identify the SRL activities discussed in this chapter.

Teacher Constraints

Many factors impact what a teacher can present in an L2 classroom. The two that stand out to us are experience related. First is the limited time a teacher may have actually been in a classroom. The first few years of teaching bring a dramatic shock of reality to most teachers just leaving a teacher training program (Farrell, 2006). As a consequence, the more stability novice teachers have in the classroom, the better. This stability can be achieved in a number of ways, one of which is having well-developed and defined materials. The second experiential challenge teachers may face is limited facility with and/ or confidence in their English language skills. Some teachers, for whom English is a second language, may feel insecure with some activities, such as grammar correction in free writing activities (e.g., 10-minute paragraphs; see Chapters 3 and 4). The adaptations presented in this chapter are intended to minimize these concerns. While the workarounds for lack of experience in the classroom and insecurities with English will serve as the primary focus for the adaptations, other teacher-related constraints are addressed as necessary.

Learner Constraints

Learners come to language classes for a variety of reasons and with mixed levels of motivation, different expectations, and equally diverse levels of proficiency. Each of these variables generates constraints that need to be accounted for when considering which SRL activities to use; many of them are discussed to some degree in this chapter. However, learners' level of English is our principal focus. Learners' proficiency level can be a challenge in any language class. Seldom does a teacher have a class where all learners are equally capable with the language. The typical situation is to have a class of learners with varying levels of language ability. It may therefore be necessary to modify activities in such a way as to make them effective for all learners. In addition, the activities in this book were designed on the assumption that the primary users would be intermediate to advanced English language learners in an academic writing class (proficiency standards based on the American Council of the Teaching of Foreign Languages guidelines, 2012). Since not all readers of this book will have intermediate to advanced learners in their classes, this chapter presents ways to adapt activities to lower proficiency levels while still retaining the intended SRL impact. Other learner constraints that seem relevant to a given activity are also discussed.

Situational Constraints

Anyone who has ever taught a second language understands that the language classroom is a dynamic, complex environment in which "all sorts of things happen, quite a few of which we might not have anticipated" (Harmer, 2007, p. 364). Reid (1993) compares the ESL classroom to the "Blind Random" setting on an exercise machine (p. 107); you can never be sure what is coming next. In such a multifaceted, unpredictable context, any number of factors can contribute to or distract from the success of a lesson. Again, while various constraints are discussed, the main focus is on how activities presented in Chapters 2–7 can be modified for large class enrollments. Since large class size is a prevalent issue in many language classes around the world, the activities presented here should be of considerable help. A number of professional organizations offer recommendations for writing class sizes. For example, the position statement (2001) of the Conference on College Composition and Communication (CCCC) suggests that "in classes made up exclusively of second language writers, enrollments should be limited to a maximum of 15 students per class" (p. 2). (See also the American Council on the Teaching of Foreign Languages [ACTFL], 2012.) It must be noted that these recommendations are not always heeded nor are they always financially possible.

Finally, it is important to note that not all the activities discussed in this chapter will necessarily have teacher, learner, and situational constraints. Accordingly, only those constraints that may be necessary to consider as teachers adapt the activities to their contexts are addressed. Accordingly, the primary purpose of this chapter is to help teachers make modifications to SRL activities for successful implementation in diverse contexts.

Motive

The motive principle of SRL examines the question "why," or the purpose for learning. Motivation involves internal processes such as goals, beliefs, views, and expectations that shape and direct behavior. It is related to learners' perceptions of their abilities and how these perceptions can influence their performance.

Internal Attributions

This is one of various strategies discussed in Chapter 2 that can be used to improve learner motivation. It focuses on helping learners understand where attributions for successes and failures belong, with the aim of instilling in the learners positive feelings about themselves and their abilities to adopt behaviors that are conducive to successful learning. The concept is based on attribution theory, which suggests that when learners believe they are in control of the factors affecting their learning, they are more motivated and better able to make the changes needed to be successful (Weiner, 1986).

Unlike other activities that have been discussed, this is not a single activity but a series of actions and activities used by the teacher to reinforce learners' positive feelings about themselves. These actions include the teacher:

- leading learners through the writing process to help them see that it takes time and effort, and that they can be successful if they are willing to invest the time and effort required to be successful;
- constantly monitoring learners' expressions (both written and spoken) watching for misplaced attributions—i.e., do they attribute success to luck or failure to not being smart enough? (with this insight, teachers reinforce correct attributions in the things they say and the feedback they provide);
- encouraging learner self-assessment in such activities as surveys, writing prompts, or journal entries that help the teacher understand learners' beliefs about writing and how they view their own abilities.

Teacher Constraints

An L2 writing class is a dynamic, intricate environment composed of many variables. As such, inexperienced teachers might not recognize the internal attributions and verbal comments their learners make or how to respond to these. The first step to overcoming this limitation is being aware of what it means when learners do not understand what they can control and do for themselves. Novice teachers need to train themselves to listen for statements that indicate misdirected attribution. It may be helpful to invite an experienced teacher into the class as an observer. This could be a focused observation on the types of comments learners make specifically about attribution of successes and failures, how the teacher responds to these, and the overall interaction between the teacher and learners related to attribution. In addition, a teacher could assign each learner to write a case study about their successes and failures as a writer in English (see the case study examples in Chapters 4 and 5). These could be effective both for helping the teacher see learners' attribution tendencies, and for helping learners see these tendencies for themselves.

Learner Constraints

While all learners, regardless of their language proficiency level, must at some point understand how internal attribution affects their performance. The key to achieving this objective is using language and examples that are within learners' linguistic grasp; therefore, the concept of internal attribution will have to be presented in language that is appropriate to the learners' level of proficiency. The phrase *internal attributions* should be avoided and instead presented in terms that a low-intermediate learner would understand. Survey questions, writing prompts, and other activities that help learners grasp the idea of attribution will need to be simplified for lower proficiency learners. The focus in these activities could be on the learners' experiences with learning in general and cultural beliefs about learning. As is the case with all learners, the primary objective with low proficiency learners is to help them understand factors that affect their success or failure and that these factors are within their control.

Situational Constraints

Large classes present a significant challenge for internal attribution training. A large class creates a situation where there are fewer opportunities overall for a teacher to interact with learners individually and address the kinds of comments they make about internal attributions. Observation from a colleague, as mentioned in the Teacher Constraints section earlier, would be appropriate in a large class as long as interaction between the teacher and learner is present when the observation occurs.

An additional way that large class limitations can be reduced is to administer surveys to each learner and use the results to capture general tendencies among class members. Yet another approach would be for the teacher to use a lecture format to present information about internal attributions to the class. Lower level learners could use a teacher-prepared outline or a fill-in-the-gap exercise as they listen. Comments gleaned from SRL journals or from the case studies mentioned in the Learner Constraints section could also be used to help the teacher identify specific examples of how learners do or do not give appropriate attribution for their successes and failures. Individual identities should be removed from any journal extracts or personal case studies if these are shared with the class.

Once the teacher is confident that learners have a grasp of how internal attribution affects them, learners could be assigned to set specific goals for how they will improve. Reporting on progress could be incorporated into SRL journal entries or a simple form that consists of two columns, with goals listed in the first column and progress on each goal listed in the second column.

High Interest Topics

The more interest a writer has in a topic, the more inherently motivating the act of writing will be. This activity helps writers select and develop topics of personal interest. An issue log allows learners to select a topic of interest and then become something of an expert on this topic over the duration of the course (Nation, 2009). Learners develop this expertise by gathering information from newspapers, magazines, TV, and other sources. They provide weekly oral reports to classmates and write a weekly summary of their findings. A similar activity is for the learner to develop an authority list, which is a list of topics on which individual learners are "experts" or at least about which they have considerable background knowledge (Reid, 1993). The learners draw from this list for writing topics throughout the course.

Teacher Constraints

While writing on topics of high interest creates motivation for writers, teachers need to recognize the problems inherent in having learners write from sources. Chief among these challenges are plagiarism and proper documentation of sources. The CCCC's position statement on second language writing notes that L2 writers often use "patchwriting," wherein they inappropriately "copy sections of texts, such as phrasings and sentence patterns" (p. 2).

Teachers, particularly novice teachers, must be aware of this challenge and provide appropriate instruction on how to write from sources. Intermediate level learners will have limited success using sources unless the task is carefully structured. This may involve having everyone in class use the same source and selecting specific sentences with which to practice finding the main idea and paraphrasing. Another alternative would be to generate a class list and then vote on which topics will be pursued. Learners could take turns bringing articles on the topic to class. Autonomy and choice are limited with these adaptations and somewhat defeat the purpose of the activity. However, once learners practice paraphrasing sentences from the same source as a class, they will likely be able to follow the steps when selecting and writing about individually selected articles.

When learners do choose their own topics, teachers need to provide guidance on appropriate topic and source selection. For example, if learners choose a current news story, it may not continue in the news for more than a week or two. Teachers need to help learners identify ongoing topics that may have multiple stories, news articles, and news reports (e.g., instead of a story on a specific robbery, the topic might be crime in general, crime in a particular part of the country, or a particular type of crime). This will require that teachers carefully review learner-generated ideas or lists before learners begin writing. The teacher might also want to provide a list of online or other sources to simplify the task and ensure the use of good sources. Furthermore, activities such as issue logs and authority lists can sometimes take large blocks of class time. Teachers will need to ensure that a specific portion of a class period is designated weekly for sharing updates on stories.

Learner Constraints

Two major constraints these activities present have to do with learner proficiency level. Lower proficiency learners will have fewer choices of topics available to them, and they most likely will not have the paraphrasing and summarizing skills needed to write from sources. Several of the ideas presented under Teacher Constraints can be implemented to address this. Additionally, the kinds of topics chosen will help resolve these constraints. Having learners write about familiar topics like family, country, and personal experiences avoids the need to write from sources, which can lead to patchwriting and plagiarism. Learners can be considered an "authority" on a personal topic. They would still need to provide additional information on that topic in their weekly reports.

Situational Constraints

Large classes present substantial but not insurmountable challenges with this type of activity. For instance, if the teacher uses the variation of having the class select topics rather than having learners select individual topics, it will be more difficult to find common topics of interest or distinct sources of information so that every learner contributes content each week. One possible way to address this would be to have groups research a topic and present the information to the class and then have everyone in class write a summary. Then the next week, another group would find additional information and present it to the class. The teacher may even consider inviting guest speakers to class or showing videos related to a particular topic to help build the learners' interest and expertise in that topic. Learners would then write a summary of that week's information or use the information to write a particular style of essay with a more focused topic. A few topics could be rotated through the semester based on class choices. By the end of the course, learners would have some expertise on topics that are inherently motivating to them.

Methods of Learning

Methods of learning refer to *how* learners learn. They consist of the tools, techniques, and strategies learners use to acquire knowledge. Low achievers typically use few learning strategies and may mistakenly attribute their lack of success to ability rather than recognizing the real cause—not knowing *how* to learn.

Progressive Editing

This activity involves editing for grammatical accuracy. The advantages and disadvantages described for this activity also apply to other activities with a similar focus. Additionally, the proposed strategies outline general principles applicable across activities involving teacher response to grammar.

As explained in Chapter 3, progressive editing entails helping learners take greater responsibility for finding and correcting grammatical errors. This is accomplished by decreasing the specificity of teacher feedback on writing assignments in the course. For example, initially teachers may mark all errors, or perhaps only those that interfere with meaning, with designated correction symbols. As a next step, they might underline errors and let learners identify the kind of error the teacher has noted. Learners need to monitor their performance and practice strategies that lead to greater independence concerning error corrections.

Teacher Constraints

Similar to the learner constraints that will be discussed next, teachers may face their own challenges related to the proposed activity. This might include a lack of confidence in marking grammatical errors due to knowing what sounds right (such as in the case of a novice native-speaker teacher) or knowing all the grammatical rules but not being completely accurate in one's own use of English (as in the case of a novice non-native English-speaking teacher).

All novice native-English-speaking teachers have to learn the formal grammar of the language and be able to explain why a particular grammatical construction is incorrect and offer a rule or guiding principle that learners can rely on to increase their accuracy. This knowledge and skill comes gradually and by finding the answers to questions that learners ask. It also involves use of the social environment—asking more experienced teachers about grammar questions posed by learners.

Novice non-native English-speaking teachers need to recognize the assets they can contribute to the learning process. They generally know the formal rules and grammatical features of the language but may not be completely accurate in their usage. Learners typically recognize them as role models and this should be emphasized. If teachers are not comfortable knowing they may have missed errors in the learners' writing, they can require that learners have at least one native speaker read through final drafts and underline, and possibly help with, remaining errors. Another approach is to focus mainly on errors that interfere with meaning or errors that learners make most frequently. Learners are unlikely to achieve complete accuracy in any case, and they will still get sufficient feedback from the teacher to make improvements.

Learner Constraints

Teachers can anticipate that learners typically like and expect to have all of their errors called to their attention. They want to know what they are doing incorrectly and may see it as the teacher's role to point this out. This is a characteristic of students accustomed to a teacher-centered educational philosophy. Thus, learners may feel a lack of needed structure when faced with finding and correcting their own errors. They may also feel that teachers are not fulfilling their responsibilities when this feedback is not provided. Another challenge is that learners may simply not be able to find their own errors unless they have specific hints. This is particularly true with lower level learners or those who are unfamiliar with the terminology that is used to describe language use. The following suggestions may be of help in meeting these challenges:

1 Ensure that learners are properly introduced to the concept of SRL at the beginning of the course, understand related expectations, and are involved in ongoing goal setting, monitoring, and reflection. This will help them understand their purpose for learning and their responsibility in the learning process.
2 Make sure that learners have sufficient structure—at least in the beginning. This is reflected by initially greater amounts and specificity of feedback that is gradually decreased. Help learners gain confidence in their ability to make corrections by pointing out and having them track their progress in making appropriate corrections.
3 Introduce learners to specific strategies for editing, such as the flowchart concept discussed in Chapter 3 (see Figure 3.1). This should be implemented for high frequency errors in the learner's writing, which can be determined through use of a tally sheet (see Table 2.5).

4 Consider alternate types of feedback for learners who are unfamiliar with grammatical terminology. This might include focusing on meaning and questioning learners in ways that help them revise their sentences in order to be understood. In such cases, progressive editing may not even be an appropriate activity, particularly if the majority of learners do not have a formal grammatical foundation. Another approach would be to point out online and print-based resources for gaining familiarity with grammar basics and helping learners identify goals in this area.

5 Limit the marking of errors to those that have been discussed in class or are most common across learners. This will make the task of understanding and correcting errors more manageable and structured for learners with intermediate and lower levels of language proficiency.

Situational Constraints

Teachers with large classes may want to require shorter pieces of writing or less frequent writing samples, or to implement peer and group editing techniques (see Chapters 3 and 6). They could also transition more quickly from marking errors with symbols to underlining, using checkmarks, or providing summary comments about types of major errors than they might in a smaller class. Although none of these are ideal, large classes present a significant challenge to language learning. Teachers will need to be strategic with the feedback they provide and encourage use of the social environment. A positive factor of a large class is that, in many respects, learners are more likely to be independent out of necessity. The best teacher strategy may be to help learners focus on the advantages of being self-regulated and teach them how this can be best accomplished.

Reformulation

In this activity the teacher rewrites a paragraph or sentence from a learner's assignment by making changes in content, organization, grammar, or a combination of these (Harmer, 2007). The learner then compares the reformulation with the original, and revises the writing without looking at the reformulation. Once the reformulation is completed, the writer summarizes how the teacher's reformulation influenced the changes made (see also multiple versions in Chapter 3 for a variation of this).

Teacher Constraints

Such an activity may present some challenges for less experienced teachers. For instance, they may have difficulty determining what to change or being selective about what to change. Inexperienced teachers may make such extensive changes that they appropriate the writing and take away the writer's voice (Ferris, 2003). They may also feel overwhelmed by the task, especially if they have a large class (see Situational Constraints later in the chapter).

An effective way to resolve these concerns is to keep a clear focus on what is being taught. Said another way, a teacher should always be guided by lesson objectives. For example, if the focus is writing a topic sentence or certain types of transitions, the reformulations should focus on these features of writing. If the focus of a lesson has been grammatical structures, such as making sure each sentence has a subject and a verb, the sentences can be reformulated to reflect this focus. Keeping a focus on limited features also helps avoid writing appropriation. Our experience has taught us that focused feedback facilitates learning and makes teaching much less daunting for the novice teacher.

Learner Constraints

The challenges this activity may present are highly correlated with the learners' proficiency level. Intermediate learners, for instance, may not have sufficient language skills to see the nuanced differences between the original and the reformulated versions. Similarly, they may not be able to write a full summary describing the differences between the two versions, the changes they made, and why.

Solutions to these language limitations include limiting the focus and modeling how reformulation works. As noted before, overwhelming amounts of text makes feedback difficult for the teacher to provide and the learner to process. This is especially true at the intermediate level. For this reason, we suggest that reformulations be concentrated on the sentence or paragraph level. Keep the language simple and the changes focused on what has been studied (see above—teacher experience – such as topic sentences, transitions, sentence structure, verb tenses, etc.). Modeling has been shown to be a useful practice when teaching writing (Ferris & Hedgecock, 2005). This is certainly the case with this activity. Learners should be shown how reformulation works. For instance, they may not understand that they need to create their own version, not simply copy the teacher's version. This misunderstanding can be avoided by showing learners examples of all three versions—the original, the teachers' reformulation, and the learner's revision. A further use of modeling would be to show learners examples of a learner summary. Alternatively, teachers could create a checklist for learners to complete when they submit their reformulation rather than having them generate their own summary.

Situational Constraints

Without a doubt, large class size is a challenge for an activity like this. A teacher simply may not have sufficient time to rewrite a portion of each learner's assignment. This obstacle could be overcome by having learners exchange and rewrite paragraphs or sentences from their peers' writing. This too has its challenges since any number of errors could be introduced in the reformulation without the teacher being aware. An alternative would be for teachers to select an example from two or three papers and share the reformulations with the class by projecting them on a screen or providing a handout. The class could identify as a whole or in small groups what the changes are and why the teacher made them. In doing this, the teacher would want to make sure to select writing samples from each learner over the time of the course and to illustrate a variety of types of reformulation (e.g., content, grammar, organization, vocabulary, etc.). Teachers could have learners present their own effective reformations—what they changed and why. This would emphasize the importance of revision. Finally, the teacher could prepare a handout with two versions of a paragraph or sentence and have learners choose the most effective one and state their reasons.

Time Factors

The time principle of SRL determines *when* and for *how long* learners apply themselves to learning tasks. A major aspect of this principle is learning how to estimate and budget time with the end objective of being a more successful learner.

Case Study

Many disciplines use case studies as a tool for teaching and assessment. While case studies have been included in this book as a way of reinforcing time management (Chapter 4) and physical environment skills and strategies (Chapter 5), they could also be used to reinforce other SRL principles as well. The main objective of the case study activity is for learners to see in a personal way how well or poorly others use time or how some people select appropriate physical environments for writing. To take learners beyond reading about others, teachers might ask learners to write case studies about themselves. This type of metacognitive writing helps learners see themselves as managers of their time and physical environments.

Learner Constraints

This activity, which is described in Chapters 4 and 5, should be reasonably straightforward for teachers of any experience level to apply. The one aspect that may need extra attention is the scaffolding that is provided for intermediate learners. First of all, case study is not likely a familiar genre for students. The example case studies in Chapter 4 and Chapter 5 can be used as models for students to follow. In addition, the teacher may want to add several more to serve as models (see Messerschmitt & Johnson Hafernik, 2009, for sample case studies). A teacher could write additional case studies from personal experiences. Another helpful practice is for a teacher to collect good examples from learners each time this activity is used, and, with the learner's permission, use them in subsequent classes. Again, these exemplary case studies should be used only with the original author's written permission and with any identifying information removed.

As with other activities discussed in this chapter, the vocabulary used in case studies may be a challenge for low proficiency learners. Vocabulary profilers such as Lextutor or RANGE can help resolve this problem. The two case studies in Chapter 4—"Victor" and "Marinoa" (see Table 4.1)—were intentionally written to be accessible to the intermediate learner. Running the text from these two studies through a vocabulary profiler revealed that 93% of the text comes from the first 2,000 words on the General Service List (West, 1953); 2% of the words come from the Academic Word List (Coxhead, 2000); and 5% of the words are proper nouns. With such a high percentage of words being so frequent, the text is generally quite useable for intermediate learners (Nation, 2008). The case study found in Chapter 5 is a bit more challenging, with only 84% of the words coming from the first 2,000 most frequently used words. Vocabulary profilers can be used to identify which specific words are most infrequent, thus allowing a teacher to modify and substitute vocabulary when necessary.

In addition to simplifying the vocabulary of case studies, it is also helpful if the models shown to the intermediate learners be kept relatively short—no more than one page. This will reassure the learners that writing a case study is well within their writing ability. A case study should be kept to no more than two paragraphs for intermediate writers. Longer cases could be expected of the advanced learners.

Situational Constraints

Case studies work well in large classes since they can be kept relatively short, thus limiting the quantity of writing that a teacher has to read and respond to. Furthermore, since case studies are usually a page or less in length, they can be read and discussed in pair or group work during class time. Several ways to use case studies in pairs is to have partners or small groups of three or four first read each other's cases and then offer suggestions for revision to clarify ideas. Once this has been accomplished, the case studies are revised accordingly. Subsequent readings could be an opportunity for the learners to explain to their group members how the suggested changes were made. It is also possible to have the team members focus their attention on other features of the writing as the teacher deems appropriate. Multiple drafts and group work such as this also lightens the teacher's load since the case study that finally gets submitted has been revised and edited. Typically, the cleaner the copy, the less time a teacher has to spend providing feedback.

A final note about the purpose of case studies needs to be made. Keep in mind, writing case studies has two primary purposes: (1) helping learners improve their writing, while (2) improving their SRL skills. To help learners keep SRL principles in focus as they share case studies, they should be asked to discuss the principle of time and how it impacts them as learners and writers of English.

Timeline Cover Sheet

This activity is intended to address two issues related to poor time management: being overwhelmed by the size of a task and lacking the ability to estimate how much time will be needed to complete it. This cover sheet is an effective way to help learners break a task into manageable parts and learn how to estimate time needed on the task. The cover sheet is divided into two parts. Part 1 contains the assignment title, a brief description of the assignment, a length requirement, a statement on how the assignment will be evaluated (rubric), and the submission due date. Part 2 consists of three columns. Column 1 breaks down the assignment into subtasks such as research the topic, develop a thesis statement, and write a first draft. Column 2 provides a brief description of the subtask and a space to write in the estimated time it will take to complete the subtask, and column 3 has a space to write the due date for each subtask.

Teacher Constraints

As noted in Chapter 5, the cover sheet can be modified for almost any multifaceted writing task. In fact, it will need to be modified for each assignment since the tasks and subtasks vary from one assignment to another. An L2 writing teacher just starting in the profession will, of necessity, have to create cover sheets for each assignment. These will likely have to be modified with each use to make the assignment better, but this is what any reflective teacher does to make an activity better the second time around. In addition, a scoring rubric may need to be created, so learners know how their work will be evaluated. A number of sample rubrics can be found in textbooks or online, or borrowed from colleagues. However, generally the best scoring rubrics are those created by the teacher for the context in which it will be used. For this reason, the novice teacher could find a sample that is close to what is needed and then modify the rubric categories and point totals to meet specific class needs.

Learner Constraints

The topic used as an example in the sample cover sheet illustrated in Chapter 4 (see Figure 4.4) is obviously designed for advanced-level language learners preparing for university study—"Natural disasters around the world." A much simpler assignment for intermediate learners could be substituted. For instance, a cover sheet could be created for the case study activity just discussed. The title could be "Personal Time Management Case Study." A description could be written to explain the assignment. The subtasks in part 2 of the cover sheet would also need to be changed to meet the specific assignment. Subtasks for intermediate learners writing their own case studies might include studying vocabulary, reading other case studies provided by the teacher (this introduces the writer to the concept of research), writing a first draft, and sharing the draft with a peer for feedback on ideas.

Situational Constraints

While the timeline cover sheet (Figure 4.3, Chapter 4) helps learners divide tasks into smaller components and helps them estimate how much time a task or subtask can take, it also helps a teacher communicate expectations to a large class. In a large class setting, the chances for misunderstandings are magnified by the number of students in the class. A tool such as the timeline cover sheet, with all the assignment details and due dates clearly spelled out, helps clarify the task expectations to everyone in the class, thus minimizing the chances for misunderstandings. The more detail that is included, the better learners will understand what is expected of them. A principle that has worked well for us when providing directions for L2 learners is to be abundantly and redundantly clear; the timeline cover sheet makes this possible in a large class setting.

Common Cause and Information Gap Writing

These two activities are being presented together since they are closely linked in their purpose of helping learners understand the common causes of procrastination and how it can be avoided. The first step is to assign learners homework to view various video clips on the Internet that describe causes for procrastination. They should take notes on these clips (low proficiency learners could be provided with a partial outline or a fill-in-the-blank form). The information taken from these clips can then be used for classroom discussion and writing tasks. The idea of an information gap is that one participant knows something that the other does not, thus creating the need for authentic communication to bridge that gap. In this case, one group of students watches one video while another group watches another video. This sets the context for meaningful oral and written exchanges in the class. In addition, the content allows for learning and improving the SRL principle of time.

Teachers with some experience and general facility with English should be able to successfully incorporate this activity into the classroom. The real challenges with these two activities will likely be with the learners and classroom variables.

Learner Constraints

Two learner factors that must be considered when using these activities are the linguistic difficulty the video clips may present and the complexity of the writing tasks that follow the video discussions. While it is possible that level-appropriate video clips can be found, it is also quite possible that such clips may be difficult to locate. Assuming materials on the Internet suitable for lower proficiency learners are difficult to find, the teacher can look for ideas elsewhere that discuss common causes for procrastination. Many books and "how-to" manuals are available on this very popular topic. This information could then be used to create two mini-lectures that present different aspects of procrastination. The teacher could present the lectures to students in different groups, thus creating an information gap that could be used for level-appropriate writing tasks.

The second challenge this activity may present for lower proficiency learners is the nature of the writing task that is assigned following the video activities. In Chapter 4, the writing tasks suggested for this activity are academic in nature and may therefore be challenging—compare and contrast, cause and effect, and problem solution. It is important to point out that these are only suggested tasks. It is possible and appropriate to simplify and narrow the focus of the tasks to meet the learners' abilities. For instance, learners could be assigned to write just one paragraph discussing only differences (contrasts) between the two lectures. Similarly, a paragraph that focuses only on the causes of procrastinations would make the writing task much easier for an intermediate learner. Another assignment might focus only on possible solutions for procrastination. While these writing tasks may be simplified, the purpose of reinforcing the SRL principle of time can still be achieved.

Situational Constraints

Two aspects of this activity that may present problems have to do with the Internet. First, some learners in a class will not have computer or Internet access outside of the school. The second Internet-related issue involves finding video sites on the Internet that are stable enough to be sure the clips will be available for future use. There is always the risk that what is available on the Internet today may not be there tomorrow.

Solutions to these two Internet problems can be overcome with some planning and alternate resources. First, a teacher must always be aware of the technological resources any given assignment may require. In addition, learners need to be aware of computer and Internet availability within the school, local libraries, and other venues. While viewing these videos might generally be given as an out-of-class assignment, if computer access is limited, the activity can be restructured to use the technology available in the classroom. One group could leave the classroom while one video is watched. The groups trade places while the second video is watched, thus creating an information gap.

Because the availability of video clips on the Internet may change, to ensure that video clips are available for subsequent use, teachers can use technology that captures online videos to be saved to a computer desktop for future use. Copyright restrictions must be carefully observed when using this technology, however.

As an alternative or follow-up activity, learners could be assigned to create their own video clips that demonstrate common causes for procrastination. This assumes that learners have the resources to create their own videos. Most cell phones now have a video camera built in, which would provide adequate video quality for this activity. Some models would need to be presented initially to give learners ideas. Also, as noted with case studies, once the activity has been used in class, the teacher can collect sample videos for future use.

Physical Environment

The physical environment principle of SRL focuses on location, or *where* learners primarily study and write. Learners who are able to structure their writing environment appropriately tend to perform better. The three activities discussed here help learners understand and apply this principle.

Ask an Expert

The purpose of this activity is to help learners understand how experienced writers locate and create a writing space that is conducive to study and writing. In this activity, learners interview teachers or other experienced writers to find out how they establish a suitable physical environment for writing and study and how that location contributes to their effectiveness.

Teacher Constraints

The primary reason this activity might be problematic for an inexperienced teacher is his or her limited acquaintances in a new teaching environment. First, it is conceivable that the novice teacher does not know other teachers well enough to ask if students can interview them. While many teachers, especially those in ESL departments or intensive language programs, tend to build strong relationships and are very supportive of each other, it is still true that some teachers have a strong "culture of individualism" that leaves novice teachers on their own (Farrell, 2006, p. 216). Even if teachers do not intentionally exclude a new teacher, it may be awkward to approach others who are still not well-known, especially to ask a favor that may seem to be an imposition on their time. This can be even more problematic if the new teacher has a large class and needs many interviewees. This may require asking students to interview teachers outside of the novice teacher's department, which exacerbates the situation further.

A solution to having a limited number of teachers to interview is to look for interviewees outside the teacher pool. Depending on the context, it may be possible to have learners interview advanced-standing students if the program is associated with or located near a university. Another possible source of interviewees would be individuals in the professional workforce who spend part of their time writing.

Learner Constraints

While the novice teacher may lack sufficient acquaintances, learners—especially low-intermediate learners—often lack language skills, interview skills, and confidence to conduct an interview with an authority figure in a second language. Not only is the task of interviewing an unknown teacher a potentially frightening function in a second language, but also it is particularly intimidating because of the unpredictable nature of an interview. One question can trigger responses that take the interview beyond an intermediate learner's linguistic limits. While it is possible in some settings to send students to other language teachers who are generally sympathetic participants, this may not always be possible, especially if the class is large.

To help reduce learners' concerns, class time can be used for learners to practice interviewing one another on various topics but especially on the topic of physical space as it relates to SRL. The teacher could even model several interviews in front of the class. This in-class practice serves several purposes: it helps build learners' confidence as interviewers, it helps learners build the language and vocabulary needed for the interview, and it reinforces their understanding of the SRL principle of physical environment.

Situational Constraints

As noted in the teacher and learner constraints, large classes can be a challenge with this activity. In the first place, there may not be enough teachers for the students to interview. As noted earlier, if the class is large and learner levels are limited, it may be difficult to find sympathetic interviewees. While challenging, these constraints are not insurmountable. Workarounds can be designed to make this activity a useful SRL experience for teachers with large classes.

If a class is so large that there simply are not sufficient interviewees, learners can be grouped to interview a teacher. Groupings could be set according to the number of available interviewees. Keeping the groups small will allow for increased participation by each of the learners; pairs or threesomes would be ideal. If this approach is used, the teacher could make it part of the assignment to divide the questions equally among the learners.

Another solution for large classes would be to conduct the activity in class using a role-play. With this model, the teacher provides half the class with a list of general questions that can be added to as the learners wish. The other half of the class is provided with a list of possible answers to the questions. These answers are based on the teacher's personal experiences and on the experiences of other individuals who use their physical environment well. These questions and answers can be modified to the learners' proficiency level. The students with these answers are the "experts" who will then be interviewed by classmates who do not have the answers. Such a model creates an information gap that can facilitate language development and, at the same time, provide both the "expert" and the interviewer with insights into how physical space can be useful to good writing. Regardless of which option is used, the SRL principle of physical environment is still being taught even though the interviews are conducted in a controlled classroom environment.

Physical Environment Inventory: What Distracts You?

Because of the similarities between these two activities, they are discussed together under each constraint. The physical environment inventory presented in Chapter 5 (see Figure 5.2) is an instrument used to draw the learners' attention to what their writing/study space is like as they consider the external environmental elements of view, noise, lighting, furniture, cleanliness, materials, temperature, and time of day. The learners are asked to actually go to the site where they spend most of their time studying and writing to evaluate each of these external features on a scale of 1–5. A score of 5 indicates it is an excellent location; a 1 suggests the site is poor for studying and writing.

What distracts you is an activity based on a worksheet presented in Chapter 5 (see Figure 5.6) that helps learners identify common internal distractions, recognize how those distractions may affect them, and determine solutions for overcoming them. The worksheet consists of 12 statements that reflect either an external or internal distraction. For instance, "Someone walks into the room where I am studying" is an example of an external distraction, and "I have a slight headache" is an example of an internal distraction. The learners are asked to identify if the statement reflects an external or internal distraction; rank that thing as to how distracting it would be to them, based on a scale from 1 (*not distracting at all*) to 5 (*very distracting*); and offer possible brief solutions for overcoming the distraction.

Teacher Constraints

Both of these activities should be rather straightforward for a teacher just starting out in an ESL/EFL classroom. Consequently, no teacher constraints will be presented. However, any teacher who steps into a classroom should have worked through an activity prior to asking learners to do so. This simple prepararatory step is essential to these activities running smoothly. The teacher completing the two forms prior to asking the learners to do so will facilitate the discussion and allow the teacher to offer personal insights to the learners.

Learner Constraints

Learners with limited language proficiency may find certain aspects of these activities somewhat challenging. The principal concern is likely the vocabulary used in the physical environment inventory and what distracts you forms (Figures 5.2 and 5.6). For example, words like *distracting, glaring, interruptions, commotion,* and *messy* are not frequently used words based on the General Service List (West, 1953). Also, the 12 distraction statements have been written for an intermediate to advanced-level learner. A low-intermediate learner may have difficulty understanding what is being described, thus limiting the activity's usefulness to teach the SRL principle of physical environment.

There are several ways these activities can be adjusted. The teacher could simply use the forms as they are illustrated in Chapter 5. If this approach is used, then the teacher will need to take time to introduce the vocabulary in the context as it is used on the forms. Depending on the number of words and their difficulty, this pre-activity work may consume more class time than the teacher wants to spend. Alternatively, the physical environment inventory and what distracts you forms could be revised and simplified for lower level learners. As previously noted, a number of online vocabulary profiler programs are available to help teachers identify words located on the General Service List (West, 1953) and other corpora. Any words that fall outside of the 3,000 most common words should probably be replaced with simpler, more frequently used synonyms (Nation, 2008). Most vocabulary profilers are quite easy to use; within a few minutes, a novice user can learn how to find the functions and information needed. Once a teacher is familiar with a vocabulary profiler, the forms can be revised to suit the learners' proficiency.

Finally, teachers should introduce the forms in class and illustrate how to use them before asking the learners to complete them. In this process, teachers need to help the learners keep focused on why these activities are being used—to teach them how important an appropriate physical environment is to successful learning and writing.

Situational Constraints

The follow-up activities as they are presented in Chapter 5 suggest that learners report in groups what they discovered about the spaces where they work. After completing the what distracts you form (Figure 5.6), they work in groups to reach a consensus on various solutions to the distractions. Such follow-up activities work well in large class settings, but the teacher will want to be sure to reinforce the SRL principles these activities are intended to teach. Group reports to the entire class would be helpful. The teacher may want to give a personal report on what he or she learned while completing the inventory and distraction worksheets. This could then be used to compare with findings from each of the groups.

In large classes, the teacher may also want to ask learners to summarize their impressions of the importance of a positive physical environment in their SRL learner journal. While journals can be read and responded to, they are typically used for developing writing fluency without being constrained by grammatical and formal correctness. This allows the learner to express feelings and impressions freely, and a teacher does not need to spend extensive amounts of time providing feedback. A quick read of a journal is usually sufficient to determine if a learner has grasped the purpose for these two activities: seeing the importance of writing and studying in an environment that is conducive to the task at hand.

Social Environment

The social environment principle of SRL focuses on the people *with whom* learners engage in relation to their studies. This includes the interaction of learners with peers, teachers, tutors, and others to improve learning. Self-regulated learners recognize that when they are having difficulty learning or achieving goals, they can seek assistance from others who can help them improve their performance.

Team-Based Learning™

This activity consists of assigning learners to teams for the duration of the course. Learners do the assigned readings or class preparation activities and take individual and group readiness tests. This allows teachers to focus class time on clarifying what learners have not understood from the readings and on application activities and language practice.

Teacher Constraints

Regardless of the amount of experience a teacher has, the concept of team-based learning may be unfamiliar and require some initial rethinking of procedures and practices. It involves initial planning in order to design group projects that focus on application of the writing skills studied, the creation of tests for each unit or subunit of study, and the formulation of group evaluation methods. Teachers must plan carefully so as to have all of these elements in place; this classroom approach is not something one can do only once or twice during a semester. It potentially changes an entire course and the way instruction is provided. It also strongly reinforces SRL. Demonstrating to learners that they have higher levels of performance when working with each other (e.g., through the sharing of performance graphs) will help convince learners of the efficacy of the approach and the advantages of the social environment. Reinforcing the importance that the purpose of writing is communication and that learners can help each other accomplish this goal through combined efforts with the writing process, including brainstorming, content development, organization, revision, and editing, also helps learners recognize that they are writing for an audience. Team-based learning supports the practice of learners working together to develop writing skills and share their strengths.

Learner Constraints

Readings, or textbook instruction, may be beyond the learner's language level even if the learner is correctly placed. Additionally, ESL/EFL learners are often not accustomed to preparing for class by reading in order to be familiar with information from the textbook or to have questions prepared about what they did not understand. Because learners typically take a passive approach to learning, their tendency more often is to expect the teacher to explain the contents of a textbook selection, writing technique, or other material in the book. Team-Based Learning is designed to help them take greater responsibility for coming prepared to class.

To accommodate situations in which the learner's proficiency level may not match that of the identified textbook for the course, teachers can simplify the readiness test questions to get at only the most central points—those that stand out in the chapter. Often these questions may be listed as summary points in a chapter or a section of a chapter, and teachers can help learners recognize these textbook features to help them focus their preparation on the most important points. Also, teachers can break the chapter reading into manageable sections so that learners are responsible for reading and understanding a limited number of pages or concepts. As Readiness Assurance Tests are implemented consistently, learners' levels of class preparation increase.

Situational Constraints

At some point during the course, learners in Team-Based Learning classrooms will invariably complain that some members of a group are doing more work than others. Personality problems may emerge, with some learners indicating they do not want to work with others in the class. The Readiness Assurance Tests help learners recognize that all have something to contribute—not just those who are most vocal—but these tests must be administered regularly to have the desired effect. Performance graphs provide a summary of individual and group scores and indicate the value of group work. The graphs also reiterate to learners the importance of the social environment.

Another solution to working through these issues is for the teacher to not step in to solve group problems but to turn them back to the group. This can be accomplished with evaluation forms (see Chapter 6) so that discussions about the performance of individual group members are objective and open. Group evaluation techniques are critical in helping groups recognize that they are responsible for giving each other feedback and solving problems.

For effective Team-Based Learning to occur, there must be a consistent effort on the part of the teacher to implement the entire concept including expectations for pre-class preparation, regular Readiness Assurance Tests, reporting of individual and group performance, group evaluation procedures, and planning a variety of group projects. With these regular practices, Team-Based Learning will have the desired effect.

Communication Strategies; Group Roles; Flowchart Analysis; Steps for Seeking Help

Chapter 6 contains a variety of ideas for helping learners recognize the importance of the social environment and ways to manage it as they work toward becoming SRL writers. As with activities in other chapters, many of them share commonalities in terms of possible constraints. Several of these activities can also be used together in order to achieve the end goal of SRL. The four activities presented next can be logically grouped together; possible constraints in terms of the teacher, learner, and situation related to these activities and how these activities work in combination. Before doing so, however, a brief review what these activities involve may be helpful.

- Communication strategies: teaching learners appropriate language for owning their message by stating their views in terms of their own feelings rather than in a confrontational way (e.g., "I feel left out when you talk to each other in Spanish" versus "You shouldn't talk in Spanish with each other").
- Group roles: assigning group members to various roles—such as facilitator, presenter, summarizer, and recorder—in order to provide structure for and accountability in group activities.
- Flowchart analysis: examining what information is needed, where it can be found, and the advantages and disadvantages of each source.
- Steps for seeking help: preparation for seeking help, identification of strategies, and anticipation of possible problems.

Teacher Constraints

A theme woven throughout the activities related to the social environment is helping learners develop the skills to benefit from and see the advantages of learning from individuals other than the teacher. Teachers must adopt various strategies to help learners see the value of the social environment and specifically teach them how to use it. Any teacher who has not previously focused on this approach needs to consider how to train learners. The four activities listed above provide learners with needed skills and opportunities to practice effective use of the social environment. The constraint emphasized here is the ability to recognize how to link and sequence activities. Teachers unfamiliar with SRL and the principle of the social environment may not initially perceive these linkages.

Related to the four activities selected, learners first need to practice effective strategies for interacting with others (communication strategies). They can then practice taking responsibility for interacting and collaborating with group members (as part of Team-Based Learning or group activities in general) by adopting different roles (group roles). When working on their own and encountering difficulties, they need to identify problems and evaluate sources of help (flowchart analysis). Finally, they need to prepare for getting this help by determining what to ask and how to ask it (communication strategies), and recognizing the need to turn elsewhere for help, if needed (flowchart analysis). With experience, teachers can determine how to select activities that reinforce each other and can be sequenced in a logical way. This is one example of how a series of activities build on each other to produce the desired result.

Learner Constraints

All of the activities mentioned in this section can be adapted to various levels of learner proficiency. Communication strategies can be simplified by providing learners with specific sentences they can use to interact with each other, ask for help, and resolve problems related to their requests. This is applicable to working in assigned groups in the classroom as well as in making requests of others in learning centers, institutional offices, or social situations. These constructions can be practiced in role plays followed by an assignment to obtain help from various sources within and outside the classroom. The latter can be staged by informing those on the other end (such as teachers or staff) that learners will be approaching them to seek specific information or help. This structured approach will help learners build confidence and prepare them for seeking help on their own.

Situational Constraints

There are many variables that could affect classroom success, among which are personality differences and lack of unity. If these factors are present, they can interfere with learners working in groups and being comfortable asking each other for help. The communication strategies activity can help learners address such problems by providing them with appropriate language to resolve differences respectfully. Similarly, having assigned roles in group work supports learners taking equal levels of responsibility and giving them specific tasks. This alleviates problems sometimes encountered in terms of dominating or reticent personalities.

All of the activities can be implemented in large classes, although the methods of presenting them need to be adapted. Communication strategies, group roles, and flowchart analysis activities can be introduced on a handout or PowerPoint slide and practiced in pairs or small groups. Selected learners can illustrate effective use of these strategies in front of the class, followed by whole-group discussion. For instance, a group might be selected to re-enact their discussion for the class, with the class identifying effective communication strategies, who is playing which role, and how well the group interacted. Learners could also work together to complete the flowchart by brainstorming areas of study they need help with, where to find this help, and so on. In this way, they are helping each other find appropriate help. They can then determine needed steps. By working together, learners can help each other think through the possibilities. The main disadvantage to introducing these activities in a large class is that the teacher may not be able to circulate and give feedback and guidance to all learners as they practice. However, learners will still have the advantage of interaction with their peers and of learning to take greater responsibility for identifying sources of help, practicing appropriate language and communication strategies, and evaluating the usefulness of the help received.

Performance

The performance principle addresses the *what* aspect of SRL and refers to the practice of learners monitoring their individual level of success on a task and adjusting their performance accordingly. This principle, sometimes referred to as management skills, focuses on learners' ability to set realistic goals, evaluate progress, and make necessary changes in performance to achieve these goals. Much has already been said in Chapter 8 about adaptations to the three activities outlined in this chapter: feedback loop binder, strengths and weaknesses analysis, and monitoring performance. However, since performance is central to SRL and encompasses each of the other five principles, a brief discussion of the three performance activities within the constraints of teacher, learner, and situation seems appropriate. Furthermore, since the feedback loop binder includes the strengths and weaknesses analysis and the monitoring performance forms, the primary focus of this discussion will be on the feedback loop binder.

By way of reminder, the general purpose for such a binder is to help learners take responsibility for their own learning by systematically tracking and appropriately responding to feedback, and to assist teachers in monitoring how their feedback is being perceived and applied. In many ways, the feedback loop binder encapsulates all that has been discussed throughout this book. The binder can be designed and modified in any number of ways to meet individual teachers' preferences. However, it should be kept simple and inexpensive, and that it be limited in content to maintain its simplicity and utility. While the suggestion was given in Chapter 7 to limit the contents to the strengths and weaknesses analysis and monitoring performance forms (Figures 7.1 and 7.2, Chapter 7), as teachers begin implementing such a binder in their own classes, they may find alternatives that suit their learning style and teaching preference. The main thing to remember is that the focus of the binder is to achieve the objectives of helping learners become better writers by appropriately responding to teacher feedback, and more self-regulated learners by staying focused on the seven SRL principles.

Teacher Constraints

A valuable lesson the authors learned from their own teaching careers long before they were aware of the principles of SRL is the value of requiring learners to carefully track the feedback teachers provide. Too often novice teachers and learners alike come to a classroom with the notion that it is the teacher who keeps track of scores and grades for the purpose of a final, summative evaluation at the end of a course. While this is true, it is also true that formative assessments and records need to be kept throughout the course for the purpose of monitoring and adjusting performance. It is our position that learners need to be central in this process. The more a teacher delegates this responsibility to the learners, the more the learner will develop as a self-regulated learner. The feedback loop binder was designed with this concept in mind.

A novice teacher will certainly face limitations when providing feedback that learners then transfer to the strengths and weaknesses analysis and monitoring performance forms. These limitations were addressed in Chapters 7 and 8. However, it may be worth noting several more suggestions, since proper feedback is a core purpose for this book. First, always remember that there is no quick and easy way for a new teacher to develop the skill— and it is a skill—of providing meaningful corrective feedback (see Chapter 1 for guiding principles); it is a process. To facilitate this process, keep in mind that even experienced teachers cannot address everything, nor can learners manage overwhelming amounts of feedback. Keep feedback focused. Focus on issues that disrupt meaning—the global issues. A second guideline for the teacher just starting a career in a writing class is be "persistent and consistent" when providing feedback (Hinkel, 2012). Persistence keeps the feedback coming, and consistency makes it possible for the learners to track their most salient weaknesses over a meaningful period of time. Following these two practices will make the strengths and weaknesses analysis and the monitoring performance forms more manageable and meaningful for the novice teacher and the language learner.

Learner Constraints

Several learner factors that can be anticipated are resistance and proficiency. Many learners come from educational systems that have taught them that the teacher is in charge of learning, keeps track of scores and progress, and evaluates learning accordingly. Such an idea is, of course, completely contradictory to the concept of SRL. A teacher needs to anticipate that there may be some resistance to the learner-in-charge concept. Chapter 8 provides suggestions on working around this constraint.

As with other activities discussed in this chapter, limited language proficiency will likely present some challenges to implementing a feedback loop binder. The practices of modeling and simplifying seem like the best solutions for this constraint. A teacher might overcome this limitation by initially using the materials about Marinoa found in Chapter 7 to create a sample binder for learners to see. If low-intermediate learners are using the binders, the examples from Chapter 7 may need to be simplified to make the examples and language accessible. Subsequent models could be collected from learners each time the binder is used in a class. Again, if learner binders will be used as examples, teachers need to be sure to get permission in writing from the original writer and remove any identifying features.

Situational Constraints

The situational constraints of resources and large classes should be considered when implementing the feedback loop binder and its contents, the strengths and weaknesses analysis and monitoring performance forms. The use of the term *binder* is intentional because learners need a system for keeping their forms orderly and accessible. In addition, they will need a binder that makes it possible to add documents with each assignment that is tracked on the analysis and performance forms. A simple, inexpensive three-ring binder works best for these purposes. This should not present an undue financial burden on learners who may have very little extra money. If technology resources are available, a teacher might even set up an electronic version of the binder. More and more computer applications make this an efficient alternative.

Finally, in the case of large classes, this is an example where the activity helps overcome the constraint. One might initially think that the more binders a teacher has to manage, the harder it would be. In actuality, the binder as it has been described helps the teacher manage a large class by asking the learners to keep track of the many feedback details that accumulate with each assignment. Teachers have more time to tend to other matters when learners are responsible for keeping the feedback they are given organized and current. A few preparation checks are helpful to make sure learners are keeping their binders current. The teacher simply informs the learners that there will be a certain number of preparation checks during the course. Some checks can be announced in advance; others can be on the spot. It only takes a few such checks for learners to make sure they are using the binder for its intended purposes. Furthermore, such checks only take a few minutes of a busy teacher's time.

Conclusion

The proverb used in the Preface to this book—"Give a man a fish and you feed him for a day; teach him how to fish and you feed him for a lifetime"— was used to illustrate the idea that response to L2 writing can be founded on principles of self-regulation. L2 writers can learn these principles, and thereby systematically apply the valuable feedback they receive long after they leave the confines of a classroom. As noted at the outset, this is not a typical approach to providing feedback. However, given the less-than-compelling evidence that typical methods of feedback are effective, the purpose of this book was to apply the insights of SRL research to feedback in L2 writing.

We have now reached the end of our discussion of the six principles and the associated practices and activities that can be used to help develop self-regulated writers. We have presented approaches for incorporating these principles into a writing class curriculum as well as identified ways many of the activities that we have introduced can be modified for various contexts. Our experience tells us that feedback channeled through the six SRL principles will indeed point "forward to the student's future writing and the development of his or her writing process" (Hyland & Hyland, 2006b, p. 83), and lead to "long-term improvement and cognitive change" (Reid, 1993).

Appendix
Summary of Activities

Each chapter in this book (with the exception of Chapter 1) presents activities related to a specific principle of self-regulated learning. However, some of these activities may be applicable to or can be modified to support learner development of additional aspects of self-regulated learning. The following table lists the activities from Chapters 2–6. The primary focus of the activity is indicated by a "P." Other principles of self-regulated learning that may be supported by an activity or a modified version of an activity are indicated with an "*".

Chapter 2: Motivation Activities	Motive	Method	Time	Physical Environment	Social Environment	Performance
Instrumental versus integrative	P					*
Extrinsic versus intrinsic	P					
Beliefs and experiences	P					*
Positive self-talk	P				*	*
Internal attributions	P					*
Rewards and punishments	P					*
Survey or reflection paper	P					*
Testimonials	P				*	
A real audience	P				*	
High-interest topics	P				*	
Diagnostic tools to focus on form	P	*				*
Diagnostic tools to focus on meaning	P	*				*
Conferences	P				*	*
Choice and autonomy	P					*
Accuracy goals	P	*				*
Writing process goals	P					*
Strategic questions	P	*				*
Awareness of new approaches to writing	P	*				*
Language learning plan	P	*				*

Chapter 3: Methods Activities	Motive	Method	Time	Physical Environment	Social Environment	Performance
Reformulation		P			*	
Multiple versions and self-evaluation		P				*
Progressive editing		P				
10-minute paragraphs		P				
Scaffolding		P			*	
Hints		P			*	
Modeling		P				
Resources and guides		P				
Class and small group scoring		P				*
Whole class reflection		P				
Neutral questions		P				
Requests for help		P			*	
Choice		P				*
Preference surveys		P			*	*
Negotiation		P				*
Record of achievement		P				*
Categorization		P				*
Cover sheets		P				*
Reflective notebooks		P				*

Chapter 4: Time Activities	Motive	Method	Time	Physical Environment	Social Environment	Performance
Important or urgent	*	*	P			*
24-hour evaluation	*		P			*
A, B, C; 1, 2, 3	*	*	P			*
Reporting on success	*	*	P			*
Common causes			P			*
Information gap writing		*	P			
Case studies			P			*
Procrastination survey			P			*
Metacognitive paper			P			*
80/20 rule	*		P			*
The big red X			P			
Timeline cover sheet			P			*
Assignment time log	*		P			*
Rush writes			P			
10-minute paragraph			P			*
Instant writing			P			
Daily writing			P			
Progress conferences	*		P			*
Tally sheets			P			*
Edit progress log			P			*
Ten perfect sentences			P			*

Chapter 5: Physical Environment Activities	Motive	Method	Time	Physical Environment	Social Environment	Performance
A tale of two sites		*		P		*
Ask an expert	*	*	*	P	*	*
Physical environment inventory		*		P		*
Case study				P		*
Illustrate it				P		
Great quotes wall	*			P		
Writer at work; do not disturb			*	P	*	
What distracts you?		*		P		*
Be here now				P		*
Blinders				P		*
The spider's strategy				P		*
Worry/think time				P		*
Physical remedies				P		

Chapter 6: Social Environment Activities	Motive	Method	Time	Physical Environment	Social Environment	Performance
Guiding questions					P	*
Dialogue journals	*				P	*
Muddiest point					P	*
Team-Based Learning™		*			P	*
Readiness assurance tests					P	*
Performance graphs	*				P	*
Modeling and role-play					P	
Communication strategies					P	
Group roles					P	
Flowchart analysis					P	*
Steps for seeking help					P	
Evaluation logs					P	*
Appreciative inquiry					P	*
Peer review groups					P	*
Social networking					P	*
Writing process community activities					P	*

Chapter 7: Performance Activities	Motive	Method	Time	Physical Environment	Social Environment	Performance
Feedback loop binder	*	*	*	*	*	P
Strengths and weaknesses analysis		*				P
Monitoring performance	*	*	*	*	*	P

References

ACTFL guidelines. Retrieved from http://www.actfl.org/files/public/ACTFL ProficiencyGuidelines2012_ FINAL.pdfAndrade, M.S. (in press). Self-regulated learning activities: Supporting success in online courses. In J.S. Moore (ed.), *Distance Learning.* Rijeka, Croatia: InTech.

Andrade, M.S., & Bunker, E.L. (2009). Language learning from a distance: A new model for success. *Distance Education, 30*(1), 47–61.

Andrade, M.S., & Bunker, E.L. (2011). The role of SRL and TELEs in distance education: Narrowing the gap. In G. Dettori & D. Persico (eds), *Fostering self-regulated learning through ICTs* (pp. 105–121). Hershey, PA: IGI Global.

Angelo, T.A., & Cross, K.P. (1993). *Classroom assessment techniques: A handbook for college teachers.* San Francisco, CA: Jossey-Bass.

Baggetun, R., & Wasson, B. (2006). Self-regulated learning and open writing. *European Journal of Education, 41*(3/4), 453–472.

Bail, F.T., Zhang, S., & Tachiyama, G.T. (2008). Effects of a self-regulated learning course on the academic performance and graduation rate of college students in an academic support program. *Journal of College Reading and Learning, 30*(1), 54–73.

Bell, P.D. (2007). Predictors of college student achievement in undergraduate asynchronous web-based courses. *Education, 127*(4), 523–533.

Benson, P. (2001). *Teaching and researching autonomy in language learning.* London, UK: Longman.

Benson, P. (2007). Autonomy in language teaching and learning. *Language Teaching, 40*(1), 21–40.

Beykont, Z.F., & Daiute, C. (2002). Inclusiveness in higher education courses: International student perspectives. *Equity & Excellence in Education, 35*(1), 35–42.

Bitchener, J. (2008). Evidence in support of written corrective feedback. *Journal of Second Language Writing, 17*, 102–118.

Bitchener, J., & Knoch, U. (2008). The value of written corrective feedback for migrant and international students. *Language Teaching Research, 12*, 409–431.

Bitchener, J., & Knoch, U. (2009a). The relative effectiveness of different types of direct written corrective feedback. *System, 37*, 322–329.

Bitchener, J., & Knoch, U. (2009b). The value of a focused approach to written corrective feedback. *ELT Journal, 63*, 204–211.

Bitchener, J., Young, S., & Cameron, D. (2005). The effect of different types of corrective feedback on ESL student writing. *Journal of Second Language Writing, 14*, 191–205.

Boice, R. (1997). Strategies for enhancing scholarly productivity. In J.M. Moxley & T. Taylor (eds), *Writing and publishing for academic authors* (pp. 19–24). Lanham, MD: Rowman & Littlefield.

Boice, R. (2000). *Advice for new faculty: Nihil nimus*. Boston, MA: Allyn & Bacon.

Borkowski, J.G., & Thorpe, P.K. (1994). Self-regulation and motivation: A life-span perspective on underachievement. In D.H. Schunk & B.J. Zimmerman (eds), *Self-regulation of learning and performance: Issues and educational applications* (pp. 45–73). Hillsdale, NJ: Erlbaum.

Bowen, J.D., Madsen, H., & Hilferty, A. (1985). *TESOL: Techniques and procedures* (2nd edn). Rowley, MA: Newbury House.

Bown, J. (2006). Locus of learning and affective strategy use: Two factors affecting success in self-instructed language learning. *Foreign Language Annals, 39*(4), 640–659.

Brawner, Bevis, T., & Lucas, C.J. (2007). *International students in American colleges and universities: A history*. New York: Palgrave Macmillan.

Brown, H.D. (2006). *Principles of language learning and teaching* (5th edn). New York: Longman.

Brown, H.D. (2007). *Teaching by principles: An interactive approach to language pedagogy* (3rd edn). New York: Longman.

Bruton, A. (2009). Improving accuracy is not the only reason for writing, and even if it were … . *System, 37*, 600–613.

Bruton, A. (2010). Another reply to Truscott on error correction: Improved situated designs over statistics. *System, 38*, 491–498.

Bryne, D. (ed.). (1986). *Teaching oral English* (2nd edn). Harlow, UK: Longman.

Buck, K., Byrnes, H., & Thompson, I. (eds). (1989). *The ACTFL oral proficiency interview tester training manual*. Yonkers, NY: ACTFL.

Burge, E. (1988). Beyond andragogy: Some explorations for distance learning design. *Journal of Distance Education, 3*(1), 5–23.

Canale, M., & Swain, M. (1980). Theoretical bases of communicative approaches to second language teaching and testing. *Applied Linguistics, 1*(1), 1–47.

Candlin, C., & Byrnes, F. (1995). Designing for open language learning: Teaching roles and learning strategies. In S. Gollin (ed.), *Language in distance education: How far can we go?* (pp. 1–20). Proceedings of the NCELTR Conference, Sydney, Australia: NCELTR.

Caneiro, R., & Steffens, K. (eds). (2006). The TELEPEERS Project [Special issue]. *European Journal of Education, 41*(3/4).

Carreira, J.M. (2005). New framework of intrinsic/extrinsic and integrative/instrumental motivation in second language acquisition. *The Keiai Journal of International Studies, 16*, 39–64.

Casanave, C.P. (2003). *Controversies in second language writing: Dilemmas and decisions in research and instruction*. Ann Arbor, MI: University of Michigan Press.

Chandler, J. (2003). The efficacy of various kinds of error feedback for improvement in the accuracy and fluency of L2 student writing. *Journal of Second Language Writing, 12*(3), 267–296.

Chang, M. (2005). Applying self-regulated learning strategies in a web-based instruction: An investigation of motivation perception. *Computer Assisted Language Learning, 18*(3), 217–230.

Cohen, A.D., & Cavalcanti, M.C. (1990). Feedback on compositions: Teacher and student verbal reports. In B. Kroll (ed.), *Second language writing* (pp. 155–177). Cambridge, UK: Cambridge University Press.

Collier, V. (1987). Age and rate of acquisition of second language for academic purposes. *TESOL Quarterly, 21*, 617–641.

Collier, V., & Thomas, W.P. (1989). How quickly can immigrants become proficient in school English? *Journal of Educational Issues of Language Minority Students, 5*, 26–38.

Cook, V. (2008). *Second language learning and language teaching* (4th edn). London, UK: Hodder Education.

Covey, S.R. (1989). *The 7 habits of highly effective people.* New York: Simon & Schuster.

Coxhead, A. (2000). A new academic word list. *TESOL Quarterly, 34*(2), 213–238.

Cummins, J. (1980). Psychological assessment of immigrant children: Logic or intuition? *Journal of Multilingual and Multicultural Development, 1*, 97–111.

Cummins, J. (1981). Age on arrival and immigrant second language learning in Canada: A reassessment. *Applied Linguistics, 11*, 132–149.

Cummins, J. (1996). *Negotiating identities: Education for empowerment in a diverse society.* Ontario, CA: California Association for Bilingual Education.

Day, G. (1964). *James Michener.* New York: Twayne.

Dean, D. (2011). *What works in writing instruction: Research and practice.* Urbana, IL: NCTE.

DeKeyser, R. (2001). Automaticity and automatization. In P. Robinson (ed.), *Cognition and second language instruction* (pp. 125–151). Cambridge, UK: Cambridge University Press.

DeKeyser, R. (2007). Skill acquisition theory. In B. VanPatten & J. Williams (eds), *Theories in second language acquisition* (pp. 97–113). Mahwah, NJ: Erlbaum.

Dembo, M.H., & Eaton, M.J. (2000). Self-regulation of academic learning in middle-level schools. *The Elementary School Journal, 100*(5), 473–490.

Dembo, M.H., & Seli, H. (2008). *Motivation and learning strategies for college success: A self-management approach* (3rd edn). New York: Erlbaum.

Dembo, M.H., Junge, L.G., & Lynch, R. (2006). Becoming a self-regulated learner: Implications for web-based education. In H.F. O'Neil & R.S. Perez (eds), *Web-based learning: Theory, research, and practice* (pp. 185–202). Mahwah, NJ: Erlbaum.

Dörnyei, Z. (2005). *The psychology of language teaching.* Mahwah, NJ: Erlbaum.

Dörnyei, Z., & Skehan, P. (2003). Individual differences in second language learning. In C. Doughty & M. Long (eds), *Handbook of second language acquisition* (pp. 589–630). Oxford, UK: Blackwell.

Dweck, C.S. (2000). *Self-theories: Their role in motivation, personality, and development.* Philadelphia, PA: Psychology Press.

Ellis, R. (2005). Principles of instructed language learning. *System, 33*, 209–224.

Ellis, R., Sheen, Y., Murakami, M., & Takashima, H. (2008). The effects of focused and unfocused written corrective feedback in an English as a foreign language context. *System, 36*(3), 353–371.

Emig, J. (1971). *The composing process of twelfth graders.* Urbana, IL: National Council of Teachers of English.

Evans, N.W., Hartshorn, K.J., McCollum, R.M., & Wolfersberger, M. (2010a). Contextualizing corrective feedback in L2 writing pedagogy. *Language Teaching Research, 14*, 445–463.

Evans, N.W., Hartshorn, K.J., & Tuioti, A.E. (2010b). Written corrective feedback: The practitioners' perspective. *International Journal of English Studies, 10,* 47–77.

Evans, N.W., Hartshorn, K.J., & Strong-Krause, D. (2011). The efficacy of dynamic written corrective feedback for university-matriculated ESL learners. *System, 39,* 229–239.

Evans, N., & Henrichsen, L. (2008). Long-term strategic incrementalism: An approach and a model for bringing about change in higher education. *Innovative Higher Education, 33*(2), 111–124.

Farrell, T.S.C. (2006). The first year of language teaching: Imposing order. *System, 34,* 211–221.

Ferrari, J.R., Johnson, J.L., & McCown, W.G. (1995). *Procrastination and task avoidance: Theory, research, and treatment.* New York: Plenum.

Ferris, D.R. (1995). Student reactions to teacher response in multiple-draft composition classrooms. *TESOL Quarterly, 29,* 33–53.

Ferris, D.R. (1997). The influence of teacher commentary on student revision. *TESOL Quarterly, 31*(2), 315–339.

Ferris, D.R. (1999). The case for grammar correction in L2 writing classes. A response to Truscott (1996). *Journal of Second Language Writing, 8,* 1–10.

Ferris, D.R. (2003). *Response to student writing: Implications for second language writing.* Mahwah, NJ: Erlbaum.

Ferris, D.R. (2004). The "grammar correction" debate in L2 writing: Where are we, and where do we go from here? (And what do we do in the meantime … ?). *Journal of Second Language Writing, 13*(1), 49–62.

Ferris, D.R. (2009). *Teaching college writing to diverse student populations.* Ann Arbor: University of Michigan Press.

Ferris, D.R., & Hedgcock, J.S. (2005). *Teaching ESL composition: Purpose, process, and practice* (2nd edn). Mahwah, NJ: Erlbaum.

Ferris, D.R., & Roberts, B. (2001). Error feedback in L2 writing classes: How explicit does it need to be? *Journal of Second Language Writing, 10,* 161–184.

Flower, L. (1990). The role of task representation in reading-to-write. In L. Flower, V. Stein, J. Ackerman, M.J. Kantz, K. McCormick, & W. Peck (eds), *Reading to write: Exploring a cognitive and social process* (pp. 35–75). New York: Oxford University Press.

Gardner, D., & Miller, L. (1999). *Establishing self-access: From theory to practice.* Cambridge, UK: Cambridge University Press.

Gardner, R.C. (1985). *Social psychology and second language learning: The role of attitudes and motivation.* London, UK: Edward Arnold.

Gardner, R.C. (2004). Attitude motivation test battery: International AMTB research project. Retrieved from http://publish.uwo.ca/~gardner/docs/englishamtb.pdf

Gardner, R.C., & Lambert, W. (1972). *Attitudes and motivation in second-language learning.* Rowley, MA: Newbury House.

Gardner, R.C., & MacIntyre, P.D. (1993). A student's contributions to second-language learning. Part II: Affective variables. *Language Learning, 26,* 1–11.

Garrison, R.D. (2003). Self-directed learning and distance education. In M.G. Moore & W.G. Anderson (eds), *Handbook of distance education* (pp. 161–168). Mahwah, NJ: Erlbaum.

Garrison, R.D., & Archer, W. (2000). *A traditional perspective on teaching and learning: A framework for adult and higher education.* Oxford, UK: Pergamon Press.

Gebhard, J.G. (2006). *Teaching English as a foreign or second language: A self-development and methodology guide* (2nd edn). Ann Arbor, MI: University of Michigan Press.

Gordon, L. (2008). Writing and good language learners. In C. Griffiths (ed.), *Lessons from good language learners* (pp. 244–254). Cambridge, UK: Cambridge University Press.

Gordon, T. (2001). *Leader effectiveness training. Proven skills for leading today's business into tomorrow*. Berkeley, CA: Berkeley.

Grabe, W. (2001). Notes toward a theory of second language writing. In T. Silva & P. Matsuda (eds.), *On second language writing* (pp. 39–58). Mahwah, NJ: Erlbaum.

Grabe, W., & Stoller, F. (2006). Reading for academic purposes: Guidelines for ESL EFL teachers. In M. Celce-Murcia (ed.), *Teaching English as a second or foreign language* (3rd edn) (pp. 187–203). Boston, MA: Heinle & Heinle.

Gray, T. (2005). *Publish and flourish: Become a prolific scholar*. Springfield, IL: Phillips Brothers.

Griffiths, C. (ed.). (2008). *Lessons from good language learners*. Cambridge, UK: Cambridge University Press.

Guénette, D. (2007). Is feedback pedagogically correct?: Research design issues in studies of feedback on writing. *Journal of Second Language Writing*, *16*(1), 40–53.

Hammond, S.A. (1996). *The thin book of appreciative inquiry* (2nd edn). Bend, OR: Thin Books.

Hamp-Lyons, L. (1986). Two commentaries on Daniel M. Horowitz's "Process, not product: Less than meets the eye." No new lamps for old yet, please. *TESOL Quarterly*, *20* (4), 790–796.

Hamp-Lyons, L., & Condon, W. (2000). *Assessing the portfolio: Principles for practice, theory and research*. Cresskill, NJ: Hampton Press.

Harklau, L. (2000). From the "good kids" to the "worst": Representations of English language learners across educational settings. *TESOL Quarterly*, *34*(1), 35–67.

Harlow, J. (2007). Successfully teaching Biblical language online at the seminary level: Guiding principles of course design and delivery. *Teaching Theology and Religion*, *10*(1), 13–24.

Harmer, J. (2003). Do your students notice anything? What role does noticing play in language acquisition? *Modern English Teacher*, *12*(3), 5–14.

Harmer, J. (2004). *How to teach writing*. Harlow, UK: Longman.

Harmer, J. (2007). *The practice of English language teaching* (4th edn). Harlow, UK: Longman.

Hartshorn, K.J., Evans, N., Merrill, P., Sudweeks, R., Strong-Krause, D., & Anderson, N.J. (2010). Effects of dynamic corrective feedback on ESL writing accuracy. *TESOL Quarterly*, *44*(1), 84–109.

Hartwell, P. (1985). Grammar, grammars, and the teaching of grammar. *College English*, *47*(2), 105–127.

Hattie, J., & Timperley, H. (2007). The power of feedback. *Review of Educational Research*, *77*(1), 81–112.

Hedge, T. (1988). *Writing*. Oxford, UK: Oxford University Press.

Hedgcock, J., & Lefkowitz, N. (1994). Feedback on feedback: Assessing learner receptivity to teacher response in L2 composing. *Journal of Second Language Writing*, *3*, 141–163.

Henrichsen, L. (1981). Ten perfect sentences. *English Language Teaching Journal*, *35*(3), 307–310.

Hinkel, E. (2004). *Teaching academic ESL writing: Practical techniques in vocabulary and grammar*. Mahwah, NJ: Erlbaum.

Hinkel, E. (2012, March). *Creating effective curriculum for teaching academic writing*. Paper presented at the Teachers of English to Speakers of Other Languages Conference, Philadelphia, PA.

Holec, H. (1981). *Autonomy and foreign language learning: Council of Europe*. Oxford, UK: Pergamon Press.

Horowitz, D.M. (1986a). Process, not product: Less than meets the eye. *TESOL Quarterly, 20*(1), 141–144.

Horowitz, D.M. (1986b). The author responds to Liebman-Kleine. *TESOL Quarterly, 20*(1), 788–789.

Hurd, S. (1998a). Autonomy at any price? Issues and concerns from a British HE perspective. *Foreign Language Annals, 31*(2), 219–230.

Hurd, S. (1998b). "Too carefully led or too carelessly left alone"? *Language Learning Journal, 17*, 70–74.

Hurd, S. (2000). Helping learners to help themselves: The role of metacognitive skills and strategies in independent language learning. In M. Fay & D. Ferney (eds.), *Current trends in modern language provision for non-specialist linguists* (pp. 36–52). London, UK: The Centre for Information on Language Teaching and Research (CILT) in association with Anglia Polytechnic University (APU).

Hurd, S. (2005). Autonomy and the distance language learner. In B. Holmberg, M. Shelly, & C. White (eds.), *Distance education and languages: Evolution and change* (pp. 1–19). Clevedon, UK: Multilingual Matters.

Hurd, S. (2006). Towards a better understanding of the dynamic role of the distance language learning: Learner perceptions of personality, motivation, roles, and approaches. *Distance Education, 27*(3), 303–329.

Hurd, S., Beaven, T., & Ortega, A. (2001). Developing autonomy in a distance language learning context: Issues and dilemmas for course writers. *System, 29*, 341–355.

Hyland, F. (2004). Learning autonomously: Contextualising out-of-class English language learning. *Language Awareness, 13*(3), 180–202.

Hyland, K. (2003). *Second language writing*. Cambridge, UK: Cambridge University Press.

Hyland, K., & Hyland, F. (eds.). (2006a). *Feedback in second language writing: Contexts and issues*. Cambridge, UK: Cambridge University Press.

Hyland, K., & Hyland, F. (2006b). Feedback on second language students' writing. *Language Teaching, 39*(2), 83–101.

Hymes, D. (1971). *On communicative competence*. Philadelphia, PA: University of Pennsylvania Press.

Hymes, D. (1972). On communicative competence. In J. Pride & J. Holmes (eds.), *Sociolinguistics: Selected readings* (pp. 269–293). Harmondsworth, UK: Penguin.

Johns, A.M. (1997). *Text, role, and context: Developing academic literacies*. Cambridge, UK: Cambridge University Press.

Johns, A.M. (2003). Genre and ESL/EFL composition instruction. In B. Kroll (ed.), *Exploring dynamics of second language writing* (pp. 195–217). Cambridge, UK: Cambridge University Press.

Johns, A.M. (2009, November). *The future of second language writing instruction*. Paper presented at Symposium on Second Language Writing, Tempe, AZ.

Johnson, D.W. (2003). *Reaching out: Interpersonal effectiveness and self-actualization* (8th ed.). Boston, MA: Allyn & Bacon.

Kamimura, T. (2000). Integration of process and product orientations in EFL writing instruction. *RELC Journal, 31*(2), 1–28.

Kelly, L.G. (1969). *25 centuries of language teaching*. Rowley, MA: Newbury House.

Kimura, Y., Nakata, Y., & Okumura, T. (2001). Language learning motivation of EFL learners in Japan—A cross-sectional analysis of various learning milieus. *JALT Journal, 23*(1), 47–68.

King, S. (2000). *On writing: A memoir of the craft*. New York: Scribner.

Knaus, W.J. (2000). Procrastination, blame, and change. *Journal of Social Behavior and Personality. 15*(5), 153–166.

Knaus, W.J. (2010). *End procrastination now: Get it done with a proven psychological approach*. New York: McGraw-Hill.

Krashen, S. (1981). *Second language acquisition and second language learning*. Oxford, UK: Pergamon.

Krashen, S. (1985). *The input hypothesis: Issues and implications*. London, UK: Longman.

Kroll, B. (1990). *Second language writing: Research insights from the classroom*. Cambridge, UK: Cambridge University Press.

Kroll, B. (2001). Considerations for teaching an ESL/EFL writing course. In M. Celce-Murcia (ed.), *Teaching English as a second or foreign language* (3rd edn) (pp. 219–232). Boston, MA: Heinle & Heinle.

Kumaravadivelu, B. (1994). The post-method condition: (E)merging strategies for second/foreign language teaching. *TESOL Quarterly, 28*, 27–48.

Kumaravadivelu, B. (2006). *Understanding language teaching: From method to postmethod*. Mahwah, NJ: Erlbaum.

Lane, J., & Lange, E. (1999). *Writing clearly: An editing guide* (2nd edn). Boston, MA: Heinle & Heinle.

Larsen-Freeman, D. (2011). *Techniques & principles in language teaching* (3rd edn). Cambridge, UK: Oxford University Press.

Lay, C. (1986). At last, my research article on procrastination. *Journal of Research in Personality, 20*, 474–495.

Leki, I. (1990). Coaching from the margins: issues in written response. In B. Kroll (ed.), *Second language writing: Research insights for the classroom* (pp. 57–68). Cambridge, UK: Cambridge University Press.

Leki, I. (1991). The preferences of ESL students for error correction in college-level writing classes. *Foreign Language Annals, 24*(3), 203–218.

Leki, I. (1992). *Understanding ESL writers: A guide for teachers*. Portsmouth, NH: Heinemann.

Liebman-Kleine, J. (1986). In defense of teaching process in ESL composition. *TESOL Quarterly, 20*(1), 783–788.

Little, D. (1991). *Learner autonomy 1: Definitions, issues, and problems*. Dublin, Ireland: Authentik.

Little, D. (1995). Learning as dialogue: The dependence of learner autonomy on teacher autonomy. *System, 23*(2), 175–181.

Little, D. (2000). Strategies, counseling and cultural difference: Why we need an anthropological understanding of learner autonomy. In R. Ribe (ed.), *Developing learner autonomy in foreign language learning* (pp. 17–33). Barcelona, Spain: University of Barcelona.

Littlewood, W. (1997). Self-access: Why do we want it and what can it do? In P. Benson & P. Voller (eds), *Autonomy and independence in language learning* (pp. 79–92). London, UK: Longman.

Lynch, T. (2001). Seeing what they meant: transcribing as route to noticing. *ELT Journal, 55*(2), 124–132.

Macaro, E. (1997). *Target language, collaborative learning and autonomy.* Clevedon, UK: Multilingual Matters.

Martin, J.E., Mithaug, D.E., Cox, P., Peterson, L.Y., Van Dycke, J.L., & Cash, M.E. (2003). Increasing self-determination: Teaching students to plan, work, evaluate, and adjust. *Exceptional Children, 69,* 433–447.

Masgoret, A.M., & Gardner, R.C. (2003). Attitudes, motivation, and second language learning: A meta-analysis of studies conducted by Gardner and associates. *Language Learning, 53,* 167–219.

Matsuda, P.K. (2003). Second language writing in the twentieth century: A situated historical perspective. In B. Kroll (ed.), *Exploring dynamics of second language writing* (pp. 15–34). Cambridge, UK: Cambridge University Press.

Matsuda, P.K. (2006). The myth of linguistic homogeneity in U.S. college composition. *College English, 68*(6), 637–651.

Matsuda, P.K. (2009, April). *World Englishes and the teaching of writing.* Paper presented at the Visiting Scholars Series, Brigham Young University Department of Linguistics and English Language, Provo, UT.

Messerschmitt, D.S., & Johnson Hafernik, J. (2009). *Dilemmas in teaching English to speakers of other languages.* Ann Arbor: University of Michigan Press.

Michaelsen, L.K. (n.d.). Getting started with Team-Based Learning. Retrieved from http://serc.carleton.edu/cismi/broadaccess/teamworkshop/resources.htmlcuts

Michaelsen, L.K., & Fink, L.D. (n.d.). *Team-based learning: Two methods for calculating peer evaluation scores.* Retrieved from http://www.teambasedlearning.org/Default.aspx?pageId=1032389

Michaelsen, L.K., & Sweet, M. (2008). Team-Based Learning. *Thriving in Academe, 25*(6), 5–8.

Michaelsen, L.K., Fink, L.D., & Knight, A. (n.d.). Designing effective group activities: Lessons for classroom teaching and faculty development. Retrieved from http://tblc.camp9.org/Bibliography

Michaelsen, L.K., Knight, A.B., & Fink, L.D. (eds). (2004). *Team-Based Learning: A transformative use of small groups in college teaching.* Sterling, VA: Stylus.

Michaelsen, L.K., Sweet, M., & Parmelee, D.X. (eds). (2008). Team-Based Learning: Small group learning's next big step. *New Directions for Teaching and Learning, 116*(Winter), 7–27.

Michaelsen, L.K., Watson, W.E., & Black, R.H. (1989). A realistic test of individual versus group consensus decision making. *Journal of Applied Psychology. 74*(5), 834–839.

Michaelsen, L.K., Parmelee, D.X., McMahon, K.K., & Levine, R.E. (eds). (2007). *Team-Based Learning for health professions education: A guide to using small groups for improving learning.* Sterling, VA: Stylus.

Miller, L. (ed). (2006). *Learner autonomy 9: Autonomy in the classroom*. Dublin, Ireland: Authentik.

Muller-Verweyen, M. (1999). Reflection as a means of acquiring autonomy. In S. Cotterall & D. Crabbe (eds), *Learner autonomy in language learning. Defining the field and effecting change* (pp. 79–88). Frankfurt, Germany: Peter Lang.

Murray, D.E., & Christison, M.A. (2011). *What English teachers need to know, Vol. 1*. New York: Routledge.

Murray, D.M. (2000). The maker's eye: Revising your own manuscripts. In P. Eschholz, A. Rosa, & V. Clark (eds), *Language awareness: Readings for college writers* (8th edn) (pp.161–165). Boston, MA: Bedford/St. Martin's.

Murray, D.M. (2002). The maker's eye: Revising your own manuscript. In G. Muller (ed), *The McGraw-Hill reader: Issues across disciplines* (pp. 56–60). New York: City University of New York.

Murray, G. (2004). Two stories of self-directed learning. In H. Reinders, H. Anderson, M. Hobbs, & J. Jones-Parry (eds), *Supporting independent learning in the 21st century: Proceedings of the inaugural conference of the Independent Learning Association, Melbourne, Australia* (pp. 112–120). Auckland, New Zealand: Independent Learning Association Oceania. Retrieved from http://www.independentlearning.org/ila03/ila03_papers.htm

Murphy, L. (2005). Critical reflection and autonomy: A study of distance learners of French, German and Spanish. In B. Holmberg, M. Shelley, & C. White (eds), *Distance education and languages: Evolution and change* (pp. 20–39). Clevedon, UK: Multilingual Matters.

Nation, I.S.P. (2001). *Learning vocabulary in another language*. Cambridge, UK: Cambridge University Press.

Nation, I.S.P. (2008). *Teaching vocabulary: Strategies and techniques*. Boston, MA: Heinle Cengage Learning.

Nation, I.S.P. (2009). *Teaching ESL/EFL reading and writing*. New York: Routledge.

Nation, I.S.P., & Macalister, J. (2010). *Language curriculum design*. New York: Routledge.

Nunan, D. (1997). Designing and adapting materials to encourage learner autonomy. In P. Benson & P. Voller (eds), *Autonomy and independence in language learning* (pp. 192–203). London, UK: Longman.

Nunan, D. (1999). *Second language teaching and learning*. Boston, MA: Heinle & Heinle.

Nunes, A. (2004). Portfolios in the EFL classroom: Disclosing an informed practice. *ELT Journal, 58*(4), 327–335.

Ogbu, J.U., & Simons, H.D. (1998). Voluntary and involuntary minorities: A cultural-ecological theory of school performance with some implications for education. *Anthropology & Education Quarterly, 29*(2), 155–188.

Oller, J., Baca, L., & Vigil, A. (1978). Attitudes and attained proficiency in ESL: A sociolinguistic study of Mexican-Americans in the Southwest. *TESOL Quarterly, 11*, 173–183.

Oller, J., Hudson, A., & Liu, P. (1977). Attitudes and attained proficiency in ESL: A sociolinguistic study of Chinese in the United States. *Language Learning, 27*, 1–27.

Omaggio Hadley, A. (2000). *Teaching language in context* (3rd edn). Boston, MA: Heinle & Heinle.

O'Malley, J.M., & Chamot, A.U. (1990). *Learning strategies in second language acquisition*. Cambridge, UK: Cambridge University Press.

O'Malley, J.M., Chamot, A.U., Stewner-Manzanares, G., Kupper, L., & Russo, R. (1985). Learning strategies used by beginning and intermediate ESL students. *Language Learning, 35*(1), 21–46.

Oxford, R.L. (1990). *Language learning strategies: What every teacher should know.* Boston, MA: Heinle & Heinle.

Oxford, R.L. (1994). Language learning strategies: An update. Retrieved from http://www.cal.org/resources/digest/oxford01.html

Oxford, R.L. (2008). Hero with a thousand faces: Learning autonomy, learning strategies and learning tactics in independent language learning. In S. Hurd & T. Lewis (eds), *Language learning strategies in independent settings* (pp. 41–63). Bristol, UK: Multilingual Matters.

Oxford, R.L. (2011). *Teaching and researching language learning strategies.* Harlow, UK: Pearson Education.

Oxford, R.L., & Shearin, J. (1994). Language learning motivation: Expanding the theoretical framework. *Modern Language Journal, 78,* 12–28.

Palfreyman, D. (2003). Expanding the discourse on learner development: A reply to Anita Wenden. *Applied Linguistics, 24*(2), 243–248.

Palfreyman, D., & Smith, R.C. (eds). (2003). *Learner autonomy across cultures: Language education perspectives.* Basingstoke, UK: Palgrave Macmillan.

Paris, S.G., & Paris, A.H. (2001). Classroom applications of research on self-regulated learning. *Educational Psychologist, 36*(2), 89–101.

Perry, N.E., VandeKamp, K.O., Mercer, L.K., & Nordby, C.J. (2002). Investigating teacher–student interactions that foster self-regulated learning. *Educational Psychologist, 37*(1), 5–15.

Perry, R.P. (1999). Teaching for success: Assisting helpless students in their academic development. *Education Canada, 29*(1), 16–19.

Peters, O. (1998). *Learning and teaching in distance education. Analysis and interpretation from an international perspective.* London, UK: Kogan Page.

Pintrich, P.R., & Schunk, D.H. (2002). *Motivation in education: Theory, research, and applications* (3rd edn). Upper Saddle River, NJ: Merrill/Prentice Hall.

Polio, C., Fleck, C., & Leder, N. (1998). "If I only had more time": ESL learners' changes in linguistic accuracy on essay revisions. *Journal of Second Language Writing, 7*(1), 43–68.

Purves, A.C. (ed.). (1988). *Writing across languages and cultures: Issues in contrastive rhetoric.* Newbury Park, CA: Sage.

Raimes, A. (2004). *Grammar troublespots: A guide for student writers* (3rd edn). Cambridge, UK: Cambridge University Press.

Read, J. (2000). *Assessing vocabulary.* Cambridge, UK: Cambridge University Press.

Reid, J.M. (1993). *Teaching ESL writing.* Englewood Cliffs, NJ: Regents/Prentice Hall.

Richard-Amato, P.A. (2010). *Making it happen: From interactive to participatory language teaching* (4th edn). New York: Longman.

Richards, J.C. (2001). *Curriculum development in language teaching.* Cambridge, UK: Cambridge University Press.

Roberts, B.J. (1999). *Can error logs raise more consciousness? The effects of error logs and grammar feedback on ESL students' final drafts* (unpublished master's thesis). California State University, Sacramento.

Rubin, J. (1975). What the "good language learner" can teach us. *TESOL Quarterly, 9*(1), 41–51.

Rubin, J. (2008). Reflections. In C. Griffiths (ed.), *Lessons from good language learners* (pp. 10–15). Cambridge, UK: Cambridge University Press.

Samovar, L.A., Porter, R.E., & McDaniel, E.R. (2009). *Communication between cultures* (7th ed.). Boston, MA: Cengage Learning.

Sanford, N. (1966). *Self and society: Social change and individual development.* New York: Atherton.

Sanford, N. (1968). *Where colleges fail: A study of student as person.* San Francisco, CA: Jossey-Bass.

Savignon, S. (1997). *Communicative competence: Theory and classroom practice.* New York: McGraw-Hill.

Savignon, S. (2001). Communicative language teaching for the twenty-first century. In M. Celce-Murcia (ed.), *Teaching English as a second or foreign language* (3rd edn) (pp. 13–28). Boston, MA: Heinle & Heinle.

Scharle, A., & Szabó, A. (2000). *Learner autonomy: A guide to developing learner responsibility.* Cambridge, UK: Cambridge University Press.

Schloemer, P., & Brenan, K. (2006). From students to learners: Developing self-regulated learning. *Journal of Education for Business, 82*(2), 81–87.

Schmenk, B. (2005). Globalizing learning autonomy. *TESOL Quarterly, 39*(1), 107–118.

Schmidt, R. (1990). The role of consciousness in second language learning. *Applied Linguistics, 11*(2), 129–159.

Schmidt, R., Boraie, D., & Kassabgy, O. (1996). Foreign language motivation: Internal structure and external connections. In R. Oxford (ed.), *Language learning motivation: Pathways to the new century* (pp. 9–70). Honolulu, HI: University of Hawaii Press.

Schuette, C.G. (1989). Improving your concentration. Retrieved from http://www.k-state.edu/counseling/topics/career/concentr.html

Sheen, Y. (2007). The effect of focused written corrective feedback and language aptitude on ESL learners' acquisition of articles. *TESOL Quarterly, 41*, 255–283.

Silva, T. (1993). Toward an understanding of the distinct nature of L2 writing: The ESL research and its implications. *TESOL Quarterly, 27*, 657–675.

Smith, H. (1994). *The 10 natural laws of successful time and life management.* New York: Warner.

Snow, D.B. (2006). *More than a native speaker: An introduction for volunteers teaching abroad* (2nd edn). Alexandria, VA: TESOL.

Stevick, E. (1988). *Teaching and learning languages.* Cambridge, UK: Cambridge University Press.

Storch, N. (2010). Critical feedback in second language writing. *International Journal of English Studies, 10*, 29–46.

Sugita, Y. (2006). The impact of teachers' comment types on students' revision. *ELT Journal, 60*(2), 34–41.

Swain, M. (1995). Three functions of output in second language learning. In G. Cook & B. Seidhofer (eds), *For H.G. Widdowson: Principles and practice in the study of language.* Cambridge, UK: Oxford University Press.

Takagi, A. (2003). The effects of early childhood language learning experience on motivation towards learning English: A survey of public junior high school students. *JASTEC Journal, 22*, 47–71.

Tardy, C. (2006). Appropriation, ownership, and agency: Negotiating teacher feedback in academic settings. In K. Hyland & F. Hyland (eds), *Feedback in second language writing: Contexts and issues* (pp. 60–78). Cambridge, UK: Cambridge University Press.

Team-Based Learning: Peer evaluation. (n.d.). Retrieved from http://www.teambasedlearning.org/

Thang, S.M. (2005). Investigating Malaysian distance learners' perceptions of their English proficiency courses. *Open Learning, 20*(3), 243–256.

Tinnesz, C.G., Ahuna, K.H., & Kiener, M. (2006). Toward college success: Internalizing active and dynamic strategies. *College Teaching, 54*(4), 302–306.

Truscott, J. (1996). The case against grammar correction in L2 writing classes. *Language Learning, 46*(2), 327–369.

Tsui, A.B.M. (2003). *Understanding expertise in teaching: Case studies of ESL teachers.* Cambridge, UK: Cambridge University Press.

Tuckman, B.W. (1991). The development and concurrent validity of the Procrastination Scale. *Educational & Psychological Measurement, 51*, 473–480.

Ushioda, E. (2008). Motivation and good language learners. In C. Griffiths (ed.), *Lessons from good language learners* (pp. 19–34). Cambridge, UK: Cambridge University Press.

van den Boom, G., Paas, F., & van Merrienboer, J.J.G. (2007). Effects of elicited reflections combined with tutor or peer feedback on self-regulated learning and learning outcomes. *Learning and Instruction, 17*, 532–548.

Vanijdee, A. (2003). Thai distance English learners and learner autonomy. *Open Learning, 18*(1), 75–84.

Vygotsky, L.S. (1978). *Mind in society.* Cambridge, MA: Harvard University Press.

Ware, P.D., & Warschauer, M. (2006). Electronic feedback and second language writing. In K. Hyland & F. Hyland (eds), *Feedback in second language writing: Contexts and issues* (pp. 105–122). Cambridge, UK: Cambridge University Press.

Warschauer, M. (1995). *E-mail for English teaching: Bringing the internet and computer learning networks into the language classroom.* Alexandria, VA: TESOL.

Weiner, B. (1986). *An attributional theory of motivation and emotion.* New York: Springer-Verlag.

Wernke, S., Wagener, U., Anschuetz, A., & Moschner, B. (2011). Assessing cognitive and metacognitive learning strategies in school children: Construct validity and arising questions. *The International Journal of Research and Review, 6*(2), 19–38.

West, M. (1953). *A general service list of English words.* London: Longman, Green & Co.

White, C. (2003). *Language learning in distance education.* Cambridge, UK: Cambridge University Press.

White, E. (1994). *Teaching and assessing writing* (2nd edn). San Francisco, CA: Jossey-Bass.

Wolfersberger, M. (2008). *Second language writing from sources: An ethnographic study of an argument essay task* (unpublished doctoral dissertation). University of Auckland, New Zealand.

Yi, U. (2010). *The effect of content revision logs and student-teacher conferences on ESL writing* (unpublished master's thesis). Brigham Young University, Provo, UT.

Zamel, V. (1976). Teaching composition in the ESL classroom: What we can learn from research in the teaching of English. *TESOL Quarterly, 10*, 67–76.

Zamel, V. (1982). Writing: The process of discovering meaning. *TESOL Quarterly, 16*, 195–209.

Zamel, V. (1983). The composing processes of advanced ESL students: Six case studies. *TESOL Quarterly, 17*, 165–187.

Zamel, V. (1985). Responding to student writing. *TESOL Quarterly*, *19*, 79–101.

Zimmerman, B.J. (1986). Development of self-regulated learning: Which are the key subprocesses? *Contemporary Educational Psychology*, *16*, 307–313.

Zimmerman, B.J. (1990). Self-regulated learning and academic achievement: An overview. *Educational Psychologist*, *25*(1), 3–17.

Zimmerman, B.J. (1994). Dimensions of academic self-regulation: A conceptual framework for education. In D.H. Schunk & B.J. Zimmerman (eds.), *Self-regulation of learning and performance* (pp. 3–21). Hillsdale, NJ: Erlbaum.

Zimmerman, B.J. (1998). Academic study and the development of personal skill: A self-regulatory perspective. *Educational Psychologist*, 33(2/3), 73–86.

Zimmerman, B.J. (2002). Becoming a self-regulated learner: An overview. *Theory into Practice*, *41*, 64–142.

Zimmerman, B.J., & Kitsantas, A. (1997). Developmental phases in self-regulation: Shifting from process goals to outcome goals. *Journal of Educational Psychology*, *89*(1), 29–36.

Zimmerman, B.J., & Martinez-Pons, M. (1986). Development of a structured interview for assessing student use of SRL strategies. *American Educational Research Journal*, *23*(4), 614–628.

Zimmerman, B.J., & Risemberg, R. (1997). Self-regulatory dimensions of academic learning and motivation. In G.D. Phye (ed.), *Handbook of academic learning: Construction of knowledge* (pp. 105–125). San Diego, CA: Academic Press.

Zimmerman, B.J., Bonner, S., & Kovach, R. (1996). *Developing self-regulated learners: Beyond achievement in self-efficacy*. Washington, DC: American Psychological Association.

Index